I0041613

Mixed Reality Leadership

Leadership for Modern Organisations

Dr Maitland Hyslop

Amanda Goodger

John Greaves PPE

UNIVERSITY OF
BUCKINGHAM
PRESS

UNIVERSITY OF BUCKINGHAM PRESS,
AN IMPRINT OF LEGEND TIMES GROUP LTD
51 Gower Street
London WC1E 6HJ
United Kingdom
www.unibuckinghampress.com

First published by University of Buckingham Press in 2025

© Dr Maitland Hyslop, Amanda Goodger, and John Greaves PPE, 2025

The right of the authors to be identified as the authors of this work has been asserted in accordance with the Copyright, Designs and Patents Act 1988.
British Library Cataloguing in Publication Data available.

ISBN: 978-1-917163-18-7

All the images in this volume are reprinted with permission or presumed to be in the public domain. Every effort has been made to ascertain and acknowledge their copyright status, but any error or oversight will be rectified in subsequent printings.

All rights reserved. No part of this publication may be reproduced, stored in or introduced into a retrieval system, or transmitted, in any form or by any means (electronic, mechanical, photocopying, recording or otherwise), without the prior written permission of the publisher. This book is sold subject to the condition that it shall not be resold, lent, hired out or otherwise circulated without the express prior consent of the publisher.

About the Authors

Dr Maitland Hyslop is a Visiting Lecturer at the University of Buckingham with a focus on Security, Intelligence and Cyber.

To demonstrate an eclectic leadership experience Maitland's Non
– Executive roles include: Executive Club of Chicago (USA) (International); Durham University American Foundation (USA) (Oversight); NE Learning (Charity) (Funders); European Telecommunications Resilience and Recovery Association (EC) (Governance); European Politech Institute (Honorary Professor, Science Committee); Institute for Information Infrastructure Protection (Founder) (USA) (UK); Highlands and Islands University Council; Chair NHS South East Procurement Board (Funders); Chair Surrey and Sussex Hospital NHS Trust Turnaround Board (Funders); Chair Surrey Health CIC (Public/Private Partnership: NHS, McLaren, University of Surrey, Surrey County Council); Chair, Stoke and Staffordshire Local Enterprise Partnership (Government); Keele University Council; Staffordshire County Council (Economy); Staffordshire County Fire Service (Innovation); The Middle East Association (Bahrain Representative); Ahlia University, (Honorary Professor, Research); Provisional Chair Gulf Cooperation Council Aviation Safety and Security Committee; Thomas Organisation (USA) (International); Founding Chair and Member Buckingham New University Aviation and Security Advisory Board; Family Trusts.

Strategically and operationally he was, amongst other posts, the CEO of a worldwide oil asset management company, OES Asset Integrity Management, member of the UK NHS senior leadership cadre, and Managing Director of Tetra Pak's African and Middle East businesses. He has advised a number of oil and gas organisations including the International Oil and Gas Producers Association, a number of large Middle East organisations including the Qatari Regulatory Authority, the Abu Dhabi National Insurance Company, and taught the leadership cadres of a range of multinational organisations in the USA, UK, Europe and the Middle East. He is a former soldier with combat and anti-terrorist experience. He is an award winner in private, public, government, academic and military environments. He has previously written on Leadership, Cyber Threats, War, Trafficking, the Middle East and about both Marketing and Information Security/Resilience.

Amanda Goodger is an experienced leader in mixed reality leadership, with a career spanning local to international levels over decades. Currently, she works at the University of Hertfordshire (UH) and contributes to the UK government-funded 'Help to Grow' working group (via Small Business Charter), enhancing content delivery across accredited UK business schools. Amanda has held significant leadership roles, including working for the UK Government in the cyber/digital area, serving as a Principal Risk Engineer for ARM, collaborating with the EU on cloud security, and engaging with various universities. At UH, she imparts knowledge on the digital ecosystem/AI/emerging technologies, cybersecurity, project management and business to a diverse range of learners, including small businesses and consultancy. Amanda holds an MPhil in Engineering from Cambridge University and is completing a PhD in risk appetite calibration impacting cybersecurity and resilience in hybrid environments. Her expertise as a Cyber-Physical Resilience Risk and Systems Engineer spans Product Security Assurance, Enterprise Architecture, and Compliance across sectors such as Engineering Design, Health, Education, and Government/Defence. Renowned for her proactive, customer-focused approach, Amanda achieves business-focused outcomes.

John Greaves has led globally for over forty years in the development of innovative advances in technologies focused on Supply Chain, Logistics, retailing and manufacturing in over 200 deployments of his value orientated, ROI measurable implementations. His client list includes many of the Fortune 1000.His work has been featured at the Smithsonian, in the US Federal Government and in the EU and National Government Initiatives to improve society and ultimately enshrine a quality of life for citizens by application of his OHIO Principle (Zero Human Intervention Operations). Known for his expertise in the RFID and Blockchain sector, where he develops Mixed Reality deliverables that focus on these two pillars of the program, he is known as Dr Blockchain. Resident in Florida USA he travels extensively advising on tenets of best practice on a weekly basis and is accredited to the Florida Institute of Technology where he leads the Enterprise Blockchain Initiative.

James Royds FBCI, a leading independent UK specialist in resilience, contributed to Chapter 3.

Other contributors from the 2025 Undergraduate body at the University of Buckingham include:

Daniel White – co-author of BUSCIS' *The Invisible Apocalypse* –based at the Erasmus University, Rotterdam.

Daisie Butlin – also contributor to BUCSIS' *The Invisible Apocalypse*

Isla Johnston – also contributor to BUCSIS' *The Invisible Apocalypse*

Noha Mahamud – also contributor to BUCSIS' *The Invisible Apocalypse*

Chiago Ziem Nwocha – also contributor to BUCSIS' *The Invisible Apocalypse*

Harrison Turner Robson – also contributor to BUCSIS' *The Invisible Apocalypse*

Sofia Sumpter – also contributor to BUCSIS' *The Invisible Apocalypse*

And from the 2025 cohort:

Evie Drinkwater
Josh McManus
DeSean Pierre Dwyer
Leya Alexandria Roberts

And from Buckinghamshire New University 2024 Graduates:
Sophie Devine – now of the Royal Navy
Avtar Purewal – now of Global Situation Awareness Limited
https://global-sa.co.uk

Abstract

This book looks at the complexities of integrating mixed reality, extended reality, augmented reality, virtual reality and artificial intelligence into a leadership framework called Mixed Reality Leadership. It addresses key topics such as governance, risk management, organisational values, and strategic threats in a mixed reality context. Mixed Reality and Mixed Reality Leadership are new terms, first used by the authors on LinkedIn in 2023/24.

With an initial focus on emerging challenges such as cybersecurity and artificial intelligence, the book emphasises the importance of adaptable leadership styles and robust governance. The book also examines mixed reality leadership development, training, and its intersection with critical national and information infrastructures, Obstructive Marketing, highlighting vulnerabilities in key sectors such as defence, health, finance, energy with numerous case studies.

Acknowledgements

Professor Julian Richards, Chris Donnelly, Professor Andrew Collins, Professor David Alexander, Dr Peter Trim, Professor Ray Hudson, Professor Ian Angell, General Sir Michael Rose, General Gordon Sullivan, Professor Edward Borodzicz, Sir Peter Carr, James Royds and Robert Leitch are all thinkers to whom Maitland owes much.

Maitland studied at the Royal Military Academy Sandhurst, Durham University, Northumbria University, Huddersfield University Business School, Sloan School of Management, the IMD, Concord University, and Harvard University. He owes those institutions a debt of gratitude for expanding his knowledge and implanting a continuing desire to learn. He also owes Amanda Goodger and John Greaves thanks for co-authoring parts of this book; as he does to all the undergraduates who contributed, from a different generation, in their essays and class discussion to the thinking behind this book.

Saxton Bampfylde are thanked for their permission to use their Board model.

ICAO are thanked for their permission to use some governance information.

The UN, UNDRR, and Declan Kirrane are thanked for helping all of us develop some themes in our presentations to the UN Science Summit over the last three years (2022, 2023, 2024).

Gulf Oasis Training (Bahrain) are thanked for giving the opportunity to lecture/teach in the Middle East on some of the issues contained herein.

The International Oil and Gas Producers Association are thanked for stimulating some of the thought behind this book.

Contents

Chapter 10: Training and Development for Mixed Reality Leadership   176

Chapter 18: The Foundational Economy and SMEs 275

Preface

For Dr Maitland Hyslop, this book is a result of a lifetime of interest in leadership, starting at the Royal Military Academy, Sandhurst, some fifty years ago, and a much more recent association with the University of Buckingham's Centre for Security and Intelligence Studies (BUCSIS) with an emphasis on national security in a cyber age and cyber challenges.

This book builds upon, and looks anew at some of the issues raised in six previous works but concentrates on the issue of leadership in the current 'mixed' world of the physical, virtual and metaverse. Leadership is an important issue. Many leaders do not understand the virtual world, for some this ignorance has cost them their job and sometimes their liberty. It is a serious shortcoming, particularly by MBA/Business Schools, and needs to be addressed.

Just as business continuity and resilience did not feature much in tertiary education courses a decade ago, the same is true of Mixed Reality Leadership today. This situation is partly brought about by the automation paradox, whereby there is an overconfidence in the ability of technology to solve problems and a parallel perception that the traditional disciplines needed in the human world do not apply. It is also brought about by the way current CEOs, particularly in the USA, are appointed and trained. It should never be forgotten that training, routine and discipline free up time for growth, development and creativity in all worlds. Here, co – author Amanda Goodger makes important contributions.

There is also a big data paradox which often sees diminishing returns against larger data sets – and no doubt there will be/is some form of Artificial Intelligence (AI) paradox in due course.

Hopefully a lot of this book is commonsense, or motherhood and apple pie as the Americans would say. That said it remains incredible, at times, and especially in cyber security, how often common sense is not followed. Andy Jenkinson is a rich source of such lack of common sense in this regard, on LinkedIn.

There are a few elements of the previous six publications, an occasional piece of AI, and some work from students at Durham University, Northumbria University, the University of Buckingham and Buckinghamshire New University in this book. James Royds has contributed to Chapter 3.

This book is largely written by Britons with experience of living and working worldwide. It necessarily has a western viewpoint. No excuses for that as if it was written from a Chinese or Russian point of view, it would mean little to the intended audience.

It is with delight that I am able to include Amanda Goodger and John Greaves as co-authors, with James Royds, Daniel White, and the 2nd year (2024) undergraduate students at Buckingham University's Security, Intelligence and Cyber course as contributors, It is also appropriate to thank Avtar Purewal and Sophie Devine for their input on the Aviation chapter in particular, 2024 graduates of the Buckinghamshire New University Aviation and Security School and presenters at the German Research Society conference in Amsterdam, 2023.

This book has a mixture of styles as different parts need different approaches. It is the nature of the beast that lists and checklists are important in establishing routines, aligning licences, technical equipment, behaviour, managing employees and supply chains. It is basically in two sections, the first section deals with background, introduction, enterprise cyber security, and resilience to establish a baseline. The second is a pathway to implementing Mixed Reality Leadership.

We do not expect the reader to agree with every detail in this book. Its importance lies in giving the audience a route to mixed reality leadership and the new world that awaits us, according to the World Economic Forum, by 2030, only 5 years away.

SECTION 1

Background, Introduction, Cybersecurity, Resilience – A Baseline for Progression to Mixed Reality Leadership

Chapter 1

Background and Introduction

Background

This book deals with a new term, Mixed Reality, and a new form of leadership: Mixed Reality Leadership. It is important therefore to establish the background and credentials for such. The term is original and does not rely on secondary sources, except the conversations between authors and contributors that led to its genesis.

The term Mixed Reality Leadership was coined by Dr Hyslop in 2024 and is the copyright of the author(s) and the University of Buckingham. The related thinking follows a pattern of thought developed over the last two years, see above, and also represented by Maitland Hyslop's key previous books:

Critical Information Infrastructures: Resilience and Protection (Hyslop, 2007). This was written in association with Springer and the key lesson was probably that the protection of Critical Information Infrastructures is as much about human and physical security (including HUMINT) as it is about technology. This lesson remains apposite and is part of the thinking behind this book.

Obstructive Marketing (Hyslop, 2014). This was written following the author's PhD in *Hardening Organisations (Organisational Security)* (Hyslop, 2013), with Gower, and focused on the changed nature of resilience for organisations. It identified major gaps in virtual protection, poor training of CEOs and C-Suite members, and the key threats to organisations both physical and cyber. It was and remains an organisational baseline for this book.

On War (Hyslop, 2020). In this book the author considers the shift from 'declared war' to a range of war-like and non-warlike conflicts designed to disable opponents without necessarily involving the military or large numbers of personnel in 'no rules' conflicts. Defence in the military, traditional, sense is still part of most countries' armouries. Vulnerabilities have extended to finance, critical infrastructures, and trade. So, a rounded defence strategy must now consider a military defence, defence of finance, critical infrastructures, trade and an improved general resilience. In a post-COVID – 19 and Ukraine world, the emphasis may change again

The *Elephant in the Boardroom* (Hyslop, 2023). This book followed the author's attendance at Harvard University's Cyber Security: Managing Risk in an Information Age course, where he received an outstanding result for his final project. This final project informed a large part of *The Elephant in the Boardroom*. This has also informed Chapters 2 and 3 with James Royds.

The Invisible Apocalypse (with Daniel White and others) (Hyslop & White, 2024). This book was essentially a cooperation between Maitland Hyslop, Daniel White (then a third-year history undergraduate at Erasmus University in Rotterdam en route to a first-class honours), and Dr Hyslop's first year undergraduate Cyber Challenges course at the University of Buckingham (collectively en route to top degrees) focussing on China, Russia, North Korea and Iran as hostile cyber warfare players. It was cyber challenges looked at from a contemporary and historical perspective. This has informed Chapters 4 and 9.

These books have all been part of reading for various University courses, especially Buckingham.

It is important in this day and age to be clear about the provenance of ideas and the intellectual dialectic that led to them. Even AI has occasionally to be corrected on the provenance of the term Mixed Reality, the authors having originally introduced the term to AI and been acknowledged for it. So please forgive the long introductions to the term both here and in the preambles.

Definitions and Clarifications

Mixed Reality (MR): The Integrative Lens for 21st Century Leadership

In the era of digital transformation, organisations must move beyond isolated physical or virtual strategies and adopt a **Mixed Reality (MR) mindset**—a framework that integrates **physical assets**, **digital/cyber infrastructure**, and the **emergent virtual/ metaverse domain** into a cohesive operational reality. MR is not merely a technological experience; it is a **strategic paradigm** for leadership, innovation, and resilience.

Executives and boards that fail to recognise the strategic role of MR—especially those who over-invest in physical infrastructure without digital-virtual alignment—risk obsolescence, regulatory exposure, and market irrelevance. Conversely, organisations that adopt MR as a **decision-making lens** position themselves for agility, foresight, and long-term value creation.

Understanding the New Landscape: Three Realities

Domain	Description
Physical	Tangible world: people, places, infrastructure, and assets.
Digital	Informational systems: data, algorithms, networks, and analytics.
Virtual (Metaverse)	Simulated and immersive environments, avatars, synthetic experiences.

Mixed Reality (MR) is the **strategic zone where these three realms converge**, allowing for real-time awareness, synchronised operations, and novel forms of interaction and value creation.

MR as Strategic Layer (Above XR, AR, VR, and AI)

Technology	Purpose	Strategic Role
AR	Overlays data on the physical world	UI enhancement
VR	Fully immersive digital environments	Simulation and training
XR	Umbrella term for immersive experiences	Experiential design
AI	Emulates cognitive functions	Automation and augmentation
MR (Mixed Reality)	Integrates physical, digital, and virtual systems	**Enterprise integration & situational awareness**

MR is not a subset of XR. It is the **orchestration layer—a system of systems**—that harmonises experience, data, intelligence, and physical action.

Leadership and Accountability in the MR Era

Modern CEOs and boards are being held accountable for not just financial performance, but for how well their organisations:

- **Integrate digital and physical systems,**
- **Adapt to virtual platforms,**
- **Secure operations across domains,**
- **Engage users and customers in hybrid formats**, and
- **Respond to rapid shifts in environment, data, and expectation.**

Failure to act in the MR layer is increasingly seen as **negligence—** whether in cybersecurity, digital ethics, operational continuity, or market innovation.

MR as Strategic Imperative

MR is not just a medium—it's a mindset.

It demands:

- **Cross-functional collaboration** between IT, operations, marketing, and strategy.
- **Investments in MR infrastructure**: not just headsets, but interoperable systems, APIs, AI, and secure data layers.
- **Governance models** that consider virtual and digital accountability as rigorously as physical ones.
- **Scenario planning** that blends digital twins, virtual simulations, and real-world contingencies.

Conclusion

Mixed Reality is not a niche technology—it is the **strategic domain where modern organisations must operate** to remain relevant, resilient, and responsible. Those who master MR will shape the future; those who ignore it risk being shaped by it.

In addition:

Cyber vs Digital, Cybersecurity as Resilience, and Leadership vs Management

Cyber vs Digital: Distinct but Intertwined

While often used interchangeably, **cyber** and **digital** refer to **distinct conceptual domains** that play different roles in the MR ecosystem:

Term	Scope	Emphasis
Digital	Data, code, software, systems, and platforms	**Representation and functionality**
Cyber	The dynamic, connected, and often contested environment in which digital assets operate	**Agency, security, and control**

- **Digital** refers to the **content and structure**: databases, files, analytics, cloud platforms, etc.
- **Cyber** refers to the **terrain and context**: networks, connectivity, threats, defence, and operational control.

Think of **digital** as the "what" and **cyber** as the "where and how."

Cybersecurity as a Core of Organisational Resilience

Cybersecurity is no longer just a technical function—it is a **pillar of organisational resilience** in the MR age. It protects not only data and systems but **trust, continuity, and reputation**.

"Cybersecurity is to digital trust what physical safety is to brand integrity."

Note: This is a paraphrase of Maitland Hyslop's approach to brand integrity in *Obstructive Marketing* (Hyslop, 2014).

Strategic cybersecurity ensures:

- Operational continuity across physical-digital-virtual systems.
- Legal and regulatory compliance (e.g., GDPR, NIS2, DORA).
- Protection of customer and stakeholder data across MR layers.
- Board-level oversight of digital risk, aligned with enterprise risk management.

In the MR context, **resilience means the ability to sustain function and trust across interconnected, intelligent, and immersive systems**—and cybersecurity is the active mechanism by which that resilience is enforced. There is more operational context on this in Chapters 2 and 3.

Leadership vs Management in the MR Era

The shift to MR thinking also requires a shift in **mindset between management and leadership**:

Dimension	Management	Leadership
Focus	Systems, processes, efficiency	Vision, alignment, change
Approach	Control and optimise	Inspire and transform
Concern	Today's performance	Tomorrow's readiness
Tools	KPIs, dashboards, budgets	Culture, purpose, communication
Adaptation	Systems thinking, flexibility	**Future focus, fit for purpose.**
In MR context	Operates within the physical/digital structure	**Integrates across physical, digital, and virtual realms**

Managers maintain systems. **Leaders redefine systems**—especially when new realities emerge.

To lead effectively in an MR world, one must:

- See across layers (physical, digital, virtual).
- Think in systems, not silos (this does lead to a potential conflict with ISO standards, which are often viewed as silos)..
- Be digitally fluent and cyber-aware.
- Prioritise trust and resilience as strategic assets.

Closing Thought

As Mixed Reality becomes the default environment of modern enterprise, clarity of roles, domains, and priorities become essential. Understanding the **strategic distinctions between cyber and digital**, embedding **cybersecurity into resilience**, and cultivating **true leadership over mere management** is not optional—it's critical to success.

The core of any economy is millions of SMEs that keep countries and communities 'going'. It is important that MR does not forget these. The 'Foundational Economy' is important.

The Foundational Economy & the Mittelstand: The Hidden Core of Economic Resilience

Executive Summary

Beneath the high-growth tech sectors and digital transformation narratives lies an often-overlooked engine of economic, social, and territorial stability: the **Foundational Economy**. In countries like Germany, this is epitomised by the **Mittelstand**—a network of regionally rooted SMEs that deliver long-term value beyond profit.

This segment represents over **80% of businesses** in most advanced economies. It provides **essential goods, services, and jobs**—forming the bedrock upon which resilient, equitable, and sustainable societies are built. As nations invest in AI, MR, and digital infrastructure, **rebalancing attention toward the foundational economy is no longer optional**—it is strategic necessity.

Defining the Foundational Economy

The **Foundational Economy** consists of the businesses and institutions that **provide everyday essentials**—not luxury or export-focused goods, but the services and infrastructures that underpin daily life and social well-being.

Core sectors include:

- Food production and retail.
- Housing and construction.
- Health and social care.
- Utilities, transport, logistics.
- Local manufacturing, education, finance.

This economy is **place-based, human-cantered**, and often **under-capitalised in innovation agendas**, despite its vital role.

"The foundational economy doesn't just generate GDP—it generates stability, trust, and social cohesion."

The Mittelstand: A Strategic Archetype

The **Mittelstand** in Germany represents a unique form of the foundational economy:

- Predominantly **family-owned SMEs.**
- Long-term **strategic outlook**.
- Deep **regional embeddedness.**
- Strong focus on **craftsmanship, apprenticeships, and workforce development.**
- Often **global leaders in narrow industrial niches.**

These firms combine **technical excellence with human-scale values**—flexibility, loyalty, and commitment to locality.

Strategic Value of the Foundational Economy

Strategic Theme	Foundational Contribution
Resilience	Local jobs, secure supply chains, economic shock absorption
Inclusion	Supports rural and regional economies, not just metropolitan hubs
Sustainability	Encourages circular economies, resource-conscious practices
Innovation	Focus on incremental, contextual, and applied solutions
Stability	Anchors intergenerational wealth and regional balance

While often overlooked in high-tech narratives, these sectors **protect against systemic fragility**—particularly in times of crisis or transition (unless damaged beyond repair by political vandalism).

Challenges and Opportunities in the MR Age

The Foundational Economy is **strategically vulnerable**:

- Digitally under-supported, and at risk of multiple cyber threats.
- Increasingly exposed to supply chain disruption and talent drain.
- Often excluded from innovation funding, MR adoption, and policy design.

Yet, it is also **strategically ripe**:
- High potential for AI-assisted operations (e.g., predictive maintenance, smart logistics).
- New value in MR applications (e.g., training in skilled trades, remote diagnostics).
- Enormous untapped trust and loyalty capital.

"The Foundational Economy is not behind—it's waiting to be engaged on its own terms."

Strategic Recommendations

- **Digital Equity**: Create tailored innovation programs that suit SME scale and context.
- **Resilience Strategy**: Embed foundational sectors into national resilience planning (not just GDP metrics).
- **Financial Instruments**: Offer capital models designed for long-termism and local reinvestment.
- **Cybersecurity for SMEs**: Provide regionally delivered, subsidised cyber-readiness programs.
- **MR Inclusion**: Build virtual training, visualisation, and planning tools into foundational sectors.

Conclusion: Rebuilding from the Core

The Foundational Economy—and Mittelstand-type firms—are **not a relic of the past, but a prerequisite for the future**. As we scale up AI, MR, and smart systems, we must also **scale down strategy to local economies** that quietly carry the weight of daily life.

Investing in foundational sectors is not just fair—it's **future-proofing the economy at its roots**.

Build up the digital. But never forget to anchor it in the foundational.

On 7th February 2025 Dr Cheryl Robinson wrote in Forbes magazine as follows:

'These Outdated Leadership Styles Are Ruining Careers. Don't Let Yours Be Next

Younger generations are no longer tolerating traditional workplace leadership styles.

Leadership has evolved, but unfortunately, some leaders are still stuck in the past—clinging to outdated styles that belong in a history book, not the modern workplace. If you're ruling with an iron fist like a 1950s CEO or ghosting your team like a disengaged manager, it's time for a reality check.

Autocratic and laissez-faire leadership styles aren't just old-school but career killers. Employees today want collaboration, respect, and a voice, not a boss who micromanages their every move or, worse, disappears when they need guidance. If you're guilty of these leadership missteps, don't panic. You can reinvent your approach and lead with impact.

Millennials have stepped in to replace Baby Boomers, bringing fresh innovation and more democratic leadership styles. However, 63% of Millennials feel their companies fail to support their leadership development.

The Pitfalls Of Autocratic Leadership
Autocratic leadership follows a command-and-control model where the leader makes all major decisions with little input from employees. While this style may be effective in high-stakes or emergencies, it often creates a rigid, fear-based work environment that discourages employee engagement.

Why It's Outdated
Lack of employee empowerment—Employees feel undervalued and disengage if they are never allowed to contribute ideas or take ownership of their work.

Decreased innovation—New ideas are stifled without open dialogue, limiting an organisation's ability to adapt and compete.

High Turnover—Employees, particularly younger generations, seek meaningful work and autonomy. Autocratic environments push talent away.

How To Shift To An Inclusive Leadership Style
Encourage open communication—Autocratic leaders must foster a culture where employees feel comfortable sharing their thoughts. Active listening, open-door policies and anonymous feedback mechanisms help create a psychologically safe environment.

Empower employees with decision-making opportunities—Delegation isn't a sign of weakness; it's a strategic move that empowers employees and builds trust. Leaders can start by involving teams in smaller decisions and gradually increase autonomy as trust develops.

Focus on coaching, not controlling—Instead of dictating every step, leaders should guide, mentor and support employees. Coaching helps employees develop critical thinking skills and confidence in their abilities.

The Downside Of Laissez-Faire Leadership
Laissez-faire leadership represents the opposite extreme of autocratic leadership. It involves a hands-off approach where employees are given complete autonomy with minimal guidance. While independence is essential, a total lack of structure, support or accountability can lead to disengagement, confusion and a lack of productivity.

Why It's Outdated
Lack of direction and clarity—Employees feel abandoned and unsure about expectations, leading to inconsistent performance.

Decreased accountability—Without leadership oversight, projects can stagnate and poor performance may go unaddressed.

Team dysfunction—When there's no clear leadership, decision-making becomes chaotic, creating conflict and inefficiency.

How To Shift To An Inclusive Leadership Style
Set clear expectations—Communicating clear goals, defining success metrics, and providing regular check-ins ensure employees understand the mission.

Balance autonomy with support—Employees should be free to work independently, but leaders must be available for feedback and problem-solving when needed.

Foster a collaborative environment—A leader's role is to create an ecosystem where employees feel connected and supported. Encouraging team discussions and mentorship programs help maintain engagement.

The most effective leaders today adopt a transformational or servant leadership approach. By shifting away from autocratic or laissez-faire leadership, leaders build high-performing teams that drive long-term business success. It's a balancing act between structure and flexibility, authority and collaboration, and guidance and autonomy.

This book takes this sort of thinking a stage or two further in that it believes only certain leadership styles will work in the future. The key piece missing from this scene setting quote is that there is a major disfunction in leading the physical, virtual, and metaverse worlds. Organisational leaders are still trained by business schools and higher education in 'old ways'.

This quote is not exactly what this book is about and the authors would say that it does not address the question of leadership in the same way. However, for a wide audience it gives a very good introduction to part of what this book is about.

At a strategic level this book on Mixed Reality Leadership (MRL) is about dealing with one of the great challenges of our time:

*'**Mixed Reality Leadership has the potential to democratise information and empower individuals**, but without strong governance, it could just as easily lead to **corporate feudalism**, where a few tech giants control our digital and physical realities.*

*A **decentralised, open Mixed Reality ecosystem** could prevent this, but that requires global cooperation, which is easier said than done. The big question is whether governments will **step up to regulate tech before it's too entrenched**—or if they'll just play catch-up like they did with social media.'*

At an operational level this book serves as a guide to overcoming one of the great operational issues of our time: the failure of most organisations to successfully manage the physical, virtual and metaverse worlds at great risk. CEOs and other C-suite members are increasingly being held personally to account for this, as share prices, in the business world, drop as a result of events.

N.B. The book is focussed on the physical and virtual but metaverse is added because many understand the term as being synonymous with the physical and virtual, it isn't it's a product but the term has moved into general usage, like Hoover.

Rudyard Kipling said, "I keep six honest serving men, they taught me all I knew; Their names are What and Why and When, and How and Where and Who," This quote is about the importance of asking questions and seeking knowledge. In the context of this book, briefly:

Who: This book is about the need for organisational leaders to be across the physical, virtual and metaverse worlds – mixed reality. Strangely, in an increasingly virtual world, this is by no means a norm. This is because, predictably perhaps, organisational leaders (particularly western leaders) still follow a pattern dictated by MBA courses – that completely miss, in all cases (as this is written), leadership in this new mixed reality world.

What: This book is about understanding the organisational leadership needs for the mixed reality world.

Why: This book is needed because there is very little contemporary or historical literature on this subject. Without competent mixed reality leaders our society is at risk. This further demonstrated by the World Economic Forum's view of employment in 2025 summarised thus:

"An estimated 59% (!!) of the global workforce will need reskilling by 2030 — but not everyone will get it!"

That's one of the key insights from the new *World Economic Forum – Future of Jobs Report* 2025. Based on data from 1,000+ companies, 26 industries, and 14 million workers, the report outlines what's changing — and what's coming next. *And it's loud and clear: Artificial intelligence will reshape the labour market faster than most expect.*

AI could become a general-purpose technology as transformative as steam engines were in the 19th-century Industrial

Revolution. There are clear signs that over the next 2-3 years, AI will flip business and labour upside down.

According to the report the top 10 Core Skills for 2030 (and expected to rise in importance):

1. AI and big data
2. Technological literacy
3. Creative thinking
4. Resilience, flexibility and agility
5. Analytical thinking
6. Leadership and social influence
7. Motivation and self-awareness
8. Systems thinking
9. Talent management
10. Curiosity and lifelong learning

Interesting to read that it's not just about AI and tech — but also about adaptability, creativity, and the human edge that machines can't replicate. So it's not just about mastering AI.

It's about being human — and being ready to grow.

Other standout insights from the report:
▶ There will be 170M jobs created and 92M jobs lost by 2030.
▶ 39% of current skills will be outdated.
▶ AI is both the #1 disruptor and opportunity.
▶ Main drivers for this disruption in the job market: tech adoption, climate goals, ESG, demographics.

Let's be honest here: Upskilling is no longer a perk. You're either building the future — or watching it pass you by.

How to adapt to these changes?

Start learning AI now! Understand the basics of AI and experiment with AI tools in your domain. Keep learning — AI evolves every day!

AI is bringing many challenges, but also new opportunities for people who are ready to adapt! It is not the strongest of the species that survives, nor the most intelligent that survives. It is the one that is the most adaptable to change.

Core Skills in 2030

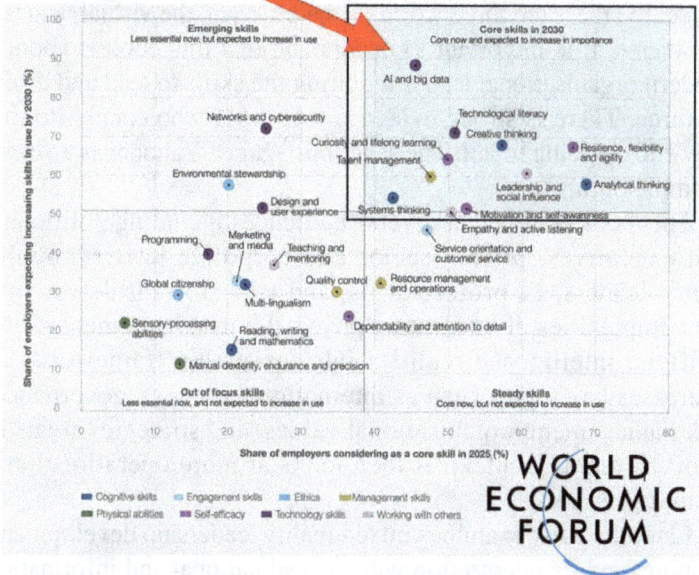

Figure 1: World Economic Forum 'Future of Jobs Report' 2025

This is from a LinkedIn piece by Andreas Horn, Head of AI at IBM. The World Economic Forum 'Future of Jobs Report' is the source of the data.

When: This book suggests there is a current leadership crisis in organisations and therefore this issue needs to be addressed now.

How: This book suggests that understanding, training and horizon scanning of the mixed reality world will help organisational leaders.

Where: This book suggests a need for higher education training courses and suggests that leadership academies of all descriptions should all carry some form of educational mixed reality leadership programme.

This book on 'Mixed Reality Leadership' therefore explores the critical leadership skills required to navigate organisations operating across physical, virtual, and metaverse environments.

A point of clarity: as briefly noted, the metaverse is a good shorthand but perhaps a little inaccurate because the two worlds–the physical and virtual–do operate independently of the metaverse. So, really, there are three worlds – the physical, the virtual, and the metaverse. It is important to understand that this book is about a modern organisational leader requiring the skills to lead and direct all three. There is strong evidence that those who cannot do this may end up going to jail. The sanctions against Yahoo was an early example of this.

This book is aimed at diverse audiences including politicians and executives, private sector and corporate leaders, public sector leaders, IT professionals, and educators. It delves into the complexities of integrating physical, virtual, augmented and artificial intelligence realities into leadership frameworks. It addresses key topics such as international context, governance, risk management, organisational values, and strategic threats in a mixed reality context. It then looks at more operational and technical issues.

Later the book examines mixed reality leadership development, training, and its intersection with critical national and information infrastructures, Obstructive Marketing, highlighting vulnerabilities in key sectors such as defence, health, finance, and energy. The book concludes with a forward-looking analysis of the next technological supercycle, underscoring the urgency of proactive mixed reality leadership in an evolving mixed reality landscape. Annexes are signposts to improvement.

Mixed Reality Leadership describes the leadership mindset required to manage organisations operating across physical, virtual and metaverse realms. In today's interconnected world, where most organisations navigate environments combining physical operations with virtual technologies such as artificial intelligence (AI) augmented reality (AR) and virtual reality (VR), leaders must adapt to this evolving landscape. Effective governance in this blended environment is crucial.

Trust in employees, especially those assuming leadership roles, is vital for organisational safety. Furthermore, the outdated division between managers and workers must be replaced by a more cooperative and trusting relationship. This book advocates fostering collaboration among leaders, managers, and employees to enhance security and resilience in a mixed reality world. The pace is fast, adaptation and agility in encompassing change will be critical.

But first it is useful to look at existing leadership styles. These are the ones that Mixed Reality Leadership seeks to either reform or replace.

Existing Leadership Styles

There are about ten recognised major leadership styles. Each has their own key characteristics, advantages, and potential drawbacks:

Transactional Leadership

Definition: This leadership style is based on structure, rewards, and punishments to drive employee performance. Leaders set clear goals and monitor progress closely.

Key Characteristics:

- Emphasis on tasks, rules, and procedures
- Clear chain of command
- Performance-based rewards and penalties
- Short-term focus

Advantages:

✓ Increases efficiency and productivity
✓ Works well in structured environments (e.g., military, manufacturing)
✓ Provides clear expectations

Challenges:

- ✗ May discourage creativity and innovation
- ✗ Focus on compliance rather than employee development

Example (Nation-State): China – The Chinese government operates with a highly structured, rule-based approach, emphasising discipline, efficiency, and economic performance.

Example (Organisation): McDonald's – The fast-food giant follows strict operational procedures, with rewards and penalties tied to employee performance and adherence to corporate policies.

Transactional leadership is not an appropriate style for Mixed Reality Leadership.

Transformational Leadership

Definition: Transformational leaders inspire and motivate employees by creating a compelling vision, encouraging innovation, and fostering professional growth.

Key Characteristics:

- High levels of motivation and enthusiasm
- Visionary and future-oriented
- Focus on individual and organisational growth
- Encourages innovation and adaptability

Advantages:

- ✓ Boosts employee morale and job satisfaction
- ✓ Encourages creativity and long-term success
- ✓ Strengthens company culture

Challenges:

- ✗ Requires strong communication and charisma
- ✗ Can be demanding for leaders and employees

Example (Nation-State): New Zealand (Jacinda Ardern's leadership) – Ardern's leadership during crises (e.g., COVID-19, Christchurch attacks) focused on empathy, inspiration, and collective vision.

Example (Organisation): Tesla (Elon Musk's leadership, at least initially) – Tesla pushes the boundaries of innovation in electric vehicles and space travel, inspiring employees to achieve revolutionary goals. (Although this is changing as this is written).

Transformational leadership is an underpinning trait for Mixed Reality Leadership.

Servant Leadership

Definition: This leadership style prioritises employees' well-being and development, ensuring their needs are met before focusing on organisational success.

Key Characteristics:

- Focus on empathy, listening, and support
- Encourages collaboration and shared decision-making
- Promotes ethical leadership and social responsibility

Advantages:

- ✓ Builds trust and strong relationships
- ✓ Improves employee engagement and satisfaction
- ✓ Fosters a supportive workplace culture

Challenges:

✗ Can be time-consuming and less efficient in fast-paced environments

✗ May struggle in highly competitive industries

Example (Nation-State): Finland – Finland's government priorities social welfare, education, and sustainability, focusing on the well-being of its citizens.

Example (Organisation): Patagonia – The company prioritises employee well-being and environmental responsibility, actively involving employees in decision-making.

The British Army has, traditionally, been an example of servant leadership The book 'Serve to Lead' used to be given to every cadet. The subject of current leadership styles in the British Army requires another book.

Servant leadership is an underpinning trait for Mixed Reality Leadership.

Autocratic Leadership

Definition: The leader makes decisions independently with little input from employees, expecting strict compliance and control.

Key Characteristics:

• Top-down decision-making
• Clear hierarchy and authority
• Strict rules and enforcement

Advantages:

✓ Effective in crisis situations requiring quick decisions
✓ Works well in industries requiring precision and discipline

Challenges:

- ✗ Can lead to low employee morale
- ✗ Limits creativity and team input

Example (Nation-State): North Korea – The government maintains strict, centralised control, with little input from citizens.

Example (Organisation): Foxconn – The Apple supplier has been known for its rigid management structure, strict rules, and high-pressure work environment.

Autocratic Leadership should be avoided, if possible, in implementing Mixed Reality Leadership; but elements may be required because of the pace likely to be needed.

Democratic (Participative) Leadership

Definition: Leaders encourage employees to contribute ideas and participate in decision-making while providing guidance.

Key Characteristics:

- Open communication and teamwork
- Collaborative decision-making
- Encourages creativity and innovation

Advantages:

- ✓ Boosts employee engagement and motivation
- ✓ Encourages diverse ideas and innovation

Challenges:

- ✗ Decision-making can be slow
- ✗ Requires a high level of trust and communication

Example (Nation-State): Switzerland – Switzerland's direct democracy allows citizens to vote on key policies, emphasising collective decision-making.

Example (Organisation): Google (Alphabet Inc.) – Encourages open communication, collaboration, and employee participation in major projects.

Democratic Leadership is a trait of Mixed Reality Leadership.

Laissez-Faire Leadership

Definition: Leaders provide minimal supervision, allowing employees to take charge of their tasks and decisions.

Key Characteristics:
- High degree of autonomy for employees
- Limited involvement from leadership
- Encourages self-management

Advantages:
✓ Empowers skilled and self-motivated employees
✓ Encourages innovation and independent thinking

Challenges:
✗ Can lead to lack of direction or accountabilit
✗ May not be suitable for employees who need guidance

Example (Nation-State): Estonia – Estonia embraces minimal government intervention in business, allowing digital entrepreneurs to operate freely.

Example (Organisation): GitHub – Encourages self-directed work, allowing employees to manage projects independently.
    In an ideal world Laissez-Faire Leadership would define Mixed

Reality Leadership. However, it is likely that other leadership styles with be required to achieve the needed aims.

Charismatic Leadership

Definition: Leaders rely on personal charm, vision, and persuasive communication to inspire employees.

Key Characteristics:

- Strong personal influence
- Inspires enthusiasm and loyalty
- Highly effective in motivating teams

Advantages:

✓ Creates strong emotional connections with employees
✓ Drives organisational change and innovation

Challenges:

✗ Success depends on the leader's personal influence
✗ Can lead to over-reliance on one individual

Example (Nation-State): France (Emmanuel Macron's leadership) – Macron's leadership style relies on personal charisma, communication, and persuasion to influence policies and people.

Example (Organisation): Virgin Group (Richard Branson's leadership) – Branson's enthusiastic, bold leadership style energises his companies and employees.

Charismatic leadership may be required to get Mixed Reality Leadership off the ground in some organisations. However, it is likely to be unhelpful in building a true Mixed Reality Leadership organisation.

Situational Leadership

Definition: Leaders adapt their style based on the situation and the needs of employees.

Key Characteristics:

- Flexible and adaptable
- Adjusts leadership approach based on employee competency and motivation
- Focuses on development and coaching

Advantages:

- ✓ Highly effective for dynamic environments
- ✓ Supports employee growth and performance

Challenges:

- ✗ Requires strong emotional intelligence
- ✗ Can be difficult to apply consistently

Example (Nation-State): Germany (Angela Merkel's leadership) – Merkel adapted her leadership style based on different crises, from economic challenges to the refugee crisis.

Example (Organisation): Microsoft (Satya Nadella's leadership) – Nadella transitioned Microsoft from a traditional tech company to a cloud-driven, innovative business, adapting strategies over time.

Mixed Reality Leadership addresses leadership in the physical, virtual and metaverse worlds. These are rapidly evolving environments. Situational leadership is a required subset of Mixed Reality Leadership.

Bureaucratic Leadership

Definition: Leaders follow strict policies, rules, and procedures to maintain order and consistency.

Key Characteristics:

- Structured and rule-based approach
- Focuses on hierarchy and formal procedures
- Emphasises compliance and standardisation

Advantages:

- ✓ Ensures stability and consistency
- ✓ Works well in government and large corporations

Challenges:

- ✗ Can be rigid and resistant to change
- ✗ Limits creativity and innovation

Example (Nation-State): Russia – The Russian government maintains a highly bureaucratic structure, focusing on formal policies and hierarchical decision-making.

Example (Organisation): The U.S. Department of Defence (Pentagon) – A strict chain of command, adherence to policies, and structured decision-making define its operations. (At least historically, who knows under Trump?).

Bureaucratic Leadership would be wholly inappropriate for Mixed Reality Leadership.

Strategic Leadership

Definition: Balances long-term vision with short-term operational goals, ensuring that the organisation remains competitive.

Key Characteristics:

- Forward-thinking and goal-oriented
- Balances innovation with practical execution
- Considers external market trends and internal capabilities

Advantages:

✓ Helps organisations stay ahead of competitors

✓ Encourages long-term success and adaptability

Challenges:

✗ Requires strong analytical and decision-making skills

✗ Can be challenging to implement in rapidly changing environments

Example (Nation-State): Singapore – Singapore's long-term vision for economic growth, sustainability, and innovation makes it a global strategic leader.

Example (Organisation): Amazon – Jeff Bezos led Amazon with a long-term vision, expanding the company into multiple industries while maintaining a strong strategic focus.

Strategic Leadership is a key trait of Mixed Reality Leadership.

Final Thoughts on Existing Leadership Styles

Each leadership style has its strengths and weaknesses, and effective leaders often blend multiple styles depending on their organisation's needs. Mixed Reality Leadership needs to take the best from Transformational, Servant, Democratic, Laissez Faire, Charismatic, Situational and Strategic Leadership styles.

Defining Mixed Reality Leadership

Mixed Reality Leadership refers to the leadership approach necessary for leading and managing organisations that operate across physical, virtual, and metaverse worlds. With most organisations now navigating blended environments involving technologies such extended reality (XR), augmented reality (AR), virtual reality (VR), artificial intelligence (AI) and other immersive digital platforms, leaders must effectively integrate and govern these complex systems. Thus, Mixed Reality Leadership is defined by an eclectic understanding of leadership applied in an equally eclectic manner, value driven, at pace and with agility to the physical, virtual (cyber and digital) and metaverse worlds.

Governance in Mixed Reality looks like:

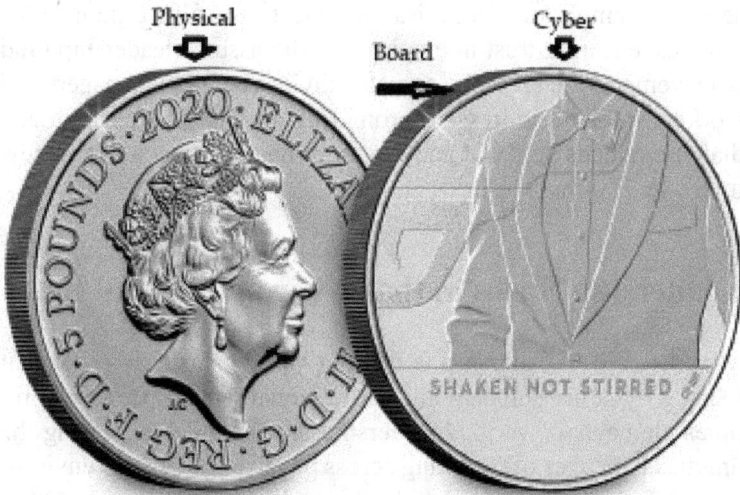

Figure 2: Governance of the Mixed Reality World

In Figure 2 the physical world is one side of the coin, the virtual (cyber and digital) the other, the rim represents governance and the whole coin is the physical, virtual, metaverse, or cyber/digital (the conjoined world) under appropriate governance.

A core element of this leadership model is the emphasis on values, particularly in the context of cybersecurity. Ensuring IT safety and cybersecurity is not merely a technical task—it is fundamentally a human issue shaped by cultural values. This should never be forgotten.

Different regions approach this issue in varying ways; the USA emphasises individualism and innovation, Europe prioritises privacy and data protection, leading to distinct responses to cybersecurity threats. Moreover, the automation paradox, where increased reliance on automated systems reduces necessary discipline in system management, has contributed to a rise in cyberattacks and ransom-ware incidents. In today's world, warfare is no longer confined to physical battlefields but extends to technical control, social control and manipulation by virtual means.

Consequently, values are critical to organisational success in the mixed reality environment. Maitland Hyslop's 2007 work on Critical Information Infrastructures highlights the enduring relevance of the USA's founding values, which is interesting in the second Trump term. Organisations must re-evaluate their value systems, ensuring trust in employees who assume leadership (and management) roles. Lastly, outdated divides between managers and workers must be addressed, promoting a collaborative approach that strengthens personal and organisational resilience in this new mixed reality era.

Leadership Styles in the Cyber and Digital Era

Mixed Reality Leadership is distinct and increasingly critical in today's dynamic personal and professional landscape, as it combines elements of various leadership styles while addressing the unique challenges of operating across physical and virtual environments. Transformational Leadership, which focuses on inspiring innovation and driving change, is vital in the mixed reality realm, where constant technological evolution demands visionary thinking. Democratic Leadership characterised by entrusting tasks to team members, plays a crucial role in fostering autonomy within geographically dispersed teams in virtual spaces. Similarly, Autocratic Leadership, which provides clear direction and confidence, is necessary in high-stakes decision-making, particularly when managing cybersecurity and IT crises, the change to Mixed Reality Leadership being one. Transactional Leadership, emphasising structured rewards and discipline, ensures that operational goals are met in environments where routine management is often overlooked due to automation. Laissez-Faire Leadership is equally important, as collaboration across diverse, cross-functional teams enhances adaptability and problem-solving in mixed reality settings. Servant Leadership, which prioritises the growth and well-being of employees, helps build trust in virtual teams and fosters loyalty in a MR workforce.

Conversely, the lack of leadership in virtual spaces can result in disarray, increasing spaces of vulnerability and destruction in relation to cyber threats and diminishing organisational cohesion. Mixed Reality Leadership integrates the strengths of these styles, offering a balanced approach that navigates both human and technological complexities. This is increasingly important because organisations now operate in a mixed reality where the physical, virtual and metaverse intertwine, requiring leaders to adapt swiftly, inspire innovation, and foster trust, ensuring long-term resilience and success.

An author's own definition of leadership is as follows:

Leadership is the ability to persuade individuals and teams to go in a particular direction by establishing a set of shared values, demonstrated by personal example and professionalism, with a consequent belief, communicated to and accepted by all, that life will be better for the experience. (© MP Hyslop 2021).

In a Mixed Reality context this can be modified for the particular use:

Mixed Reality Leadership is the ability to persuade individuals and teams to engage with the Mixed Reality and XR, AR, VR, AI worlds by establishing a common trust based on a set of shared values, epitomised by personal example and professionalism, communicated to and accepted by all that personal and professional lives will be better for the experience. (© MP Hyslop 2025).

Mixed Reality and Modern Agile Conflict in Information Technology (IT)

Mixed Reality Leadership and Modern Agile Conflict, particularly in the realm of IT, require a nuanced understanding of geopolitical dynamics, technological capabilities, and cybersecurity threats across regions.

The USA leads in innovation and technology (so far), with significant investment in AI, cloud infrastructure, and cybersecurity. Mixed Reality Leadership here involves balancing innovation with national security, especially against cyber threats from foreign adversaries and non-state actors.

Europe prioritises privacy and data protection, as reflected in General Data Protection Regulations. Its approach to Mixed Reality Leadership emphasises ethical governance, digital sovereignty, and cybersecurity cooperation across member states to counter evolving IT threats.

The Middle East and Russia often engage in hybrid and mixed reality warfare, including cyber operations and disinformation campaigns. Mixed Reality Leadership focuses on defending against state-sponsored cyberattacks and securing critical information infrastructures in a volatile geopolitical landscape.

India, as a growing tech powerhouse, faces challenges in scaling cybersecurity and managing a vast IT workforce. Mixed Reality Leadership here involves fostering innovation while strengthening cybersecurity frameworks to protect critical sectors. As in the physical world India adopts a neutral stance in the virtual and metaverse worlds.

China, with its advanced technological ecosystem and focus on digital control, emphasises blockchain, AI development and cyber offense capabilities. It competes directly with the USA in a number of virtual areas, AI being the latest as this is written.

Iran conducts sophisticated cyber operations and is a regional cyber power. Leadership involves managing cyber threats and responding to sanctions that limit access to global technology.

North Korea is known for state-sponsored cybercrime, including ransomware and financial hacking, leadership in countering North Korea involves strategic defence and international coordination.

Non-State Actors such as **technology companies, large corporates,** cyberterrorists and hacking groups pose unique challenges.

Dark and Deep Web platforms facilitate illegal activities, including data breaches and weapon sales. Leadership requires constant vigilance, law enforcement collaboration, and technological solutions to counter these threats.

Mixed Reality Leadership must navigate the delicate balance between state control, corporate innovation, and global cybersecurity cooperation. It must focus on intelligence sharing and proactive cyber defence. That said, it should be a competitive advantage to those who successfully adopt it.

Strategic Challenges and Opportunities

The term, pneumonic, MADMENACE highlights critical strategic issues with widespread global implications, requiring immediate attention. Modern Agile Conflict, involving multi-vector warfare with diverse and simultaneous threats, challenges traditional leadership and defence models and affects everyone.

An Invisible Apocalypse, the potential collapse of Western IT systems, threatens global stability, commerce, and communication. Ideological tensions among Democracies, Plutocracies, and Non-Aligned states shape governance models and international relations.

Migration, driven by conflict, climate change, and economic disparity, poses significant political and humanitarian challenges worldwide.

Core societal pillars like Education, Freedom, and Free Speech face increasing threats from authoritarian regimes and internal pressures, endangering personal liberties.

Nuclear Proliferation remains a critical concern, with potential for catastrophic conflict.

The rise of Artificial Intelligence is transforming industries and raising ethical issues around privacy, surveillance, and inequality.

Meanwhile, Climate Change, combined with crises in Fossil Fuels, Food Security, and Water, pose interconnected risks to human survival.

Evolution, both biological and technological, forces humanity to adapt to rapid innovations. Together, these issues form MADMENACE, underscoring the need for coordinated leadership and cooperation.

Threats stemming from these challenges include organised cyber warfare and crime. Cyberwarfare is central to adversaries' strategies. Key players include Russia, with its history of cybercrime and geopolitical tensions, China, driven by hegemonic ambitions, Iran, with its disruptive and religious motivations, and North Korea, known for criminal cyber activities. Other actors also engage in organised cybercrime (such as recently seen in scamming factories in Cambodia etc.), posing further risks to global security.

Global and Organisational Context

Modern Agile Conflict involves 42 distinct conflict vectors, many of which are cyber-related, making it a complex and evolving threat landscape. In the international context, organisations must navigate both the virtual and real worlds, yet they often struggle with effective virtual governance, resulting in poor oversight of digital and cyber operations. Risk management for virtual assets tends to be inadequate, with organisations either underestimating risks or failing to properly address them. (As readers of the 'Hitchhikers Guide to the Galaxy' will be aware 42 is the answer to everything).

A clear risk appetite—the level of risk an organisation is willing to accept—becomes crucial in making informed strategic decisions. Additionally, virtual compliance is frequently overlooked due to costs, leaving many organisations vulnerable to breaches and regulatory penalties. Adopting a systems thinking approach is essential to understanding interconnected risks and ensuring that digital and cyber defences are robust. Hybrid hardening, the process of securing both physical and virtual assets, is critical to counter modern threats. Despite the rise of virtual zero-trust frameworks, organisations still need total employee trust to operate effectively, making human factors key.

The complexities of managing all these aspects highlight the challenge of Mixed Reality Leadership, which requires balancing innovation, security, and trust. Cyber threats from state actors like the USA, China, Russia, Iran, and North Korea dominate modern conflict, each employing unique strategies to disrupt and destabilise opponents. The UK, while reasonably well advanced in cybersecurity, faces persistent threats from these adversaries. Looking ahead, future-proofing systems and addressing emerging cyber issues will be vital for maintaining resilience in an increasingly digital world.

The Fragility of the Global Virtual Technical Infrastructure

The global virtual technical infrastructure is increasingly fragile due to its complexity and dependence on interconnected and often unprotected (physical and virtual) systems. This infrastructure comprises critical components such as data highways, which can be mapped in correlation with old trade routes, and essential frameworks, which reflect the hegemonic history of nations. Among the most critical elements is DNS server security, whose vulnerability can disrupt global internet operations. (Jenkinson, 2025) The infrastructure spans across key regions, including the USA, UK, Europe, the Middle East, the Far East, and Africa, each with varying levels of technological development and security readiness. A PESTEL analysis highlights the primary factors influencing this fragility.

Politically, government backdoors and national cybersecurity policies, such as the UK's approach, pose both risks and opportunities. In the USA the tech giants are dominating the political agenda.

Economically, the USA is experiencing a boom driven by a new supercycle in artificial intelligence, biotechnology, and convergent ecosystems, while other regions strive to keep pace.

Socially, technology exerts significant influence on various aspects of life, including psychological impacts, criminal activities, education, and the dissemination of information, where distinguishing real from fake news becomes critical. These social changes necessitate heightened IT safety and security at national, organisational, and personal levels, particularly in regard to DNS servers.

The interplay of political, economic, and social factors underscores the need for robust and resilient virtual infrastructure to safeguard global stability and technological progress in an era marked by rapid digital transformation.

Environmentally there are challenges from XR, AR, VR and AI.

Legal structures remain well behind the technical innovation curve and with different rules in different regions.

The next chapter looks at what an organisational baseline might look like in order to progress to a Mixed Reality led organisation. It also includes a diagram on global context which supports the context comments above. The baseline itself is a challenge. That being said, most organisations do need to have met it by now, if they are to progress.

Chapter 2

Establishing a Baseline for Mixed Reality Leadership

This chapter opens by asking the obvious question: 'Where to start in order to create a Mixed Reality led organisation?' All organisations are different but all need, and should have, an Enterprise Information Security Plan (EISP). This is a complicated and complex issue. It needs some detailed attention by the Board, Directors and Management. This Chapter (and Chapter 3) is basically a copy of the plan an author developed for an Enterprise Information Security Plan at Harvard University. This can be interpreted as a baseline for moving to Mixed Reality Leadership. If an organisation has not yet got such a plan in place, and operating, then moving to a Mixed Reality Leadership structure will be difficult because the culture of the organisation is unlikely to be mature enough to cope with the shift. This brings us to pace. Pace is required both to institute the plan below, if there is not one, and/or to move to Mixed Reality Leadership. This is involves Extended Reality (XR), involving Artificial Intelligence (AI), Extended Reality (XR) blending the physical and virtual. Mixed Reality (MR), Extended Reality (XR), Virtual Reality (VR), Augmented Reality (AR), and Artificial Intelligence (AI))and Mixed Reality (MR) are moving at such a pace that unless organisations re-organise around the plan and a leadership model they will be quickly overtaken by events. Even this book is being written at pace to try and get it published before events overtake it.

This is not a leadership chapter. This chapter sets out a series of management tasks to be completed before an organisation can move to becoming a Mixed Reality led organisation. It is a precursor to

Mixed Reality leadership. It provides the discipline, routines and checks necessary to provide the freedom to lead.

This plan is written for a notional Middle East insurance business XXX. However, if an organisation's name is inserted in place of XXX then a good baseline plan, with sensible and obvious amendments for the new target organisation, is established. This is a detailed, time consuming, and expensive, piece of work. It is a necessary precursor to developing a Mixed Reality Leadership approach for an organisation – and the authors would say any organisation these days.

	Title: Project Amin	Date: 1st February 2025
Revision: Final	Author: Maitland Hyslop	Approved: xxx
Security Classification	Confidential: Commercial in Confidence	

Briefing Paper: Project AMIN (Notional Middle East Insurance Business)

Cybersecurity Risk Mitigation, Cybersecurity Attack Simulation, Cybersecurity Emergency Response Plan and Associated Business Resilience Plan.

Reference A: Minutes: Project Amin Project Briefing Meeting, XXX.

1. Project Name

Project AMIN (Notional Insurance Business)

2. Introduction and Vision

Project AMIN has, initially, four key sections and objectives. The XXX organisation does not have a Cybersecurity plan of any kind – and thus these are also seen as strategic objectives of the organisation.

- Project AMIN Cyber Risk Management Strategy.
  - Project AMIN Context and Reconnaissance.
  - Project AMIN Cyber-Risk Management.
- Project AMIN Cyber-Security Attack Simulation.
- Project AMIN Cyber-Security Emergency Response Plan.
- Project AMIN Associated Business Resilience Plan.

The project will be approached in that order.

Vision: XXX will create and maintain an initially secure and ultimately resilient Cybersecurity ecosystem permitting the core insurance business to thrive in a protected environment, that also safeguards the owners, shareholders, stakeholders and partners.

3. XXX Background

XXX is the National Health Insurance Company.

XXX offers a comprehensive range of health insurance solutions for both citizens and residents.

The Government/Rulers own 80% of XXX shares, with the remaining 20% owned by European based YYY, who is also a strategic partner. XXX is part of a wider Government/Ruler investment portfolio. XXX covers more than 3 million members.

XXX provides Health Fund Management and administration services on behalf of several Government entities, with the main one being the Government.

XXX offers several private insurance products across the country under a separate portfolio

XXX has contracted 3,000 healthcare providers in the country (with more elsewhere), with direct billing services across the country.

XXX has specific relationships, and IT connections, with over 20 clinics both within and without the country.

XXX supplies a Health Insurance product to Government, Residents, non-residents (largely European and South Asian expatriates) and others on a bespoke basis.

In 2021, XXX launched its digital branch services, which allowed members to access XXX's entire portfolio of services online. Following the successful launch of the service, XXX has now made its digital branch offering available to all its 3 million members across the country.

XXX competes within a competitive international marketplace and within a regional marketplace which suffers from military conflict, religious conflict, economic downturn, economic crime, and cyber-crime. Cyber-crime is rising and is under-reported. A specific issue is the protection of information regarding senior personnel within the region.

The company has recently moved into a purpose-built new office and has 12 outlier offices within and without the country. The COVID-19 pandemic has made managing the business from a personnel and IT perspective very difficult.

4. Project Requirements

The initial requirements are for:

- Project AMIN Cyber Risk Management Strategy.
  - Project AMIN Context and Reconnaissance.
  - Project AMIN Cyber-Risk Management.
- Project AMIN Cyber-Security Attack Simulation.
- Project AMIN Cyber-Security Emergency Response Plan.
- Project AMIN Associated Business Resilience Plan.

These are to assist in the development of XXX key strategic goals of:

- The leading and most profitable regional medical insurance business.
- The leading and lowest cost regional medical claims organisation.

By:

- Defending the organisation from cyber-attack by state and non-state actors.
- Safeguarding owners, partners, staff and data from virtual, physical, social and legal compromise.
- Cultivating relevant talent and expertise.
- Creating market, business, and virtual opportunities by way of excellence in Cybersecurity.

This document describes how the organisation can **start** to address these goals and objectives.

5. Proposed Approach Cyber Risk Management Strategy

5.1 Context and Reconnaissance

The idea of context and reconnaissance in Cyber/IT/Business Continuity was introduced some ten years ago. This has now spread to include network security and associated issues. Context and reconnaissance are the starting points of every strategic decision. In military terms, 'What is the situation?' This becomes increasingly important in a data centric age. Context has become critical to the managing of businesses over the last few years.

The following is the Godfearing Model which is an attempt to visualise context at high level in a geopolitical and multinational arena. (N.B. Godfearing has nothing to do with God, just a reflection of the first letter of key words).

This model depicts on the left-hand side a 'western based' approach to a number of political, economic, social, technological, environmental and legal issues. On the right-hand side are the 'antitheses' to such an approach. In the middle, a potential helpful compromise position. In the background is the omnipresent IT environment and the omnipresent Organised Crime environment. Also noted is the relative decline of the North and West of the world, and the relative rise of the South and East. This is a suitable model for XXX.

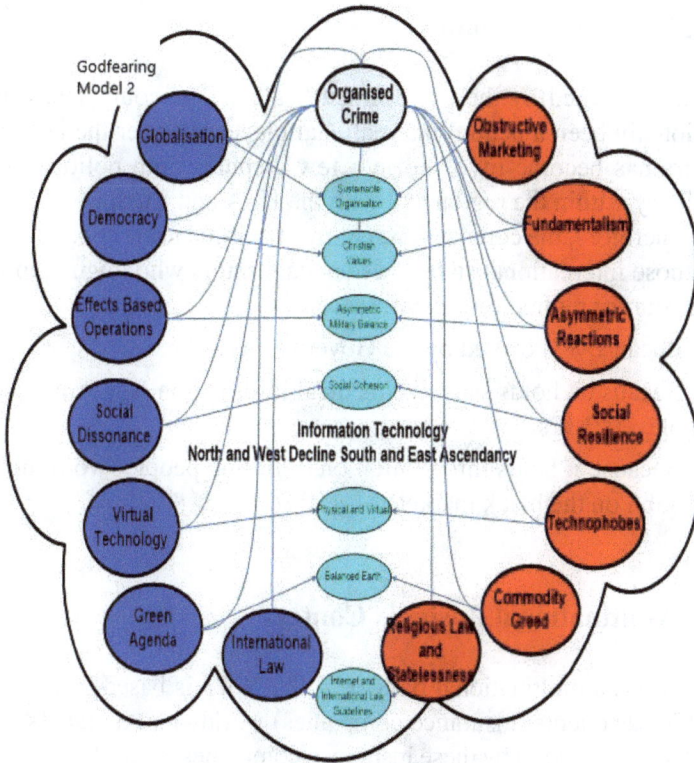

Figure 3: Godfearing Model 2 (© Maitland Hyslop 2011 – 2025)

Against this model XXX operates in a country:

- That operates in a global environment.
- That is an effective dictatorship in a Muslim region.
- That practices asymmetric responses against larger players.
- That is a regional leader in virtual technology.
- That relies heavily on two commodities to generate income.
- That practices Muslim religious law (Sharia) nationally; but participates in various international legal frameworks.
- That is highly connected nationally and internationally from an IT perspective and sits on an international data hub.
- That is known to harbour significant Organised Crime elements of an international nature.

5.2 Geopolitical Context

XXX is owned by the Government/Rulers. The country has traditionally been a neutral international player but over the last few years has become involved in a few disputes both political and military within the region and with the USA and Russia.

Therefore, the company, XXX, must assume itself to be a target of those international state and non-state actors who might oppose the country regime for several reasons, e.g.:

- Because it is owned by the Government/Rulers.
- Because it holds sensitive medical information on key national players/VIPs.
- Because it holds information on 3 million people (worth up to $3bn on the black market).

5.3 Multinational Business Context

XXX has a multinational partner YYY. YYY is based in Europe. YYY has clients (insurance companies) worldwide. It assures part of the risk covered by these insurance companies, as well as providing comprehensive advice on the insurance business. YYY has more than 50 Business Units around the world. YYY provides reinsurance cover for life, health, casualty, cyber, transport, aviation, space, fire and engineering business. In 2018, gross premiums written in the reinsurance segment amounted to around $50bn.

YYY's direct insurance arm serves 35 million clients.

YYY is a serious target for organised crime.

5.4 National Political Context

The national political context is that the absolute ruler is ill, and the current power base lies with a nominated successor. Data is sought on both these individuals. The country is otherwise relatively stable but is a target for two major regional powers.

5.5 National Business Context

The national business context is stable except for the impact of COVID-19 which has, as with everything else, had a significant impact on the economy and, in relation to XXX, an increase in health insurance claims. In 2025 the Trump tariffs threaten to destabilise the situation if no bi-lateral deals are resolved quickly.

5.6 Compliance

Compliance issues are an important part of the risk landscape.
The compliance environment for XXX is complex.

- Financial compliance is driven by USA HIPAA and Sarbanes Oxley type reporting.

- Payments are taken by Credit Card, but the company does not absolutely conform to PCI Standards.

- European Partner compliance, on the other hand, is driven by European legislation such as the General Data Protection Regulations.

- Some health clinic partners conform to the HIMSS 7 standard of information management.

- Insurance Compliance is based on recommendations from the UK's Chartered Insurance Institute and can be best summarised by the Qatari Financial Centre Regulatory Authority. (XXX is not in Qatar, but these regulations formalise an approach to the market by insurance companies that is very similar to the approach that needs to be adopted by XXX).

5.7 Strategic Business Cybersecurity Context

At a strategic level the business has a Board, appointed largely by patronage, and a relatively new CEO. It does not have a CISO.

- The Board needs to establish itself along the lines of the Saxton Bampfylde model (qv).

- The Board needs upgrading in terms of its understanding of Cyber Threats.
- The CEO has recently taken over from a long serving expatriate CEO; and is collegiate in nature. The CEO's knowledge of cyber needs improving.
- The Board needs to appoint a CISO.
- The Board needs to create an Executive Committee with oversight of Cybersecurity.
- There is no Enterprise Information Security Plan.

5.8 Operational and Tactical Reconnaissance

Data and data privacy are defined differently in different parts of the world:

- The USA harvests data for corporate and government purposes with scant overall regard for the individual, although this is changing.
- Europe has introduced GDPR to protect individual data.
- Europe and the USA are constantly in battle regarding data and personal privacy.
- Apple has a pro-individual privacy policy (in the main); Google/Android do not.
- Clouds acquire information and data, not always with the permission of the client; care must be taken as to where clouds are based.
- China has an authoritarian view on data.
- In Russia, the Middle East and India, data is bought and sold openly.

XXX sits in the middle of these views on data. Therefore, it has to manage approaches in all of these environments. (See Compliance).

- At Director/Management level there are gaps in understanding the above issues and risks.
- At Operational level there are gaps in operational understanding

and lack of precise understanding of the systems, networks and data of the business.

- The company has an 'adequate' post – COVID-19 ISO 22301 business continuity plan.
- The CEO takes an interest in resilience and business continuity and the Business Continuity Manager is a direct report.
  - The IT Manager and the Business Continuity Manager do not 'get on'.
  - The Business Continuity Manager is someone who knows the business.
- The Business Continuity Manager reports directly to the CEO and is clearly trusted to protect the business.
- The company has recently launched a mobile app which is not fully secure.
- COVID-19 has exposed the risks to the company of employees working from home.
- The company recently moved into multi-storey office block housing 1000 employees which is less used since COVID-19.
- The company has 12 outlier sites with another 600 people, some of these are in other countries. These have been less used during COVID-19.
- The company operates 2 call centres one in the main building one in an outlier.
- There are resilient communications, apparently, between HQ and outliers, especially between call centres.
- The company is a Microsoft house, but this may change.
- Mission Critical Systems, Business Critical Systems and Safety Critical Systems are about to be replaced by an IBM based model (see Para 5.9.3).
- RFID access badges are issued to personnel – they are not zoned.
- There are stated strong firewalls.
- The company has an internal East European ethical hacker.
- The only digital information that is supposed to leave building is CEO's tablet!
- There is a USB policy – not a USB ban.

- Laptops are not allowed out of the building.
- Desktops have no local drives: but USB ports are not plugged.
- There are no network 'sniffers'.
- Personnel are not allowed to hold personal info on PCs.
- Insurance handlers can't have access to external emails only internal.
- The company has ISO 22301 at HQ – and has been tested – but not in new buildings or covering working from home. The company does not have ISO 27001 (although the website says it does?).
- The company has not undertaken an electronic sweep of building.
- The company does not have a Near Field Communication policy.
- The clean desk policy is not fully enforced.
- The company does not seem to have PCI standards – but should probably adhere to them.
- Security is outsourced.
- Cleaning is outsourced.
- Some facilities management is outsourced (building maintenance etc.).
- Customer service area, entered via main entrance but inside office not fully secure – customer discussion tables and service points are accessible.
- There has been no thought to known unknown, or unknown unknown risk issues.
- No Business Impact Analysis has been undertaken outside of the rudimentary Business Continuity Plan, which is very much facilities oriented.
- There is no Enterprise Information Security Policy and no consequent policies.

It follows from the foregoing that XXX has a wide variety of risks, external and internal pressures, and an upcoming change in systems and networks which need to be reflected in an appropriate Cybersecurity plan.

The following is an initial guide/plan to turning XXX into a first-class Cybersecurity focussed company.

5.8 The Owners and Board Geopolitical/Multinational/ National/Board/Risk Management

Geopolitical and related risks, as confirmed by the Owners and Board, must be managed. Therefore, a formal means of dialogue with the ruling family and associates must be established in order that they can be managed from the XXX perspective.

Similarly, discussions with the European partner, regional partners, clinics, and national bodies need to take place to create a similar risk scorecard to the above.

The Board, before it drives any company policies, has to re-educate itself from a Cybersecurity perspective, form an appropriate Board/ Executive Committee and appoint a CISO who should have the ultimate responsibility for Cybersecurity within the organisation, and personal responsibility for the creation of the Enterprise Information Security Policy.

The Board should formally record its values along with any Mission Statement and Objective.

The Board should record its appetite for risk in different scenarios within a Scorecard.

This is the backdrop to the creation by the Board, CISO (to be appointed) and a Cybersecurity Executive Committee (owned by the CISO) of the Enterprise Information Security Policy.

5.9 Enterprise Information Security Policy

This policy is a Board Document owned by the CISO, to be reviewed every 3 years. It is concerned with the Confidentiality, Integrity and Availability of the business' intellectual property, systems, networks, processes and procedures and, above all, data. There are some detailed notes on some of the policy items. This is because they may be new to being managers. This is a Board policy and covers:

5.9.1 Risk Management

Introduction

Managing Risk
Directors and Managers will work together to, in detail:

Establish a Governance Framework that enables and supports information risk management

To sufficiently address the security of information systems, the governance of Cybersecurity programs aims to:

- Strategically align Cybersecurity efforts with business strategies to support organisation objectives.
- Support risk management by enforcing necessary controls to mitigate risk.
- Reduce the impact of security breaches on information resources; and
- Improve resource management by efficiently managing Cybersecurity knowledge and infrastructure.[2]

Some of the broader benefits of effective governance, with a focus on risk mitigation, include:

- Increased predictability of business operation.
- Greater control over the confidentiality, integrity, and availability of data, resulting in less potential for civil or legal liability.
- More cost-effective allocation of security resource.
- Improvements in risk management, business process, and effective incident response in the case of a breach.
- The ability to make critical decisions based on clear, valid information; and
- Greater safeguarding of sensitive information during important business activities, such as acquisitions and mergers, regulatory responses, and business process recovery.
- Understand the organisation's appetite for risk (a Board decision).
- Maintain the Board's engagement.
- Produce supporting policies. In particular, a Board risk policy.

- Adopt a lifecycle approach to business and information risk management.
- Apply recognised standards of security management.
- Educate users and maintain their awareness.
- Promote a risk management culture.

A suggested approach is as follows:

Approach

- **Risk Assessment:** All risks within the scope of this EISP are identified, considering XXX organisation's culture and technical systems. Gap analysis is important.
- **Risk Analysis:** Risks in XXX policy are prioritised based on impact, likelihood, and potential cost. This can be done on a qualitative, quantitative, or hybrid basis with the goal of performing a cost-benefit analysis/return on mitigation for potential security measures.
- **Risk Treatment:** Based on the results of the previous two steps, an outline of the concrete steps of how to treat (and minimise) those risks should be written. XXX policy should state how each risk will be mitigated, transferred, or accepted based on the analysis.
- **Risk Monitoring:** In this final phase, controls are continually monitored for changes in risk levels or new deficiencies or weaknesses that may rise to the surface over time. Metrics reporting is to be put in place, in addition to periodic auditing, so that risk level is constantly adjusted to the appropriate level.

These issues are brought together, initially, for presentation and management in a:

5.9.2 Risk Scorecard

<u>SCORECARD AND RISK REGISTER</u>

Risk – the uncertainty of outcome, whether positive opportunity or negative threat, of actions & events
I – impact   L – likelihood (within a 3-year period)

1 LEADERSHIP (Category) *(Governance & Board)*				SCORECARD:		External Risk (Red, Amber, Green)		Internal Risk (Red, Amber, Green)
Date	Risk Identified	I	L	Risk Factor	Response (Track or Treat)	Action agreed	Responsible Officer	Timescale For Action

Figure 4: Risk Scorecard

Source: Wood (2000). Managing Complexity. London. Economist Books.

Potential sub-headings for the risk scorecard include, in addition to Leadership:

- Organisational Values.
- Business Design.
- Business Ecosystem.
- Business Environment.
- Performance Measures.
- Knowledge Management and Data Systems.
- Management Processes including IT Systems.

This scorecard is probably a good starting point for an organisation that has not looked at risk in such a manner before.

From the Cybersecurity perspective all of these are important, but Leadership, Values, Performance Measure, Knowledge Management and Data Systems and Management Processes including

IT Systems are key to this project. (Measuring progress is one way of looking at a success metric for Cybersecurity).

Leadership is something that has to be demonstrated by the owners, partners, Board, Executive Committee, CISO and Managers.

Leadership is defined:

Mixed Reality Leadership is the ability to persuade individuals and teams to engage with the Mixed Reality world by establishing a common trust based on a set of shared values, epitomised by personal example and professionalism, communicated to and accepted by all that personal and professional lives will be better for the experience. (© MP Hyslop 2025).

Organisational values flow from the owners' positions, articulated by the Board and CEO to managers and staff. They should be codified.

From a Cybersecurity point of view these are the starting point for the Enterprise Information Security Policy.

The Board, once the scorecard is created, should consider its appetite for risk. Risk appetite should be the determining factor, in due course, for managing risk. However, at XXX, a better understanding of risk all round is required. Thereafter the approach can be improved by looking more closely at Risk Appetite and, in particular, how AI (Artificial Intelligence) is married to EI (Emotional Intelligence).

This in turn informs Management Processes and Procedures which are to be developed for:

5.9.3 The New Architecture

The proposed new architecture for XXX looks like:

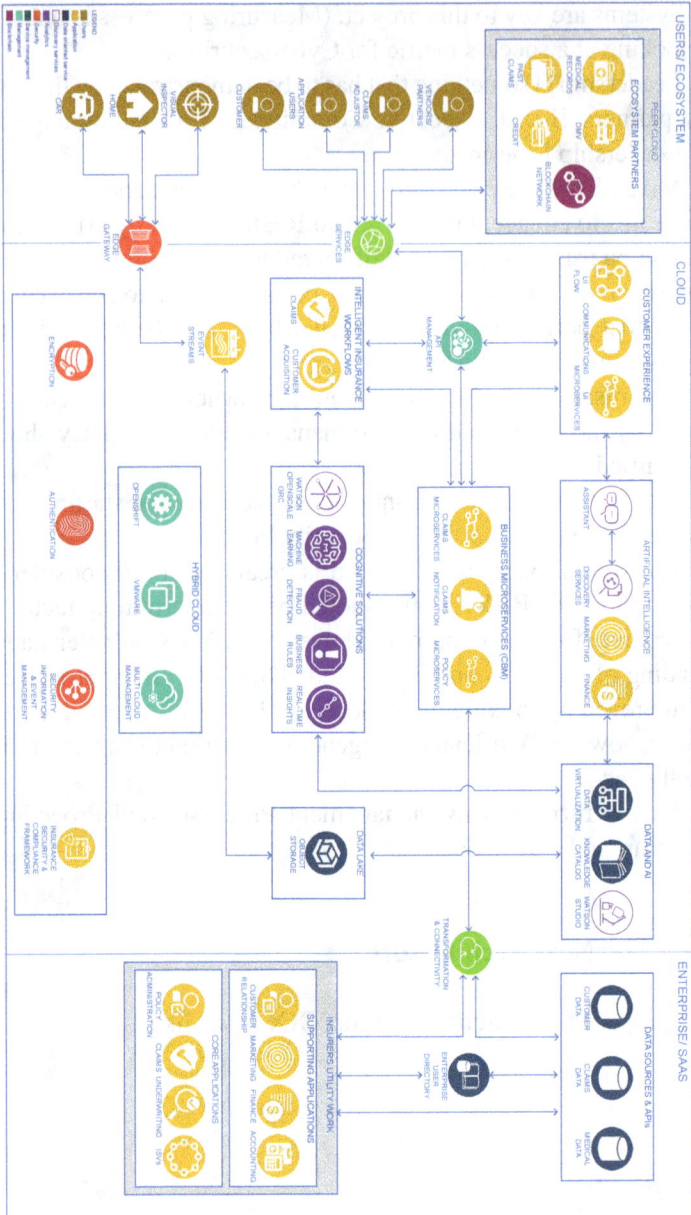

Figure 5: Reference Architecture

Source: IBM Cloud Architecture: A Visual Representation of Insurance Reference Architecture

Managers are to familiarise themselves with the proposed Architecture and ensure that it is fit for purpose. Workshops will provide opportunities for understanding and amendment.

A short examination would suggest that data needs to be more strongly defended and network segmentation improved. Monitoring the new architecture design is part and parcel of this policy.

5.9.4 Secure Configuration

It is important from the beginning to make sure the configuration of the architecture is sound and therefore managers must create policies and pay attention to the following:

- Policies to update and patch systems (this is extremely important).
- Create and maintain hardware inventories.
- Lock down operating systems and software.
- Conduct regular vulnerability scans.
- Disable unnecessary input/output devices and removable media access.
- Implement whitelisting and execution control.
- Limit user ability to change configuration.

5.9.5 Network Security

Managers must create policies/routines and pay attention to the following:

- Patching and patch management (this is extremely important).
- Password checks.
- Conduct regular vulnerability scans.
- Updated Security Applications (firewalls, proxies, antivirus software, etc.).
- Network Architecture Design (and review), including appropriate network segmentation preferably based on a risk appetite model.
- Endpoint Controls & Analysis.

- Create and maintain hardware inventories.
- Include a similar analysis for Wi-Fi (in regard to which attacks are becoming more frequent and more sophisticated).

5.9.6 Application Security

Managers must create policies/routines and pay attention to the following:
- Application structure and layer review.
- System development lifecycle.
- Penetration testing.
- Source code review.
- Patch management (this is extremely important).

5.9.7 Compliance Management

Managers must create policies/routines and pay attention to the following:
- Relevant National Regulations.
- Central Bank Regulatory Authority Standards for Finance and Insurance Businesses.
- Payment Card Industry Standards.
- HIPAA.
- HIMSS 7 etc, where appropriate.
- Sarbanes Oxley.
- General Data Protection Regulations (Europe).
- UK Court of Appeal.
- European AI Act.

5.9.8 Legal/Litigation

Managers must create policies/routines and pay attention to the following:

- The amount of data held (up to 38 million records in XXX and partners) and its black-market value ($38 billion +/-); distributed across 4 countries.
- HIPAA check lists.
- Cyber – insurance: These days premiums are rocketing, self-insured retentions rising, policy terms narrowing, and defence coverage only increasing, to avoid claim payments.
- Minimising risk from data processors.
- Minimising risks from third parties especially vendors.
- Protecting from known unknowns e.g.: poor processes, poor documentation, poor contracts (across several jurisdictions).
- Securing employment contracts.
- Determining purchasing policies and contracts to obviate Lenovo/Huawei-type scenarios where spyware is installed in hardware.
- Promoting employee awareness.
- Preventing 'suicide' clauses in contracts; particularly with the Chinese.

5.9.9 Reputation

Managers must create policies/routines and pay attention to the following:
- Reputational risk is everyone's responsibility and must be addressed as such.
- Control processes to be in place in in each area of the business.
- Understand actions by all personnel can affect public perception.
- Understand shareholder and stakeholder expectations – in country and abroad.
- Focus on a positive image and communication – but understated.
- Create response and contingency plans for when good and bad news breaks.

5.9.10 Physical Security

Managers must create policies/routines and pay attention to the following:

Physical security is often overlooked; but should be an integral partner of Cybersecurity planning. This includes things like hardware (computers/servers/routers/etc.), facilities, media, people, and paper/physical data. Controls typically outlined in this respect are:

- CCTV.
- Fire extinguishers.
- Water sprinklers.
- Smoke detectors.
- Fencing.
- Building management systems (BMS).
- Physical locks.
- Security guards.
- Adequate lighting.
- Access control cards issued to employees.

Where these are controlled/monitored by IOT devices these latter must be treated in the same way as other system hardware devices.

5.9.11 Managing User Privileges

Managers must create policies/routines for and pay attention to the following:

- Secure the network perimeter.
- Install firewalls.
- Prevent malicious content.
- Protect the internal network.
- Segregate network assets.
- Secure wireless devices.
- Protect internal IP addresses.

- Monitor the network.
- Test the security controls.

5.9.12 User Education and Awareness

Managers must create policies/routines for and pay attention to the following:

- Produce a user security policy.
- Establish a staff induction process.
- Maintain user awareness of the cyber risks faced by the organisation on a continuous basis:
- Against existing shortcomings:
  - ◦ Enforce a clean desk policy.
  - ◦ Zone RFID access.
  - ◦ Enforce the ban on personal information on company equipment.
  - ◦ Introduce a Near Field Communication policy.
- Support the formal assessment of Information Assurance skills.
- Carry out pre-employment vetting and screening very carefully.
- Monitor the effectiveness of security training.
- Promote an incident reporting culture.
- Establish a formal disciplinary process (in this case also deal with the issue between the IT Manager and the Business Continuity Manager).
- Include third parties in education and awareness.

5.9.13 Malware Prevention

Managers must create policies/routines for and pay attention to the following:

- Develop and publish corporate policies.
- Ensure DNS security and management.

- Establish anti-malware across the organisation.
- Manage all data import and export.
- Blacklist malicious websites.
- Deploy anti-virus and malicious code-checking solutions to scan objects at the perimeter/edge, on internal networks and on host systems.
- Install firewalls on the host and gateway devices.
- If possible, disable Windows scripting (Active X), VB Script and JavaScript, and disable the auto run function on removable media.
- Regularly scan every network component and apply security patches.
- Remember the importance of layers and layering, and of network segmentation.
- Apply the secure baseline build to every network device and mobile platforms.
- User education and awareness.

5.9.14 Monitoring

Managers must create policies/routines for and pay attention to the following:
- Establish a monitoring procedure.
- Monitor all ICT systems.
- Monitor network traffic.
- Monitor all user activity.
- Monitor third parties.
- Fine tune monitoring systems.
- Ensure there is sufficient storage.
- Train security personnel.
- Align incident management policies.

5.9.15 Removable Media Controls

Managers must create policies/routines for and pay attention to the following:
- Produce a corporate policy.
- Limit the use of removable media (N.B. USB sticks and ports).
- Scan all removable media for malware.
- Audit media regularly.
- Encrypt the information held on the media.
- Lock down access to media drives.
- Monitor systems.
- Actively manage the reuse and disposal of removable media.

5.9.16 Home and Mobile Working

Managers must create policies/routines for and pay attention to the following:
- Assess the risks and create a mobile working policy.
- Educate users and maintain their awareness.
- Protect data at rest.
- Protect data in transit.
- Review incident management plans.
- Currently this is a major risk.

5.9.17 The Digital App

Managers must create policies/routines for and pay attention to the following:
- Assess the risks and create a Digital App working policy.
- Educate users and maintain their awareness.
- Protect data at rest.
- Protect data in motion.

- Review incident management plans.

Currently this is a major risk.

5.9.18 Third Parties

Managers must create policies/routines for and pay attention to the following:
- Creating a general management policy for third parties.
- Maintain a Vendor Assessment and Monitoring Programme.
- Maintain a Contractor Assessment and Monitoring Programme.
- Have a specific policy for any Cloud Providers with stringent monitoring requirements bearing in mind the organisation is responsible for all data held by the Cloud Providers. Note that Cloud Providers are notorious for mission and cost creep.

5.9.19 Out of Country Offices, Outlier Offices, Travel

Managers must create policies/routines for and pay attention to the following:
- Assess the risks and create a policy for Out of Country Offices, Outlier Offices and Travel.
- Educate users and maintain their awareness.
- Protect data at rest.
- Protect data in motion.
- Review incident management plans.
- Focus:
    - Do I really need to take my PC?
- Logons, passwords and removable hard disks.
- USB Pen Drive: storage and more.
- Encryption.
- Wi-Fi.
- Commercial encrypted Email.

Currently this is a major risk.

5.9.20 Incident Management

Managers must create policies/routines for and pay attention to the following:
- Obtain Board, senior management approval and backing.
- Establish an incident response and disaster recovery capability.
- Provide specialist training to the incident response team.
- Define the required roles and responsibilities.
- Establish a data recovery capability.
- Test the incident management plans.
- Collect and analyse post-incident evidence.
- Conduct a lessons learned review.
- Jurisdiction Compliance.

This is covered more specifically by the example in Annex B to this chapter, and by the Business Continuity approach at Annex C.

5.9.21 Business Continuity Planning

Managers must create policies/routines for and pay attention to the following:

Business Continuity Planning (BCP) deals with how the business potentially deals with a successful breach or attack, but generally from the non cyber specific perspective. The EISP need to integrate the BCP and outline how a Business Impact Assessment (BIA) should take place during planning and also after a security incident, measuring things like downtime and data loss after (and during) a disaster scenario. For XXX guidance a suggested approach is at Annex C to this document.

5.9.21 Integration With Other Organisational Policies

Managers must create policies routines for and pay attention to the following:

It is important that the EISP does not sit in isolation from other organisational policies. To this end it is important that all other parts of the business are consulted regarding impact, either way, of the EISP with other policies and procedures. These include, but are not limited to, quality policy, information policy, business continuity policy, environmental policy, hiring policy, assessment policies. All of these can impact the EISP.

5.9.23 Dependency Modelling

Once all policies/plans/routines have been created and there is an awareness of how things relate to each other an organisational dependency model is to be created. This will apply probabilities to events and let the organisation understand what might be worst case scenarios and catastrophic events. To help understand this consider the following:

Within the foregoing EISP planning guidelines will be found dependencies as each management process and procedure is worked up to comply with the policies,

Dependencies are related to risks, and to an effective response plan. Dependency modelling works like this:

The formal parts of an organisation are those most often emphasised.

It is unfashionable to speak much of uncontrollables since they lead to feeling uncomfortable and helpless. Yet every organisation on the planet is susceptible to certain combinations of things all going wrong at the same time.

Risk analysts understand that they depend on things over which they have little or no control. These things constitute the essential luck needed to continue functioning. The analyst's job is to arrange things so that the organisation relies on as little of this luck as possible.

This leads to the following additional definitions on risk:

- Risk is sensitivity to those things that cannot be controlled.
- Risk Management is the science of understanding and optimising sensitivity to those things that cannot be controlled.

Understanding Risk involves understanding why there are dependencies on things that cannot be controlled, through an understanding of what are called Dependency Relationships.

In simple terms dependency modelling is to risk as a spreadsheet is to a business plan.

Dependency Relationships (Example)

A failure of the public electricity supply cannot be prevented. If depended upon and it fails then power continuity is lost.

PowerContinuity depends on PublicSupplyOK.

The entities PowerContinuity and PublicSupplyOK are shorthand for the ideas of continuity of the source of electricity, and the effectiveness of the public electricity supply in providing continuity of electric power.

The public electricity supply cannot be controlled by the organisation, it is at its mercy. If the public supply fails the organisation loses electric power. The organisation depends on something it cannot control. This may or may not be serious depending on the extent to which the organisation depends on continuity of electricity supply. The public electricity supply is an uncontrollable. The organisation depends on the good fortune that it will not fail, but it cannot be forced to be reliable.

If, however, the organisation has a standby generator suitably configured to take over in such a timely manner as to provide continuity of power when the public supply fails, then the organisation can reduce its dependency on the public supply which cannot be controlled.

PowerContinuity depends on PublicSupplyOK OR StandbyGeneratorTakesOver

The / symbols mean OR in dependency maps. The entity StandyByGeneratorTakesOver is shorthand for the effectiveness of the standby generator in taking over the continuity of electrical supply if the public supply fails.

The standby generator is a countermeasure. It too can fail, but the organisation is still better off than without it since to lose power continuity will now require two, simultaneous failures – the public supply and the standby generator.

Providing these events are statistically independent, (i.e., providing there is no common cause which will take out both at the same time) risk is greatly reduced.

If, however, there is some common component, such as a transformer, which is used both by the public supply and the standby generator, and if this component is potentially unreliable, then this constitutes a common cause which prevents the reduction in risk being as great as it would otherwise have been.

So now:

ViaPublic depends on PublicSupplyOK AND TransformerOK.

ViaPublic is shorthand for the contribution of the combination of public supply and transformer in attempting to provide power continuity.

Similarly now:

ViaStandby depends on StandbyGeneratorOK AND TransformerOK.

ViaStandBy is shorthand for the contribution of the combination of standby generator and transformer in attempting to provide power continuity if the public supply fails.

It is easy to turn these into actual measures of risk. To every issue there corresponds an exposure. The ideas from this simple example can be extended to cover the whole range of business activities.

Every organisation is a rich network of dependency relationships. An organisation depends on the availability of its key staff, its buildings, its telecommunications, its records, its data processing facilities and so forth. These things in turn depend upon other things, and so on. For example:

- The availability of key staff depends on recruitment processes, on industrial harmony, on their state of health, on the workload, absence of overtures from predatory rivals etc.

- Telecommunications depends on availability of a public electricity supply, on the integrity of cabling and optical fibre networks, on freedom from various faults, on the availability of standby systems and so on.

- The availability of records depends on the integrity of computer memory systems, on backup procedures, on the correct functioning of software, and of course on the availability of telecommunications.

These could be represented in dependency diagrams.

Moreover, it is not just various forms of availability that

organisations depend on. They depend on good will, on freedom from litigation, on confidentiality of records, on health and safety factors and so on. All of these can be analysed into dependency relationships.

Due to the interdependencies in the organisation, the effects of failures of various combinations of the uncontrollables can lead to highly unpredictable, and possibly very damaging chains of events.

These chains of events show up particularly well on dependency maps.

The formal part of the organisation can be thought of as being under constant attack by the uncontrollable part. Risk Management is about designing the former to be maximally resilient to the latter. While root causes cannot be controlled – the uncontrollables – nevertheless the effects are more under control through management of the dependency relationships within the organisation.

Interdependency relationships are unique to the particular organisation, and only by coming to terms with the actual relationships in that organisation can anything really valuable be done to understand, manage and reduce risks.

Dependency Modelling was developed to capture these interdependencies in a highly visual model so that the consequence of failures could be uncovered in the safe, virtual environment of the computer.

Having created the model it is relatively easy to:

- Infer the risk to the organisation implied by the model. (Each part can be given a statistical value).
- Illustrate the risk graphically in easy-to-understand terms.
- Find which scenarios are the most dangerous to the organisation.
- Find variations of the organisational structure which carry less risk.
- Evaluate the effectiveness of any countermeasures.
- Determine which factors are important and which can be ignored.
- Support management proposals with evidence.
- Avoid spending money on measures which are likely to be ineffective.
- Find ways of reducing risk without necessarily spending money.

A key benefit of Dependency Modelling for Cybersecurity Policy is that it helps to identify key weaknesses in the organisation that may make it vulnerable to either virtual or physical attack. It is also risk-based – and can complete the loop back to Risk Appetite and the Risk Scorecard mentioned in para 5.9.2. This can also be used as a metric.

As can be seen from this document so far protecting an organisation from a Cybersecurity attack is a complex, detailed and mathematical issue.

5.9.24 Return on Mitigation

Return on Mitigation is to the EISP as the Return on Investment is to the Business Plan. It describes in terms understandable to the C-Suite what measures have been implemented, how effective and efficient those measure have been, and the impact on the business. At its best Dependency Modelling gives the organisation a very good idea of the concept of Return on Mitigation.

It is useful to remember that C-Suite members other than the CISO will need to have the benefits of Cybersecurity explained to them in terms of: cost or margin, risk, customer satisfaction, employee efficiency and other strategic initiatives (Cybersecurity is but one).

5.9.25 Moving to Zero Trust

The organisation must take the opportunity of new systems and network infrastructure to move to a Zero Trust environment.

A Zero Trust environment is defined:

> *'The main concept behind zero trust is that devices should not be trusted by default, even if they are connected to a managed corporate network such as the corporate LAN and even if they were previously verified. In most modern enterprise environments, corporate networks consist of many interconnected segments, cloud-based services and infrastructure, connections to remote*

and mobile environments, and increasingly connections to non-conventional IT, such as IoT devices. The once traditional approach of trusting devices within a notional corporate perimeter, or devices connected to it via a VPN, makes less sense in such highly diverse and distributed environments. Instead, the zero-trust approach advocates mutual authentication, including checking the identity and integrity of devices without respect to location, and providing access to applications and services based on the confidence of device identity and device health in combination with user authentication.'

The CISO will work with Managers to create this environment.

5.9.26 Horizon Scanning

Managers must create policies/routines for and pay attention to the following:

- Develop antennae for trouble – be a little paranoid.
- Odd events – look for things out of context
- Quirky tasks – an example from elsewhere: e.g. members of the Finance Department may be trading illegally.
- Weird queries/Obvious queries – may be phishing attacks.
- New products. E.g., Blockchain will become important in the insurance industry. And it is in the IBM Architecture above, but no one knows anything about it.
- Etc.

5.9.27 Understanding Threat Vectors

Managers are to meet regularly to understand the evolving threat landscape. Cyber-criminals are agile the organisation needs to keep permanently aware of offensive developments.

5.9.28 Sequence of Events

Clearly not everything can be done at the same time. So, the sequence of events will be informed by initial risk analysis and initial dependency modelling which will inform the organisation of the key risks and pressure points. These will be dealt with first; with every manager being responsible for ensuring their own department is managed in line with this EISP as new systems and networks are brought online in the meantime.

5.9.29 What To Do With The EISP.

This document will help to create an interim EISP which will be reviewed after the new systems and networks are finally agreed. In the meantime, use it as the corporate guide to the who, what, when, why and how of your managerial approach.

5.9.30 Metrics

The Risk Scorecard and the Dependency Model are two metrics. The first identifies progress on identified risks (plus known unknowns and unknown unknowns in due course) and the second overall system stability. Added to these are the Cybersecurity measures of Time to Detect and Time to Recover. Costs and budgets are yet to be properly set but progress against related financial metrics will also be introduced. It is important to note that as the organisation moves to become a Cyber Resilient organisation then the relevant continuity metrics (see Annex C as a starting point) become relevant.

6. Cyber-Attack Simulation Plan

This attack simulation plan will help the EISP clarify action plans and sequence of events. It will also help to bring more cyber awareness to the organisation.

In summary this will initially look at:

- A 'phishing' attack.
- Suspicious 'phone calls.
- USB drives.
- Suspicious customer activity.
- Wi-Fi.

In addition, a third party may use the timings of the above and the confusion it creates to attempt to penetrate the network.

Detailed plan for these scenarios is attached at Annex A.

7. Cyber-Attack Emergency Response Plan

In summary XXX follows the USA's National Institute for Standards and Technology Methodology as amended by XXX for its own use:

7.1 Govern(ance) and Context

In February 2024, the National Institute of Standards and Technology (NIST) released Version 2.0 of its Cybersecurity Framework (CSF), introducing a new core function: **Govern**. This function emphasises the importance of establishing and overseeing an organisation's cybersecurity risk management strategy, ensuring alignment with its mission and stakeholder expectations.

The **Govern** function encompasses several key areas:

- **Organisational Context**: Understanding the internal and external factors that influence cybersecurity decisions.
- **Cybersecurity Strategy**: Developing and implementing a comprehensive plan that integrates cybersecurity into the organisation's overall risk management.
- **Roles, Responsibilities, and Authorities**: Clearly defining and communicating the duties and powers related to cybersecurity within the organisation.
- **Policies**: Establishing and maintaining policies that guide cybersecurity activities and behaviours.

- **Cybersecurity Supply Chain Risk Management**: Identifying and mitigating risks associated with third-party suppliers and partners.

By integrating the **Govern** function, NIST CSF 2.0 aims to provide a more holistic approach to cybersecurity, ensuring that governance and strategic oversight are foundational elements of an organisation's cybersecurity efforts.

Context was a previous addition to the framework and reflects work by the author and James Royds in 2008. It informs all plans of the organisation's geographical, geopolitical, national, economic, virtual etc. positioning.

7.2 Identify

- To protect the organisation, the organisation must know what's worth protecting;
- This initial step involves accounting for all the organisation's assets, including personnel, systems, machines, users, endpoint devices, networks, and both stored and transmitted data. That accounting, as well as the risk assessment and vulnerability testing of those assets, will be unique for everyone.

7.3 Protect

- Once the organisation is aware of what is valuable, it will be able to take immediate protective actions. This involves everything from patching systems to implementing two-factor authentication to locking down employee mobile devices; and eventually moving to a zero-trust environment.
- This step includes bringing all of those identified assets up to the security standard set by the organisation. Based on the risk assessment and vulnerability testing done in Step 1, each organisation can create a unique formula for protection and close any loopholes.

7.4 Detect

- The organisation next needs to put the tools in place to monitor for threats, including everything from managed firewalls, intrusion detection and protection, antivirus/malware protection, distributed denial of service protection, threat analytics and insider threat–and, for government agencies or government related entities, security tools such as Einstein (or equivalent).
- These tools work continuously to detect threats, monitoring the network, systems and people to spot anomalies that could cause harm.

7.5 Respond

- What happens when those tools detect a threat? That's where the organisation's response plan comes into play. In some instances, the security tools themselves will respond to the threat automatically. In others, the organisation or a third party must respond manually.
- To respond correctly, the organisation must have a standard operating procedure for each type of potential threat. These procedures should identify what actions a threat should trigger, which people take what steps and who gets notified.

7.6 Recover

- Even with excellent security in place, breaches can occur. Therefore, building a recovery plan is crucial. The plan should address what tools, actions or partner will be responsible for recovering systems and applications. Business units specialising in marketing and public relations also have a role to play in recovery as breaches can be detrimental to any brand's reputation and public image. These departments should know ahead of time what messages to publicise and how to best spread the word.
- Organisations should also take steps to understand how the same situation could be avoided in the future. Part of the recovery

process involves updating the organisation's response plan with any lessons learned.

7.6 A Living Document

- While these five steps may work as a framework for an organisation's Cybersecurity plan, putting them in place is just the beginning.
- Maintaining the plan requires regular drills to test for weakness and continual updates based on new threats, as well as changes to the organisation itself including changes in endpoint devices, networks and users.
- An organisation's security plan is a living document. Cyber criminals are constantly learning and changing their strategies, so security documents must evolve just as quickly. But with constant vigilance, it is possible for organisations to stay one step ahead of their attackers.

The detailed plan is attached at Annex B.

8. Rolling Organisational Resilience Plan

The World Economic Forum (2021) suggests it is wise to move from Cybersecurity to Cyber Resilience. As XXX is at the start of both a proper Cybersecurity and Resilience journey then it is appropriate to include a link to Resilience. IT also ee, 2025, disinformation as the World's No. 1 risk.

In order to deliver the EISP XXX will work with a facilitator to train managers in what they are required to do to provide a rolling approach to improving Resilience/EISP, the management processes and procedures, training and improving defences; the practicalities of building a resilient organisation in line with the objectives of the EISP and the Response Plan.

A general resilience planning document is attached at Annex C (mainly for confidentiality reasons) which will be modified to assist XXX become a first-class Cybersecurity organisation by developing an aligned comprehensive resilience plan.

In summary the purpose of the resilience planning document is:

- To outline what it means to be a resilient organisation.
- To explain what a resilience team does.
- To highlight the advisory and training propositions.
- To demonstrate some of the advisory options on offer delivered via a flexible methodology that will meet the organisation's requirements.
- To provide a sensible route map through business continuity and resilience to comprehensive cyber risk management aligned to the EISP.

An example approach is attached at Annex C.

9. Projection Initiation and Milestones

XXX has to convert these series of policy actions and plans into a Project Initiation Document and comprehensive series of milestones. A way to do this is outlined in Annex C in the Business Continuity context.

10. Board and Management Advisory

This document and the Annexes that follow are not totally comprehensive as there are gaps in knowledge that must be addressed. However, it is clear, and one of the reasons why Annex C is included, that the amount of time required to implement an EISP (and a resilience plan if followed through) is enormous. Therefore, either an internal task team must be formed or an external team sought to assist in the process. On balance, it is better to employ an internal team as the team stays and has consistent personnel (as long as they have the knowledge). External advisors will eventually leave, and do not always have consistent personnel.

Annex A: Simulated Cyber – Attack

Situation: The company's Help Desk will issue a series of warnings relating to attack scenarios outline below. N.B. Although these may seem a little outdated they do, because they represent human failings, account for a good proportion of cyber- attacks. Access via DNS servers accounts for a significant part of the remainder.

Task: To identify if those warnings are followed by the company employees.

Scenario 1.

Help Desk issues a warning about potential phishing attacks.

Action: Various company employees are identified and sent an email containing a web link. If 'clicked', the web link will take the individual to a generic 'website under construction' page, information on those 'landing' on that page can be collected by Google Analytics.

Result: How many of those receiving this suspicious email actually report it? How many of those receiving this suspicious email actually access the web page?

'Phishing' attack scenario.

This scenario will consist of two attempts, while the basic scenario and set up will be similar, the contents of the emails will be significantly different; the first email being a generic large-scale phishing email, and the second being an email that includes specific information about the organisation.

Set Up

As this is a 'black box' attack, it must be assumed that all emails will be received by their specified recipients, that our web server is reachable, and that the binary [included with the phishing email] will be able to send data through the organisation's firewall. For each attempt a SMTP server (Postfix) and a HTTP server (Apache) will need to be set up.

The attack will be carried out as follows.

The Postfix SMTP server sends a 'malicious' email to each employee. Every email has a unique link to the Apache HTTP server. An employee clicks on the link in the email and reaches our HTTP server. The HTTP server will be set up to:

- Log user information through a PHP script, and
- Automatically serve the 'malicious' binary to anyone browsing its contents.

The HTTP server sends the 'malicious' binary to the employee. The binary does not install anything on the system – it will serve as a one-time SMTP client. When it is executed, it will read the name of the system and the logged-in user, and then send this information to the email account of the individual conducting the attack. When the binary has read the system variables and sent the email it will end, displaying an error message to the end-user.

First Attempt

This will consist of an update for a well-known software for displaying, printing and managing documents. Naturally we will need to identify which type of software is used by the organisation. But for demonstration purposes let's assume it is Adobe; the product must be updated through a service which is installed along with the application. NB: this attempt is not targeting at any particular user; for the benefit of this attempt a recipient is the only information that is required. The domain (www.adobedownloads.com) will be used to point to our 'malicious' HTTP server. The email will be spoofed from support@adobe.com and the user is requested to download the latest version of their software. Example email below:

<from>support@adobe.com</from>
<subject>Adobe PDF Reader Update</subject>

Dear Adobe Reader Customer,

A new version of Adobe Reader (version XX.**) was recently released.

This update includes new enhanced features for viewing, creating, editing, printing and sharing of PDF documents.

It also includes several important security improvements.

The update is available for download on the following location:
http://www.adobedownloads.com/?reader=XX**

Regards,
Adobe Support

The domain (www.adobedownloads.com) will be used to point to the 'malicious' HTTP server. The email will be spoofed from support@adobe.com and the user is requested to download the latest version of their software.

Second Attempt

This is a targeted attack. The context of the email involves the updating of the organisation's antivirus software with a temporary add-on as the current antivirus version does not cover the virus that has infected some of the organisation's computer systems. The user will be asked to click on a link and update the current antivirus software with the temporary add-on. The email will use the IT managers' actual email addresses. N. B. there are some specific aspects of this attempt that make it more demanding.

Firstly, the email will have to be specifically customised for the organisation. Secondly, is this type of request undertaken by a centralised IT administration or by individual IT managers? Lastly, without some detailed knowledge of individual IT managers, the email may not reflect how IT managers typically express themselves via emails.

In order for this attempt to succeed, we will need to find the email details of the organisation's IT managers and be able to 'link' those individuals to the organisation's employees. However, such information should be easily accessible; for example, from information gathered from the company website or from social media sites such as Facebook, LinkedIn.

Scenario 2

Help Desk issues a warning about suspicious phone calls. Action: Harassed mother [baby crying in the background, with emergency services siren going off] calls asking for login details for one the accounts. N.B. – this requires some extensive intelligence gathering; we need to understand the account access protocol (e.g., what is the username; email address, etc.). Result: How many receiving these suspicious phone calls actually respond? How many receiving these suspicious phone calls report them?

'Suspicious' Phone Calls.

This scenario will use a series of phone calls to customer care agents to try and gain access to personal information. This scenario is based on the assumption that senior management of the organisation are all registered with the organisations health care provider. User registration consists of: a card number; this is the number that uniquely identifies the individuals' membership number with the health care provider. An active policy number; this is the number that uniquely identifies the individuals' policy with the health care provider.

This is the type of information sought:

User registration also uses a mobile number, and an email address. This type of information can be identified using social media accounts such as Facebook and LinkedIn. For this scenario to be successful, detailed information on individual senior managers will need to be acquired; difficult, but not impossible. In addition, a female social engineer is required, or at least a female who is very talented in persuasion. Furthermore, an ANI-spoofing [giving the appearance of dialling from the mobile number of the target individual] will be necessary. For the benefit of this scenario, let's assume the individuals name is 'John Smith', the steps in this scenario are as follows:

The mobile number of 'John Smith' is 'spoofed' in a call to the customer care centre – masking the real number being called with what a customer service representative would see as being 'John Smith's' number.

A YouTube video of babies crying is playing in the background, making it appear that the caller is distraught and calling from a hectic household – once the female is talking to a customer service agent, she claims she is John Smith's wife. Example dialogue below:

"I'm so sorry, can you hear me OK? My baby, I'm sorry. My husband is like, we're lost our medical card, and we just had a baby, and he's like 'Get this done today,'" setting the scene for the agent that she's a busy mother, who really needs help. "I'm trying to log in to our account for policy information, and I can't remember what the username is."

If the customer service agent provides this information, then the scenario would continue, with the female asking for the card number and policy number. A successful conclusion would be the customer care agent, refusing to provide this information.

Scenario 3.

Help Desk issues a warning about suspicious USB drives. Action: This will also require some intelligence gathering; in particular we need to identify those areas where company employees congregate for a cigarette. Once these locations are identified, a specific number [say 2-3] of USB drives are left in place. Result: How many of the known USB drives are handed in?

USB Scenario

This scenario is relatively simple, and will test the organisations' 'no USB policy'.

A portable USB hard disk drive is handed in to Reception at a number of Customer Service areas. The USB drive has a sticker attached, asking anybody who finds it to please call the mobile number supplied, with the instructions such as – *'If found, please call 01234 567890.'*

The investigation team then wait for a call. As in the suspicious calls scenario, the call is answered by a distraught female, with a YouTube video of babies crying in the background, giving the impression the harassed woman is living in a hectic household. She would explain the situation as follows:

"I'm so sorry, can you hear me OK? My baby, I'm sorry. My husband is like, we're have applied for a loan, and we just had a baby, and he's like 'Get this done today,'" setting the scene for the Receptionist that she's a busy mother, who really needs help, *"and the loan details are on the portable USB drive, the baby isn't well, and I don't want to travel back into the city centre, could please email me the loan agreement."*

This scenario attempts to work at two levels, firstly they may have children of her own, and empathises with the caller, and secondly our innate insatiable curiosity – what is the loan for, how much?

A successful outcome of this scenario would be the Receptionist refusing to plug the USB into their machine and accessing the loan documentation.

Scenario 4.

Help Desk issues a warning about suspicious activity customer receptions. Action: This is a technical attack, in which the individual will attempt to gain system access via the service points in the customer receptions. Again, some intelligence gathering will be required; what are the service ports? Are they LAN ports? Are they open or closed? Result: Does anybody ask us what we are doing?

Suspicious Customer Activity

This is a technical attack and may be performed in two ways; using any computer terminals reserved for customer use in the reception are, and/or making use of any identified LAN ports.

Customer Computer Terminals

In this attack, the investigation team will try to gain SYSTEM level access to the customer terminal, otherwise known as a privilege escalation attack. Given the organisations' 'no USB policy' it is highly unlikely, that a USB drive would be allowed access to the terminal. So instead the investigation team will make use of a little-known aspect of Windows OS; namely PowerShell. Please note, given that the organisation uses Windows OS, I'm assuming that they will be using Windows 7 and above.

This attack will make use of Windows PowerShell, and Power-Sploit. PowerSploit is a collection of Microsoft PowerShell modules that can be used to compromise Windows 7 and above operating system versions. This is because PowerShell comes installed on Windows 7 and above. PowerShell is an ideal exploitation utility in Windows due to its ability to perform a wide range of administrative and low-level tasks without the need to install malicious execut-ables onto the hard disk drive – it works at the physical memory [otherwise known as RAM], and is therefore able to evade antivirus applications. More details on the modules can be found at: https://github.com/PowerShellMafia/PowerSploit. The module used in this attempted escalation is Exfiltration (to steal sensitive data from a compromised machine), using Mimikatz (identify credentials), Privesc (identify misconfigurations), and GPPPassword (retrieve encrypted passwords) scripts.

The scripts would be downloaded from a repository, either from github.com, but given the internet browser on the customer terminal may not allow access to github.com, then it would be better to use a HTTP server controlled by the investigation team. Once downloaded into the physical memory, the scripts will be invoked and then run.

Obviously, the intention is not to compromise the customer

terminal, but to ascertain if any of the office staff identify the behaviour of the investigation team as being suspicious and challenge them.

Identified LAN Ports

This attack will try to make use of an any identified Local Area Network [LAN] ports but is dependent on those ports being open and accessible. The attack will mimic an investigate of the network for any exploitable vulnerabilities [this would be classed as a reconnaissance exercise and is not particularly subtle] with the intention of establishing whether anybody challenges the investigation team.

Firstly, Nmap would be used to map the network. Nmap [Network Mapper] is a security scanner used to discover hosts and services on a computer network, thus creating a 'map' of the network. To accomplish this task, Nmap sends specially crafted packets to the target host and then analyses the response. Secondly, a vulnerability scanner such as Nessus, would be used to aggressively interrogate the network to find any vulnerabilities in a network.

All this activity would take considerable time, and create an enormous amount of network traffic. Assuming the network is being monitored, then this increased level of network traffic should alert the network administrators, and hopefully they would investigate.

Scenario 5

Help Desk issues a warning about unusual WiFi traffic. Action: In one of the main offices a wireless de-authentication flooding attack (otherwise known as a Wi-Fi DOS attack) is attempted. Result: How long does it take the IT team to identify the attack, locate the source, and come ask us what we are doing? NB – this type of attack is technically difficult, and if successful could result in some serious disruption for the office under attack.

Wireless DOS Masquerading Scenario

Understanding that the organisation has a Wireless Local Area Network [WLAN], then the open medium of wireless networks makes it relatively easy to undertake a masquerading attack (such as de-authentication flooding and de-association flooding) at the Media Access Control (MAC) level. In addition, this open medium aspect of wireless networks allows for the attacker to 'sniff' traffic in order to find devices on the network.

De-authentication Flooding attack

Before any communication between a client and an Access Point [AP] can begin, the client has to authenticate itself with the AP. The de-authentication message is part of the normal authentication process, by which clients and APs can de-authenticate from each other. Unfortunately, there is no secure authentication method, so consequently an attack can 'spoof' a de-authentication message. The attack proceeds as follows:

The investigation team sends a spoofed de-authentication message to an AP with the MAC address of its clients.

On receiving this message an AP de-authenticates and de-associates the client whose MAC address is specified in the de-authentication message.

The above scenario is a typical example of how a de-authentication message is spoofed when the MAC address of client is found via WLAN sniffing. Please note, this attack is used to target a particular client, which could be the CEO's tablet.

However, it would more effective to target multiple clients, in which case the attack would focus on sending a de-authentication message from an AP to all its clients – this essentially means the AP is terminating the connection. This will require the investigation team to spoof the MAC address (or the BSSID) of the AP.

Such a sustained attack on multiple clients, may result in loss of employee productivity, sometimes such an attack may result in the loss of revenue or business. But more importantly, a de-authentication flooding attack is a pre-emptive stage of a much more serious multi-level attack, and as such the organisation's IT team should detect, identify and investigate this type of attack very quickly.

Please note, while this scenario appears relatively straightforward, it is technically quite challenging, and its success cannot be guaranteed.

Annex B Cyber-Attack Emergency Response Plan

The following is a schematic to follow for the preparation of the Cyber-Attack Response Plan based on the NIST Framework.

NIST Cybersecurity Framework (CSF) 2.0 – Updated Structure

GOVERN (GV)

Category	Subcategory
Organisational Context (GV.OC)	GV.OC-1: Understand internal and external organisational factors affecting cybersecurity.
GV.OC-2: Define cybersecurity roles, responsibilities, and decision-making authority.	
Cybersecurity Risk Governance (GV.CR)	GV.CR-1: Develop a cybersecurity risk management strategy aligned with business objectives.
GV.CR-2: Establish clear policies and procedures for cybersecurity governance.	
Supply Chain Risk Management (GV.SC)	GV.SC-1: Identify and assess supply chain cybersecurity risks.
GV.SC-2: Monitor and manage supply chain security practices.	

IDENTIFY (ID)

Category	Subcategory
Asset Management (ID.AM)	ID.AM-1: Inventory physical devices and systems.
ID.AM-2: Inventory software platforms and applications.	
ID.AM-3: Map organisational communication and data flows.	
ID.AM-4: Catalogue external information systems.	
ID.AM-5: Prioritise resources based on classification, criticality, and business value.	
ID.AM-6: Define cybersecurity roles and responsibilities for all stakeholders.	
Business Environment (ID.BE)	ID.BE-1: Identify organisational role in the supply chain.
ID.BE-2: Understand position within critical infrastructure and sector.	
ID.BE-3: Establish priorities for organisational missions and objectives.	
ID.BE-4: Define dependencies and critical functions for service delivery.	
ID.BE-5: Establish resilience requirements for critical services.	
Governance (ID.GV)	ID.GV-1: Establish organisational cybersecurity policies.
ID.GV-2: Align cybersecurity roles and responsibilities internally and externally.	

ID.GV-3: Manage legal, regulatory, and privacy requirements.

ID.GV-4: Address cybersecurity risks in governance and risk management processes.

Risk Assessment (ID.RA)	ID.RA-1: Identify and document asset vulnerabilities.

ID.RA-2: Receive threat and vulnerability information from external sources.

ID.RA-3: Identify and document internal and external threats.

ID.RA-4: Identify potential business impacts and likelihoods.

ID.RA-5: Use threats, vulnerabilities, and impacts to determine risk.

ID.RA-6: Prioritise risk responses.

Risk Management Strategy (ID.RM)	ID.RM-1: Establish and manage risk management processes.

ID.RM-2: Determine and express organisational risk tolerance.

ID.RM-3: Inform risk tolerance through sector-specific risk analysis.

PROTECT (PR)

Category	Subcategory
Access Control (PR.AC)	PR.AC-1: Manage identities and credentials for authorised users.

PR.AC-2: Manage physical access to assets.

PR.AC-3: Manage remote access.

PR.AC-4: Implement least privilege and separation of duties.

PR.AC-5: Protect network integrity.

Awareness and Training (PR.AT)

PR.AT-1: Inform and train all users.

PR.AT-2: Ensure privileged users understand roles and responsibilities.

PR.AT-3: Train third-party stakeholders.

PR.AT-4: Educate senior executives.

PR.AT-5: Train physical and information security personnel.

Data Security (PR.DS)

PR.DS-1: Protect data at rest.

PR.DS-2: Protect data in transit.

PR.DS-3: Manage asset lifecycle.

PR.DS-4: Maintain availability capacity.

PR.DS-5: Implement protections against data leaks.

PR.DS-6: Use integrity-checking mechanisms.

PR.DS-7: Separate development and production environments.

DETECT (DE)

Category	Subcategory
Anomalies and Events (DE. AE)	DE.AE-1: Establish a baseline of network operations.
DE.AE-2: Analyse events to understand attack methods.	
DE.AE-3: Aggregate and correlate event data.	
DE.AE-4: Determine the impact of events.	
DE.AE-5: Establish incident alert thresholds.	

RESPOND (RS)

Category	Subcategory
Response Planning (RS.RP)	RS.RP-1: Execute response plan during or after an event.
Communications (RS.CO)	RS.CO-1: Define roles and operations for response.
RS.CO-2: Report events according to criteria.	
RS.CO-3: Share information per response plans.	
RS.CO-4: Coordinate with stakeholders.	
RS.CO-5: Facilitate voluntary information sharing.	

RECOVER (RC)

Category	Subcategory
Recovery Planning (RC.RP)	RC.RP-1: Execute recovery plans during or after an event.
Improvements (RC.IM)	RC.IM-1: Incorporate lessons learned into recovery plans.
RC.IM-2: Update recovery strategies based on experience.	
Communications (RC.CO)	RC.CO-1: Manage public relations post-event.
RC.CO-2: Repair reputation following an incident.	
RC.CO-3: Communicate recovery status with stakeholders.	

This updated framework reflects the integration of the new "Govern" function in NIST CSF 2.0 and enhances the existing categories and subcategories for a more holistic approach to cybersecurity.

Chapter 3

Towards A Resilient Organisation

In this Chapter the same company. XXX. as in Chapter 2 is addressed but this time the subject is resilience. This Chapter is written from the perspective of a resilience provider. This provider could be an internal team or an external consultant.

The Resilience Proposition: the delivery of risk, crisis and continuity management (Disaster Planning).

Please note that the embedded tables have been disabled.

XXX has a Business Continuity Approach, more or less based as follows. This document and those in Chapter 2 need to be edited and integrated to create a Cyber Resilience document.

1.Introduction

1.1 Document aims and objectives

The purpose of this document is:

- To outline what it means to be a resilient organisation.
- To explain what the resilience team can offer.
- To highlight the advisory and training propositions.
- To demonstrate some of the advisory options on offer delivered via a flexible methodology that will meet requirements.
- To reassure that the organisation has the right licences, knowledge, expertise, skills, experience, personal qualities, and attributes required to provide support in this specialist area of work

1.2 Being Resilient What Does It Mean?

Of humans it is said that it is an individual's ability to cope with stress and adversity: in systems to tolerate disruption, or cope with and absorb shocks. This coping attribute may result in the individual or system "bouncing back" to a previous state of normal or improved functioning. In business it is often described as "an ability to adapt to the consequences of a catastrophic failure".

This ability or collective capabilities enable organisations to anticipate key events from emerging trends, constantly adapt to change and to bounce back or bounce forward from disruptive incidents.

Attempts to codify organisational resilience as both a discipline and a management system continue and academic research on resilience to organisational practice is still work in progress. However, what can be concluded is that resilient organisations are forward thinking and able to adapt to changing circumstances which may have damaging effects on their ability to survive and prosper. These include such things as changes to the market in which the organisation operates, competitors, legislation, technology etc., as well as incidents that disrupt the ability to deliver products and services.

The purpose of business continuity management, for example, is to make organisations more resilient: it is the discipline's unifying purpose. In other words, organisations do business continuity in order to make themselves more resilient. Similarly with risk and crisis management but too often these activities are carried out in isolation. What is needed is a coherent and integrated approach which acknowledges that organisations exist on three levels:

• Life before an event – is about risk management
• Life during an event – is about crisis management
• Life after an event – is about business continuity management

1.3 Integration is the Key

Integrating the functions of risk, crisis and continuity management help organisations to build and improve their resilience. These primary management activities provide organisations with a range of capabilities, for example, understanding threats, mitigating probability and impact, responding to events which threaten business or organisational objectives and continue in pursuit of common purpose. As such, organisations which practice risk, crisis and continuity management, as well as other mitigation activity such as physical and logical security, asset protection, fraud prevention, etc., will make the organisation more resilient.

Resilience therefore is a relative and dynamic concept and organisations can only be "more or less resilient". Being resilient is a goal or an objective and not a fixed state and is made possible by integrating many management activities into a cohesive, unifying strategy.

2. What the Team Does

2.1 Introduction

A wide range of training and advisory support services is available across the Resilience Agenda e.g. risk, crisis and business continuity management. The essence of what is normally required to be a resilient organisation revolves around two complementary outputs:

- Individual and collective competencies (e.g. planning, decision-making, managing incidents etc.)
- Documentation to demonstrate evidence of due process (e.g. we _say_ what we do and we _do_ what we say)

2.2 Training, advisory, validation, interim management

These four broad categories include:

Training, education and awareness: across the managerial and technical components of resilience management. For example:

- Management – Policy, programme and project management: risk, crisis and continuity
- Management – Embedding: a culture of resilience

- Operational – Integrating with day-to-day procedural and process requirements
- Technical – Analysis: business impacts, threats and risk assessment
- Technical – Design: risk mitigation and plans development
- Technical – Implementing: risk mitigations and crisis and continuity plans
- Technical – Exercising: risk solutions, crisis and business continuity plans
- Advisory: (e.g. knowledge transfer, mentoring, analysis, programme design and management, document development, standards certification preparation)
- Validation: (e.g. risk, crisis and business continuity team(s) exercising, IT component testing, business teams exercising, performance management, key performance indicators and continuous improvement)
- Interim management: (e.g. manpower substitution, project management, technical support – broadly speaking the placement of technical practitioners for parts or all of the resilience implementation life-cycle)

2.3 The Confidence to Cope

Threats, vulnerabilities, exposures, dependencies and expectations are all on the increase. Solutions are suggested to reduce disruption via risk, crisis and continuity management services. This also includes IT service continuity and information security / assurance consulting, training and exercising for organisations at all levels, from the strategic to the operational.

Using trusted trainers and a network of industry-approved instructors the team is focused on developing the capabilities in people to perform effectively and confidently in crisis situations. Through structured training and team building, leadership development and exercising – based around the development and maintenance of credible risk, crisis and continuity policies, plans, processes and procedures – the team ensures people are confident to cope in a crisis.

It is recognised that whilst good planning is essential, it is people who matter and make the difference – implementing, managing, maintaining and improving their capabilities across the resilience agenda.

It is people who determine the response to – and therefore the outcome of – any crisis, so they need to be well prepared and be supported by credible decision-support materials (e.g. tools, techniques, methods, doctrine etc.)

2.4 What This Means

The team is a network of proven professionals in this specialised field of expertise – specifically what is driving the adoption of risk, crisis and business continuity programmes via threat analysis; and how to prepare for, respond to, cope with and recover from disruption whenever and wherever it occurs – regardless of its cause.

The team understands the application of all aspects of risk, crisis and continuity management within complex organisations and is able to focus on developing people to integrate management systems, plans and procedures which protect staff, reputation, facilities, IT infrastructure and supply chain, thus making XXX more resilient.

2.5 Values

It is appropriate to align with core XXX values. The team is known for a no-nonsense approach when managing training and advisory assignments and strives to make organisations self-sufficient. Delivery hallmarks can be summarised as follows:

- Expert knowledge transfer.
- Trust and reliability.
- Clarity and honesty.
- Excellence in delivery.
- Projects and assignments are always delivered on time and within budget.

The working ethos is to develop a trust-relationship with each XXX team and develop a detailed knowledge of each team's strategy, objectives and business culture. Only by understanding "business-as-usual" can effective resilience policies, plans, processes and procedures be developed to make XXX more resilient and therefore more capable of withstanding disruption whenever and however it occurs.

This approach is based on the principle of a trusted partnership. It is an enabling relationship which supports each client's requirements, while deriving the maximum benefit and return on investment in these relatively new management disciplines. The style is to work closely with its XXX's internal management team(s) – in other words those who are responsible and accountable for ensuring resilience – with the emphasis on working *with* rather than for them.

These attributes are consistent across the three areas of delivery: training, advisory and validation services.

Taking each in turn:

2.6 Training

The team has a wide range of experiences of training within most business environments. The portfolio of risk, crisis and continuity training courses can be targeted at all levels of responsibility within an organisation. The team has access to the full suite of industry-approved (e.g. BCI-approved) training courses. These can be found by clicking on the link below:

BCI endorsed
courses for BCM.xls)

The training courses are tailored to meet the specific needs, objectives and culture of a client organisation and span the full hierarchy from President/Chief Executive through to operational response teams.

Capabilities currently exist (or can be designed from new) to offer a comprehensive portfolio of courses from the basic and awareness level through to expert practitioner and advanced levels in all aspects of risk, crisis and continuity management.

2.7 Advisory

Advisory services in Organisational Resilience are much in demand today and we are happy to work with any size and scale of organisation in any sector of business anytime, anywhere, anyplace.

Resilience programmes for organisations with multiple sites across multiple time zones including those with vital national infrastructure responsibilities have been delivered in many industries and business sectors, e.g. oil, gas, water, electricity etc., as well as many regional and national government departments: police, health, regional administration and authorities etc.

The team adopts an innovative and flexible approach to programme delivery that is based on a sound working knowledge of industry best practice.

2.8 Knowledge Transfer

A key part of the support provided is to ensure a timely and relevant transfer of knowledge and ideas to staff. There is little point the advisors "doing it all for you!"

By transferring proven and practical skills which have been stress-tested in real situations, staff will soon will be able to plan, do, check and act on their own. This increases self-sufficiency in these important management disciplines – particularly setting priorities during crisis management (e.g. save lives, safe environment, safe premises, safe business).

A major benefit of this transfer of expert knowledge and experience is that XXX is provided with plans which work. Plan templates, example policies and other management system documentation can be customised, rather than "re-inventing a brand-new wheel". In this way the time, effort and input required from staff is greatly reduced – thus saving time and money.

It is recognised that clients and their organisations differ in terms of their business operations, their experience and knowledge of risk, crisis and continuity issues, and their specific requirements for support. Rather than adopting a "one size fits all" approach, we offer a highly flexible service, tailored to the needs of each particular client but based on proven principles which work.

2.9 Assurance

The aim is to transfer expert knowledge throughout the life-cycle of any training and advisory assignment. The assurance our clients gain by having external practitioners in direct support means expertise is on call when the need arises.

XXX's risk, crisis, continuity training programmes are aligned with all national guidelines and international standards. This means embedding resilience into business operations and, if necessary, integrating it with existing management systems (e.g. ISO 9001, ISO 27001 etc.). This approach will enable XXX to run and manage a conformant or compliant resilience programme; respond to incidents when they arise and recover from crises long after our engagement and knowledge transfer has come to an end.

This is available on a project-by-project basis or as a renewable "managed service".

2.10 Validation

Many risk, crisis and continuity exercises and performance management programmes (KPIs) to public and private organisations have been delivered around the world. The team design and deliver exercise programmes to ensure that XXX plans are validated and their teams are well prepared to respond to unexpected disruptions.

The team can deliver desktop, workshop and simulation exercises at every scale of size and complexity – from plan walk-throughs to major national and international simulations (please note: the latter require time and resources to execute). The aim is to prepare client's staff – specifically decision-makers – to deliver a fast and effective response and therefore minimise the impact of major disruption on staff, assets, revenue and reputation.

2.11 Specific deliverables

On offer are specific deliverables as individual components or packaged together as part of a wider programme of support. For example, in order to determine what level of training support is needed it is usual to complete a Training or Support Needs Analysis. Please click on the embedded link below for the Training Needs Analysis template for BCM:

Training Needs
Analysis.xlsx

Training Needs Analyses exist for other relevant disciplines, e.g.
• Risk
• Dependency Management

2.12 How Training and Advisory is Delivered

Training and advisory support may be delivered as either help for specific phases / stages in the risk, crisis and continuity management life-cycle or support for every phase / stage. All training and advisory programmes are consistent with industry and international best practice, standards, guidelines and good practice set by ISO organisations, the British Standards Institute and the BCI (www. thebci.org).

2.13 Self Sufficiency

The team believe in helping organisations to help themselves in order that they become self-sufficient and self-reliant: self-sufficiency is a hallmark of a resilient organisation.

Once knowledge transfer is completed across one or two life-cycles of support (e.g. this could be over a three-five year time period) staff will be able to continue the legacy of what has been achieved on their own. Therefore, it is critical that they understand how risk, crisis and continuity processes work and are improved upon in order that they own all the key planning and plan outputs.

The stages of the process which require most external advisory support are usually:

- Understanding how to design and run an effective resilience management system for risk, crisis and continuity (or the integration of all three and other disciplines).
- Establishing risk registers.
- Presenting mitigation options and strategic ideas to Senior Management.
- Conducting business impact analysis and risk and threat assessments.
- Understanding how to design and complete effective Crisis and Continuity plan frameworks and populate templates.
- How to set up and run an exercise programme with credible scenarios such as loss of people, premises, business processes and supply chain partners.
- Analysing supply chain resilience.
- Integrating risk, crisis and continuity with other disciplines and systems (e.g. ISO 9001, 27001).
- Preparation towards certification such as ISO 22301:2012.
- Benchmarking, performance measurement and KPIs.
- Integrating with the EISP and ensuring alignment.

2.14 Developing Resilient Capabilities

The purpose of supporting a resilience assignment is to develop XXX capabilities across a spectrum of management activity defined as follows:

Enterprise Risk Management: a "systematic application of management policies, procedures and practices for communicating, consulting, establishing the context, identifying, analysing, evaluating, treating, monitoring and reviewing risk" in XXX.

Business Continuity: the competence and capability of XXX to continue the delivery of products or services at acceptable redefined levels following disruption.

Business Continuity Management: a management process that identifies potential threats to an organisation and the impacts to business operations those threats, if realised, might cause, and which provides a framework for building organisational resilience with the capability of an effective response that safeguards the interests of its key stakeholders, reputation and brand activities.

A Business Continuity Management System: (or a crisis and continuity management system) forms part of an overall system of governance that establishes, implements, operates, monitors, reviews, maintains and improves business continuity and business resilience.

Crisis Management: the capability of XXX to respond to an "inherently abnormal, unstable and complex situation that represents a threat to its strategic objectives, reputation or existence" and manage the consequences so disruption is kept to a minimum.

A Crisis and / or Business Continuity Plan: a set of documented processes and procedures that guides your organisation to respond, recover, resume and restore critical activities to a pre-defined level following disruption. Typically, this covers resources, services and activities required to ensure the continuity of critical business activities / functions.

A Business Continuity Program: on-going management and governance process supported by Top Management (and appropriately resourced) to implement and maintain business continuity management. This is achieved through the running of a compliant C&CMS.

Cybersecurity (and cyber resilience): a set of documented processes and procedures that helps XXX to protect via the cyber-security plan or respond, recover, resume and restore critical activities to a pre-defined level following disruption should that occur. This would link directly to the current EISP.

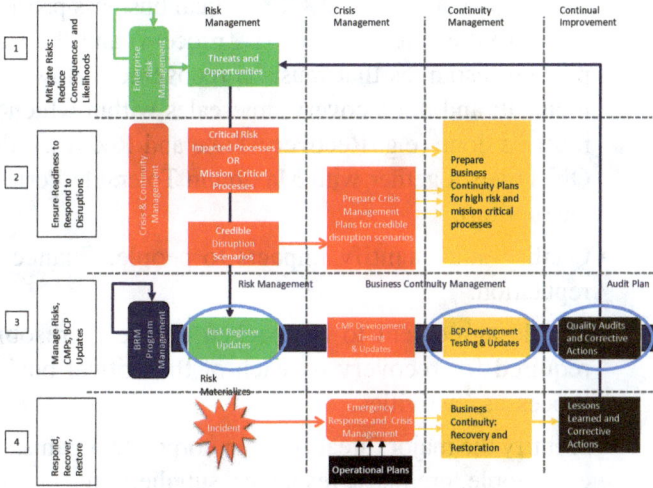

Figure 6: The relationship between Risk, Crisis and Business Continuity Management.

2.15 The Benefits of Training and Advisory Support

The benefits of resilience training and advisory support for either risk, crisis or continuity (or a combination of all three) means that staff:

- Become subject matter experts in their own right via the transfer of knowledge, best practice and proven process which works.

- Learn not just 'what' to do, but also the 'why', 'how' and 'when' of good practice / international standards.

- Are equipped with knowledge and understanding to be able to practice these complementary management disciplines – while all three are highlighted here the focus is on BCM.

- Are provided with practical insights into good practice and expertise by leading and well-respected industry professionals.

- Are able to:
  - Identify the roles and responsibilities of all personnel directly responsible for ensuring the success of the XXX programme and the running of a national standards or ISO conformant management system (e.g. the NCEMA doctrine).

- Identify and agree what XXX critical business processes and activities are (via the BIA process) and their supporting resources that must be recovered following an incident; and the recovery timescales within which this must be done (e.g. Recovery Time and Recovery Point Objectives together with Maximum Tolerable Period of Disruption).
- Qualify and quantify impacts to people, finance and reputation.
- Enable agreement to be reached on the IT resources required for recovery by each of the critical business processes / activities.
- Identify the major threats to your corporate organisation: e.g. people, premises, resources, suppliers etc.
- Provide guidance for an effective and integrated management system together with plan framework(s) for each of your business units.
- Recommend appropriate enhancements to any existing risk, crisis and continuity procedures to meet the requirements of ISO 31000 (risk) BS 11200 (crisis) and ISO 22301 (continuity). Where possible all relevant standards, e.g. including ISO 14000 and 45000. Should be brought together under a common risk process as all have potential EISP and resilience issues.

- Specifically XXX will be able to demonstrate evidence and capability across three areas of continuity and resilience planning:
  - An ability to identify risks to operations and have in place a capability to mitigate and manage those risks (via the existing Risk Management process).
  - An ability to manage uninsurable risk, such as risk to reputation (a key task implied in all Business Continuity planning).
  - A response process: effective response to major disruptions (via the existing and relative mature Crisis Management process).
  - An ability to demonstrate that the process is credible and

consistent via exercising and auditing (AE/SCNS/NCEMA 7000:2015, ISO 31000, BS 11200, ISO 22301 etc.).

○ Competitive advantages conferred by ability to maintain customer service, staff employment etc., (Business Continuity Management).

3. The Training Proposition

3.1 Overview

This section is intended to define the Training proposition (specifically training rather than advisory although they are both supportive of each other); and to whom it should be targeted within your organisation.

3.2 What is the Training Offering and What Is It For?

The training offering is a selection of structured courses, covering the spectrum of risk, crisis and business continuity management in order to focus on the development of further capabilities in resilience.

Courses can be taken individually or combined and can be tailored to meet your specific requirements. All courses are designed for in-house participation: to be hosted by XXX in an on-site location. These are not "public-facing courses" and can be tailored to XXX specific circumstances.

The objective of all training is to enhance XXX's understanding of, develop capabilities in and increase knowledge and improve competency in the primary disciplines of resilience: risk, crisis and continuity management, by using practical examples and case studies to develop practitioner and employee skills, competencies and abilities.

3.3 Targeting the Training

Training offerings are appropriate to organisations with resilience programmes of all levels of maturity.

In general, the following guidelines for suitability apply:

Induction or introduction courses: are aimed at those new to resilience. Staff who require an understanding of the subject (or specific components: risk, crisis and continuity) but who are not destined to become practitioners or subject matter experts. These may include senior managers, C-suite executives and board members: people in other words who have an input to the process but are not directly involved in its implementation or maintenance. General awareness courses are for those employees who are not assigned roles within the response hierarchy, but who need to have an understanding of an organisation's legal obligations, responsibilities, capabilities and practical arrangements

Risk and continuity practitioner courses: are aimed at those who are directly involved in developing, implementing or maintaining a risk, crisis and continuity programme. These are likely to be new risk and continuity managers or members of a risk, crisis or continuity / recovery team. They may also include business representatives who are required to play a coordination role in the implementation and long-term maintenance process e.g. business impact analysis

Crisis Management training: is aimed at members of emergency, crisis or incident management teams – especially decision-makers and first responders (e.g. emergency response and on-scene command). Crisis management leadership courses are for those individuals who may be expected to play a leadership role within such a team in the event of invocation

Crisis Communications courses: are for those who are involved in developing and delivering communications during the response to a major incident. This may include senior management, specialist public relations or customer marketing personnel

Specialist training: addresses some of the more common areas where a more detailed examination of specific issues and methodology may be of benefit. Typically, these courses will be of interest to practitioners who have responsibilities in these areas, e.g. BC managers, IT managers, procurement and supply chain managers.

Other specialist courses can be developed on demand to match a customer's specific requirements

CBCI training: is for continuity practitioners and is an exam-based course for entry into the Business Continuity Institute

3.4 Key features of Training

The following list of features are specific for XXX:

Expertise – Courses can be designed using practitioner subject matter expertise, experience and detailed knowledge of best practice

Fee structure – You know exactly what you are getting for your money before the training delivery begins

Range – Courses can be structured to suit varying knowledge levels and requirements from Executive and Senior Management to new starters. For example:

- Awareness for Executives.
- Awareness for Staff and Employees.
- Technical training for risk / CM / BC Managers.
- Technical training for risk / CM / BC Co-ordinators.
- Training for Crisis Management Teams (strategic, operational and tactical).
- Media Training for Communications teams.
- Integrated Operational Training
- Flexibility – Courses can be customised to meet XXX specific requirements and delivered by trainers who know your sector, industry or business.
- Value – Each course delivers clear benefits to participants in developing and maintaining their resilience competency and capabilities.

3.5 The Training Portfolio

The team offers a comprehensive range of outcome-based training courses designed for people new to the disciplines (e.g. risk, crisis and continuity); as well as experienced practitioners seeking to increase their knowledge of the disciplines e.g. integrating risk, crisis and business continuity management, resilience and crisis communications.

Courses provide a solid foundation of knowledge: why we do this, who is accountable and responsible, how they are achieved e.g. via the various stages of the disciplines e.g. the COSO risk framework, the ICS 3-tier crisis response structure or the 6-stage BCM lifecycle.

3.6 Risk Management

Typically these courses might include:

- What is risk management, why do we do it, who is accountable, how do we do it, when and with what resources?
- Introduction to risk management / enterprise risk management: e.g. COSO[1]
- Practitioner training e.g. risk categorisation / analysis / assessment etc.
- How to develop and maintain a risk register
- Measuring risk: probability and impact, impact and time

3.7 Crisis Management

Typically these courses might include:

- What is a crisis, what is crisis management, why do we need it, who is accountable, how do we do it, when and with what resources?
- Incidents and crises: what is the difference and does it matter?
- Leadership training in crisis management

---

1. The Committee of Sponsoring Organisations of the Treadway Commission (COSO) issued Internal Control – Integrated Framework to help businesses and other entities assess and enhance their internal control systems. That framework has since been incorporated into policy, rule, and regulation, and used by enterprises to better control their activities in moving toward achieving their established objectives.

- Integrated Emergency Management
- Generic 3-tier crisis command structures e.g. Incident Command System
- Crisis Management courses are designed to prepare individuals, teams and organisations to respond to disruption (regardless of cause) using the traditional 3-tier response process. Whether in the public, private or not-for-profit sectors there are defined processes and procedures which make managing a crisis easier through a systematic and consistent approach.
- Courses can be combined to create more comprehensive crisis management training if required by the participants. The individual courses focus on the different aspects of assessing and responding to unexpected incidents, including information management, crisis leadership and crisis communications, as follows:

Crisis Management principles – This course looks at the context and objectives of crisis management and investigates the best practice mechanisms and methodologies commonly used to manage information and record and co-ordinate the response.

Crisis leadership – Exploring team dynamics, potential pitfalls, and the characteristics of effective crisis leadership.

Crisis communications theory & practice – Examines the principles of effective communication, including audiences, content, delivery and control. Includes message preparation, live media interviews to camera and press conference hosting and presentation techniques.

3.8 Business Continuity Management

The spectrum of courses cater to different levels of knowledge, complexity and duration to suit the individual requirements of delegates. For example:

BCM fundamentals – a basic introduction to the subject and to the BCM programme elements aimed at those who need to understand BCM but do not intend to be practitioners, e.g. senior management, programme sponsors, departmental heads etc.

BCM for business unit[2] coordinators – understanding why it is important to maintain, review and improve BCM planning and plans. Aimed at departmental BC coordinators who are tasked with maintaining plans and acting as the link between the BC Manager / Team and the business unit.

BCM awareness – an overview of BCM in general and client-specific strategy and programme structure aimed at all staff within an organisation. This can be delivered via online e-learning.

Specialist courses – e.g. CBCI (for exam-based entry into the Business Continuity Institute).

Courses are aimed at those who are either existing BCM practitioners or who are planning to become one. Content is based on ISO 22301 (the International Standard for BCM) and the Business Continuity Institute's Good Practice Guidelines (GPG) (2020) which covers in detail all six stages of programme management and technical implementation. They take a modular approach, providing learning-based outcomes and are bought to life via group discussion, participation in team-based exercises and involve tools and techniques in use today from actual case studies.

Course modules follow the professional practice structure of GPG 2020 and can either be delivered as practitioner preparation / advancement courses or as a BCI-approved exam-based package:

BCM management practices:

BCM programme Management: designing the programme structure, roles and responsibilities, audit and maintenance programmes etc., based on examples of existing good practice and guidance within the ISO standard.

Embedding BCM in the Organisation: Exploring the issues behind organisational acceptance of BCM, including different audiences, resistance factors, messages and methods for increasing awareness and knowledge of BCM.

BCM technical practices:

Understanding the Organisation: learning what and how to do BIA – business impact analysis and risk assessment for business continuity. This module explains why these are essential and explores the various techniques and methodologies available to the practitioner.

---

2. A business unit is usually defined as an entity, a division, a department, a section, a team.

Designing BCM Strategies: This module demonstrates how to use the information gathered from the BIA and RA to develop a BCM strategy based on available and credible resilience and contingency options.

Implementing a BCM Response: Looking at how we turn the BCM strategy into processes for the business by creating BC and CM plans and options for implementing resilience and contingency measures, including the pros and cons of outsourced provision.

Validation: This module explores the varying types and complexities of exercises, from desktop walkthroughs to full disaster simulation exercises and examines techniques for maintaining and reviewing BCM data and documentation, including the pros and cons of specialist BCM software.

Courses can be combined to create more comprehensive or integrated training.

3.9 Specialist BCM Training

These courses are designed to address specific areas within the risk, crisis and continuity disciplines. By focusing on discrete areas, courses can address these in greater detail. These courses assist practitioners with an approach to, or methodology for, addressing specific issues around implementing and maintaining a successful resilience programme, as follows:

CBCI exam preparation (see comments above)

How to run an exercise programme – a one or two day course for exercise planners

Identifying and reducing Supply Chain risk – a one day course to examine how to identify and prioritise supply chain risk

What we do what
we offer.xlsx

3.10 BCI Approved Courses

The team have agreements with the Business Continuity Institute to deliver their approved instructor-led courses. These include:

- BCI Good Practice Guidelines Training (CBCI) – with exam or without exam
- An Introduction to Business Continuity (see links to examples below)
- BCI Business Impact Analysis (BIA) Course
- BCI Exercise Planning Course
- BCI Crisis and Incident Management Course
- BCI Supply Chain Continuity Management Course
- BCI Writing Business Continuity Plans Course

These courses are available now and only require a minimum amount of preparation to be delivered to your organisation. Please click on the links below for examples of the BCI's Introduction to Business Continuity:

BCI Introduction to BCI Introduction to   The BCI
BC Course V1.2_PRIIBC Training course fIntroduction to Busi

The BCI's certification course (the entry-level exam-based course for BCI membership – Certificate of the BCI) provides an ideal start for professionals seeking a globally recognised credential in business continuity management. The CBCI course is an exam preparation course and as such needs to focus on the GPG 2020. The suggested daily course schedule can be found below:

BCI course outline -
GPG 2013 Exam Cou

An example of CBCI content can be found in Module 1 in the embedded link which follows:

1.ModuleOne.pdf

This is Module 1 (Policy and Programme Management) of 6 modules which prepare delegates for the BCI's Certificate exam. The other BCI approved courses (listed above) can also be delivered as separate or modular courses without an exam.

More courses are scheduled for release and include:

- Embedding Business Continuity to build Organisational Resilience course
- Business Impact Analysis (BIA) – refreshed and updated
- Incident response and Crisis Management course
- Introduction to Organisational Resilience
- Writing & Implementing Business Continuity Plans
- Designing and Delivering Effective Exercises course
- Policy and Programme Management
- Validating your BCM Programme
- Cyber Resilience for BC Practitioners – to be determined
- BCM and Insurance
- Supply Chain Resilience
- Crisis Communications
- BCM for small, medium-sized enterprises
- IT Disaster Recovery and Business Continuity Management

Please visit the Business Continuity Institute website:
http://www.thebci.org/

3.11 Non-approved Courses

The team can also deliver other non-BCI approved courses which are still all about resilience, It's just that they do not carry a Business Continuity Institute endorsement.

These courses can be tailor made to fit your specific organisation's circumstances. A detailed Training Needs Analysis phase would need to be conducted before these could be delivered.

Click on the embedded link below for an example:

Examples of
Non-approved BCM

4. The Resilience Proposition

4.1 Introduction

The team's aim is to help organisations help themselves in order to make them more resilient. A hallmark of a resilient organisation is self-sufficiency – being self-sufficient across a range of complementary management activities.

It is widely accepted that organisational resilience draws on the experience and efforts of a large number of interrelated management disciplines e.g. risk, crisis and continuity. The list of contributory disciplines is extensive and may include emergency response, ICT service continuity, occupational health and safety, environment protection, physical security, supply chain management, information and Cybersecurity management and various forms of risk management (e.g. credit, market, enterprise). For this reason, no one management discipline can credibly claim 'ownership' of organisational resilience since it requires, for its success at an enterprise level, a collaborative approach. Furthermore, organisational resilience cannot be described as a subset of another management activity.

Risk, crisis and business continuity practices explain how organisations can:

- Identify threats.
- Mitigate them.
- Respond effectively (when events conspire against the status quo).
- Prioritise products, services and activities and their timeliness.
- Communicate with key stakeholders and interested parties.

Collectively these processes and procedures (and many more) help organisations to understand what is required to ensure a capability to anticipate and plan for, respond to, cope with and recover from disruption and continue to operate key priorities in the face of disruption. It is unlikely that one individual or one department has the knowledge, skills and expertise necessary to do everything required of an organisation's resilience objectives. The development and enhancement of organisational resilience capabilities, therefore, requires a collaborative effort between participants across many management disciplines.

4.2 Questions, Questions, Questions

Resilience is driven by insatiable curiosity and resilience professionals need to cultivate an enquiring mind. They must be prepared to ask awkward and uncomfortable questions – sometimes without fear of the consequences. For example:

What if: we lose key members of staff, business processes, assets and/or premises?

What if: we lose the data centre, critical information?

What if: we lose key customers and suppliers?

What if introduces a suggestion or speculation about past, present and future events. It is fundamental to resilience planners, planning and plans and applies equally to the primary management disciplines.

4.3 Management Systems

We take a management systems approach to governance or those activities germane to the development of individual and collective capability within a structured framework:

Question: what is the difference between a Risk Mitigation Plan and a Risk Management System?

Question: what is the difference between a Crisis Management Plan and a Crisis Management System?

Question: what is the difference between a Business Continuity Plan and a Business Continuity Management System?

Part of the answer is that a *plan* (noun) is one of many outputs of a *planning* (verb) process; while a management system provides the framework for the design, development, implementation, validation and continuous improvement of all management activities to support your *planning* activity.

A system provides the structure, control mechanisms and assurance (*a system of governance*) that establishes, implements, operates, monitors, reviews, maintains and improves your resilience. This underpins the Deming doctrine of PDCA (plan, do, check, act) to which the team subscribes and includes:

Context of the organisation:

- Leadership.
- Planning.
- Support.
- Operation.
- Performance & Evaluation.
- Improvement.

4.4 Delivery of Advisory Services

The key to note is that the activity of doing risk, crisis and continuity management needs a collaborative management systems approach. In helping you to develop, sustain and improve your Resilience Management System (RMS) it should differentiate between:

- Risk, Crisis and Business Continuity (XXX competencies and capabilities).
- Risk, Crisis and Business Continuity Management (XXX Process and Procedures for managing your threats and mitigations, your response and continuity of service / product).
- Risk, Crisis and Business Continuity Management System (XXX planning and management system using the universally accepted doctrine of Plan, Do, Check, Act).
- Risk, Crisis and Business Continuity Plan(s) (e.g. outputs from the process).

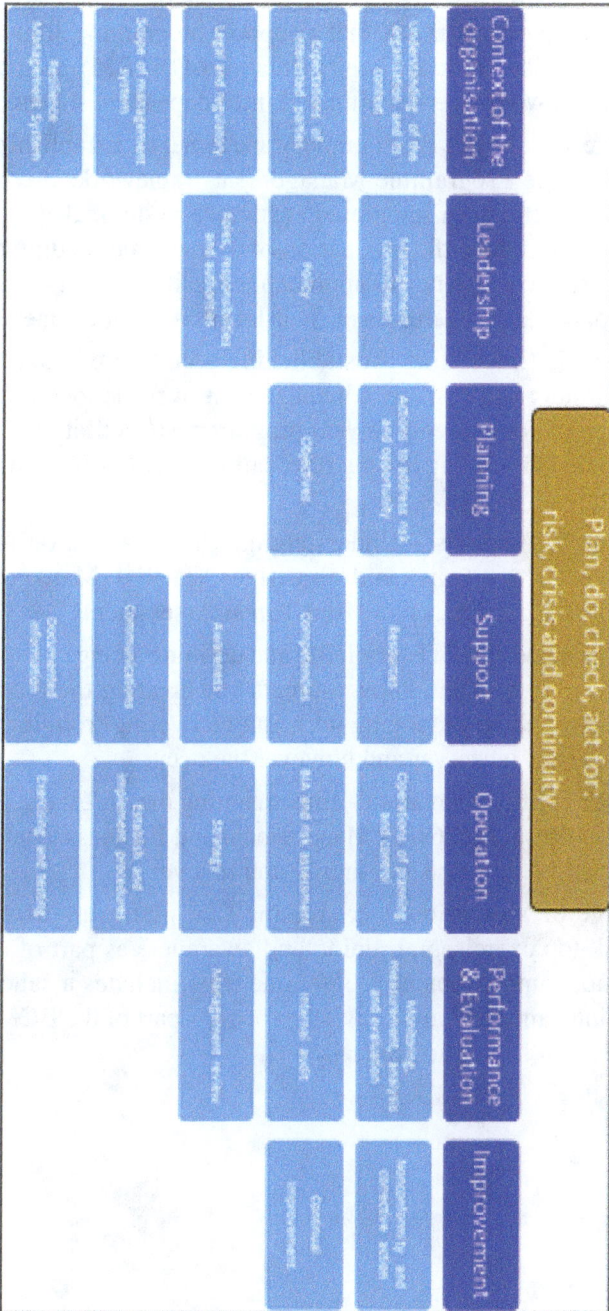

Figure 7: Plan, Do, Check, Act.

This recommends to XXX that a support programme aligns with these principles; while the implementation of any RMS programme should follow six over-lapping and inter-dependent stages:

- Stage 1: Policy & Programme Management – Establishing the Resilience Programme Management framework, the policy and designing an integrated resilience system. If necessary this will include the production of a "group defined practice" to ensure consistency of approach for resilience matters across all operations regardless of their location or time zone

- Stage 2: Embedding – establishing a culture of risk, crisis, continuity and resilience management over the long term (be prepared for a three-five year programme of activity to embed the behavioural attributes of creating a long-term resilience culture)

- Stage 3: Analysis – Understanding the organisation and its context, complexity and objectives via Risk Management, Business Impact analysis and Threat Assessments

- Stage 4: Design – Determining and defining a range of strategy options to mitigate known threats and creating the processes for responding to, coping with and recovering from incidents whenever, wherever and however the occur

- Stage 5: Implementation – Implementing measures: e.g. Emergency Response, Crisis Management and Business Continuity plans (for response, continuity and recovery)

- Stage 6: Validation – Exercising (i.e. plan walkthroughs / desk-top exercises), training and awareness as part of a continuous improvement programme (this includes a scheduled maintenance and audit review process – part of the BCMS but not a full simulation exercise)

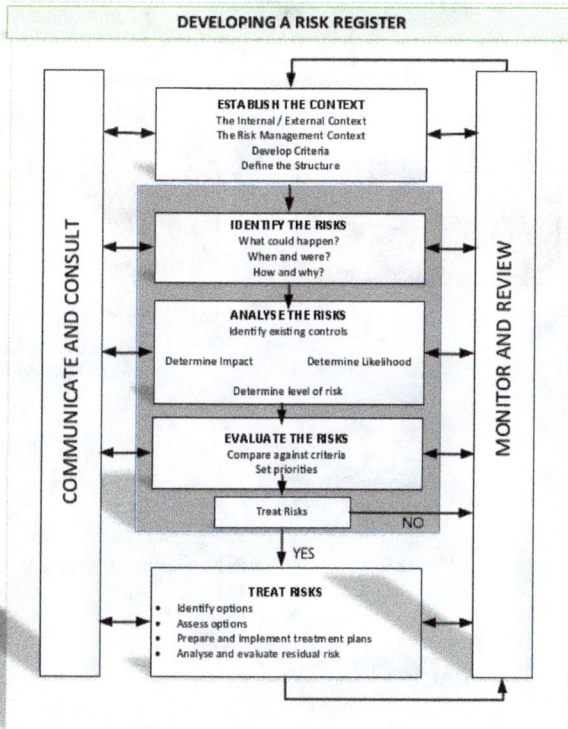

Figure 8: The Enterprise Risk Management Life-cycle.

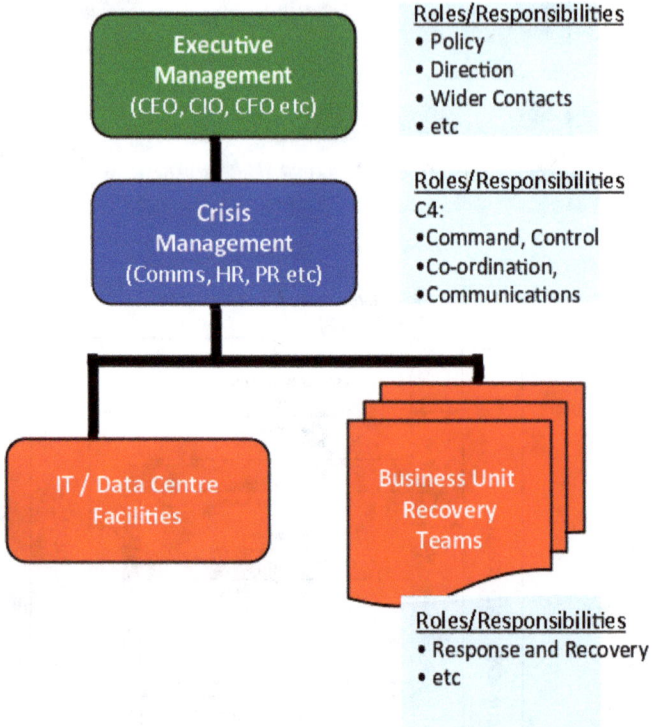

Executive Management (CEO, CIO, CFO etc)

Roles/Responsibilities
• Policy
• Direction
• Wider Contacts
• etc

Crisis Management (Comms, HR, PR etc)

Roles/Responsibilities
C4:
• Command, Control
• Co-ordination,
• Communications

IT / Data Centre Facilities

Business Unit Recovery Teams

Roles/Responsibilities
• Response and Recovery
• etc

Figure 9: The 3-tier Crisis Management Structure

Six Professional Practices (PP)

Management Practices

PP1	Policy & Programme Management
PP2	Embedding Business Continuity

Technical Practices

PP3	Analysis
PP4	Design
PP5	Implementation
PP6	Validation

Figure 10: The Business Continuity Management Life-cycle

Following proven implementation models and process life-cycles for the components of resilience ensures that you align with "good practice" and international standards. We implement your resilience programme and develop your capabilities, plans and management systems in a systematic and consistent way.

4.5 The Integrated Approach

All resilience management systems share the following attributes:
- Training, awareness and exercising.
- Document development and control.
- Management review.
- Internal audit.
- Corrective / preventive action(s).

The act of integration arises by examining existing processes and if necessary and where appropriate by adding new practices to your existing ones and hence revising, updating, refreshing your current documents or by creating new ones. The evidence for XXX resilience capabilities becomes the combined output of competent and trained members of staff and documentation to prove it.

5. How Resilience Services Are Delivered – Statements of Intent

5.1 Stage 1 – Description

Programme Management: The first stage will include: a Project Initiation Meeting (physical or virtual) to confirm the programme objectives, requirements, identify stakeholders, establish the project implementation and management principles and reporting arrangements, and refine the precise scope and content of the work, together with relevant contacts and responsibilities.

Project Initiation: This will be written up as a Project Initiation Document (PID) to capture the agreed content, scope and approach. It will also clarify timings for the work, and resources needed from your organisation (mainly about availability of staff for interviews, review of documents etc.).

The PID will confirm the detailed objectives, timescales and deliverables and establish other practical requirements for the success of the project. It will set out the project plan, key milestones, quality control criteria and any perceived risks to the project and what steps should be taken to mitigate them.

Gap Analysis: This stage will allow some time for initial investigation, familiarisation or "discovery" – to help confirm the scope of the programme and report by way of a high-level gap analysis. Once we understand "where you are now" then we can help you "get to where you need to be". We recommend that a gap analysis includes initial discussions with members of your operational management team(s) and, possibly, discussions with Directors responsible for critical activities / priority services for which continuity plans are required.

System Design: The team will help XXX to design a Business Resilience System ensuring that it aligns with (or can be certified against) the requirements specified in relevant national and international standards (e.g. see Annex A). This will include all necessary directions and high-level principles for setting up and running a resilience management system. Its scope will be defined taking into account: XXX mission, objectives, EISP, legal responsibilities and internal and external obligations; products and services; and the needs of interested parties; as well as risk appetite and how the system fits existing management systems.

Policy Development: Working on behalf of XXX Senior Management (Executive and Board), the team drafts a policy which is appropriate to the purpose of the organisation (taking into account its size, nature, complexity, culture, dependencies and operational environment). The Policy provides a framework for setting objectives; states legal and regulatory requirements and continuous improvement criteria for your business resilience system. It communicates your strategic intent to interested parties and is consistent with other management policies you may already have (e.g. for quality, H&S, environmental) and aligns, could include, the EISP.

The Policy will also provide direction on scope, limitations and any exclusions; responsibilities, incidents types and their scale and align with relevant standards, guidelines etc.

5.2 Stage 2 – Description

Embedding a culture of resilience: This phase wraps around the entire implementation programme and should aim to last indefinitely. Creating a culture of resilience can take 3-5 years. The changes which occur as a result of Continuous Improvement are subtle and must be viewed over the long term. This stage is about changing or influencing human behaviours while hardening the physical and logical attributes of your organisation: thus making it more resilient.

This does not happen overnight. As soon as a contract is awarded, however, initiatives can be begun in earnest. The primary objective of this stage is to give all relevant interested parties the ability to plan, the confidence to cope and the reassurance to recover if or when significant disruption occurs. Knowing what XXX priorities are, who will do what, how, when and with what resources becomes the focal point of a training and competency development programme. This can be targeted at individuals and teams.

5.3 Stage 3 – Description

An organisation achieves its purpose by delivering goods or services to customers. Therefore it is important for the organisation to understand the effects of impact or disruption on product or service delivery over time.

The risk, BIA and threat assessment process enables your organisation to identify measures that:

- Highlight your risk appetite and approach to risk management.
- Reduces the likelihood of disruption.
- Limits the impact of a disruption on your organisation.
- Shortens the period of disruption.

Understanding XXX business. Business Impact Analysis is the critical stage and the foundation upon which all resilience planning is dependent. BIA identifies, quantifies and qualifies the impacts of a loss, interruption or disruption to business processes, assets and capabilities while providing the data from which appropriate risk mitigation, business continuity and recovery strategies are developed and maintained.

The purpose of Business Impact Analysis is to:

- Understand your organisation's key products and services and the processes and business activities that deliver them.
- Determine priorities and timeframes for resuming activities (e.g. recovery time objective and maximum tolerable period of disruption).
- Identifying and estimating the resources likely to be required for continuity and recovery.
- Identify dependencies (both internal and external).

The BIA will identify and determine critical activities (ISO 22301 = "prioritised activities") and determine their relative priorities for recovery. It will reveal Recovery Time Objectives, Recovery Point Objectives and a Maximum Tolerable Period of Disruption (MTPD) for your time-critical activities as well as identify stake-holders, dependencies and any obvious single points of failure. It will identify and quantify the resources required for your critical activities in order to meet stated RTOs.

When assessing impacts these will relate to your business aims and objectives and any relevant interested parties. Criteria may include:

- Adverse effects on staff or public well-being.
- Consequences of being in breach of statutory or regulatory requirements.
- Damage to reputation.
- Reduced financial viability.
- Deterioration of product or service.
- Environmental damage.

In summary, the BIA will highlight:

- Products, services and activities.
- Recovery priorities.
- Significant dependencies and supporting resources.

Risk and Threat Assessment. XXX should have a formal risk

assessment process that systematically identifies, analyses and evaluates the risk of disrupting your organisation's time-critical activities and the processes, systems, information, people, assets, suppliers and other resources that support them. It is expected that your risk management process to align with ISO 31000.

Taking a structured process attempts to answer:

- What may happen and why?
- What might be the consequences?
- What is the likelihood of an event happening?
- Is there anything that might mitigate the consequences or reduce the likelihood before the event occurs?

XXX should consider financial, government and societal obligations and understand the threats to and vulnerabilities within resources required. In particular those:

- Required by an activity with high priority
- With a significant replacement lead-time

Risk identification. Risks of disruption to "prioritised activities" are the main area of focus. This means specific threats which may disrupt activities and resources, e.g.

- Fire, flood, power failure, staff loss, staff absenteeism, computer virus and hardware failure, etc.
- Disruptive incidents which may arise from vulnerabilities within resources e.g.
- Single points of failure, lack of fire protection, lack of power resilience, inadequate staffing levels, poor IT security and resilience etc.

Risk evaluation. Assess and evaluate which disruption-related risks require treatment. The focus is on resources required by activities with high priority or significant replacement lead time.

Risk treatment. Identify treatments that can deliver the business continuity objectives and are in accordance with your organisation's risk appetite.

Results or outputs of the BIA process will be delivered via a documented Findings Report which includes high level strategy options for response and recovery. Combining Stages 3 and 4 of implementation in one document *saves both time and money* and collates strategy decision-support information with its analysis in one integrated document.

A completed BIA has a significant added benefit: it also serves as an interim Business Continuity plan for the organisation, department or section which has completed it <u>before</u> plans are fully written and approved. Once a department has completed a BIA this becomes their interim BC plan thus ensuring an early quick win in the process.

5.4 Stage 4 – Description

Design: determining and selecting Strategies: Alternative risk mitigation, response and recovery options / strategies are identified and highlighted in the same Findings Report (see above) as for Stage3. This saves time and money and is consistent with a flexible delivery method.

This stage is about identifying the action needed to address the findings from the BIA and Risk and Threat Assessment in such a way that meets the business continuity objectives of your organisation, e.g.

- Carrying our production or service delivery across different premises.
- Installing backup power.

Reducing the overall impact of disruption through business continuity arrangements that shortens the period of interruption and reduce its severity (or intensity) to an acceptable level

Strategies are based on the outputs from your risk, BIA and threat assessments. Strategies include protecting, mitigating, stabilising, continuing, recovering and resuming prioritised activities and their dependent resources.

5.5 Stage 5 – Description

Implementation: developing and implementing a response: This stage formalises the analysis in Stage 3-4 and pulls together the results and decisions to enable crisis and continuity plans to be developed, written and implemented. These plans may include:

- Emergency Response and Crisis Management.
- Communications.
- Safety and Welfare.
- Damage Assessment.
- Salvage and Security.
- Recovery of ICT.
- Continuation activities for departments or business functions.
- Resumption and return to normal plans.

Plans will outline accountabilities, roles and responsibilities together with resources required for continuity and recovery, alternate work locations (if required) etc.

5.6 Stage 6 – Description

Validation: exercising, maintaining and review: the team will work with a number of trusted third partners for delivering full-scale exercises. The principle is to test systems, exercise plans and rehearse people. This is the moment when all the planning begins to make sense and is a vital part of the process. Without at least one or two exercises it is unlikely that your plans will work and so the aim of an exercise programme is to validate the plans – especially your Crisis / Incident Management Plans – and familiarise people (e.g. the Crisis Management teams) with their roles, responsibilities and accountabilities.

Exercising Crisis Management Team(s) is best left towards the end of the plan's development process but the awareness programme can begin as soon as a contract is awarded – in Stage 2 if necessary. It is recommended that awareness briefings / workshops begin early to assist with the process of organisational "buy-in". This is consistent with the team's flexible delivery methodology.

5.7 Summary of Deliverables

Stage	Lifecycle	Outputs / deliverables
1	Programme Management	Project Initiation Document
		Project Plan
		(Carry out high level gap analysis against ISO 22301 / ISO 31000 and report) – Optional
		Resilience Policy Framework
		Resilience supporting documentation (e.g. stakeholder map, policy, draft operations manual etc.)
		Process descriptors, processes, procedures, tools, techniques which align with a "standards-based approach"
		Status reports, stage closure reports, quality assurance etc.
2	Embedding Business Continuity	A long term (e.g. 3-5 years) individual and collective training and exercise programme.
3	Business Impact Analysis	Customised / completed BIA questionnaires for each key department and/or directorate / department / service within scope
		Completed BIA interviews following workshops and briefings
		Findings report including:
		confirmation of key business functions, systems and services
		RTOs / RPOs / MTPD / MBCO etc.
		Resources required

	Risk / Threat Assessment	Completed high-level assessment of threats to critical activities
		Identification of any significant single points of failure
		Risk mitigation measures
4	Resilience Strategy:[3]	Recommended risk, crisis and business continuity strategy options
		Recommended "hard-wiring" options to make organisation more resilient
5	Crisis and Business Continuity Plan Framework(s):[4]	Documented Crisis / Incident Management structure based on 3-tier ICS model
		ICT Continuity Plan framework (if required)
		IT Cybersecurity plan
		Departmental continuity and recovery plan templates / frameworks (one for each business unit / entity in scope)
6	Validation programme	Training and exercise programme
		Plan walkthroughs and training to validate plans in Stage 5.

5.8 Programme Milestones

Programme milestones and priorities are as follows:

1. Completed project plan (for all stages of implementation)
2. Completed Resilience Management System (includes policy)

---

3. The team recommends that the BIA, Risk Assessment and Strategy Options are delivered as one Findings Report. This saves money and considerable time. Client should lead delivery for this stage and be supported by consultant.

4. The team recommends that they provide plan frameworks to be finalised by individual teams within your organisation. This also saves both time and money and helps the awareness campaign. Your business / depts must "own" their plans.

3. Completed Findings Report (Business Impact Analysis + Risk Assessment + Strategy Options)

4. Completed Plan frameworks and supporting documentation for: Risk, Crisis and Business Continuity and Crisis / Incident Management etc.

5. Completed first round of Crisis / Incident Management / Executive desktop walk-through(s).

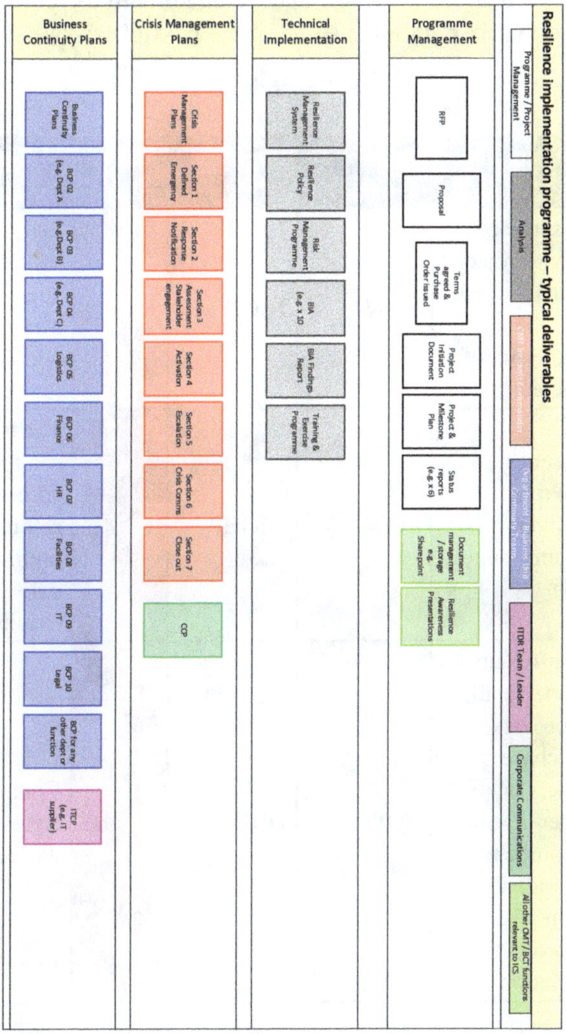

Figure 11: Deliverables

5.10 Project Risks

There are a number of potential risks to any resilience programme. These should be discussed during contract negotiations, at an initiation meeting, addressed where possible, and managed throughout the life of the project. We will also consider any potential new risks during the programme's life-cycle and will bring these to the programme board's attention and manage them as required. The following matrix highlights some of the possible risks:

ID	Description	Probability	Impact	Priority	Mitigation Notes
01	Absence of client Project Manager and / or client lead Point of Contact.	LOW	HIGH	1	Lead for resilience to be appointed (e.g. merge existing with Risk function).
02	Absence of Project Delivery Team – supply side	LOW	HIGH	1	The team can arrange access to extra resources for a multi-functional delivery team if required.
03	Insufficient scope detail, approvals, purchase orders or other pertinent resource not provided or in place at project initiation	LOW	HIGH	1	Contract signed. Scope is defined.

ID	Description	Probability	Impact	Priority	Mitigation Notes
04	Insufficient access (remote or physical) to systems	LOW	MEDIUM	2	Security clearance? The team do not usually require physical access to IT systems unless Cybersecurity is a key deliverable
05	Insufficient access to relevant personnel	LOW	HIGH	2	Workshops and BIAs will be scheduled in advance.
06	Insufficient physical access to sites	LOW	HIGH	2	A client project manager acts as a point of contact.
07	Failing to meet deadlines	LOW	MEDIUM	3	None anticipated.
08	Assignment "creep"	LOW	MEDIUM	3	Project Initiation Document defines Terms of Reference.
09	Insufficient budget	LOW	HIGH	3	Budget agreed. There will be a fixed element and a variable element.

ID	Description	Probability	Impact	Priority	Mitigation Notes
10	Insufficient education & awareness programmes linking with risk management approach.	MED	HIGH	6	Establish an E&A programme linking with risk management

Key	Probability >		Low	Medium	High
		High	Low / High	Medium / High	High / High
	Impact	Medium	Low / Medium	Medium / Medium	High / Medium
		Low	Low / Low	Medium / Low	High / Low

Probability is defined as the likelihood that the impact of a risk will be incurred.

Impact is defined here as a risk's ability to prevent an objective or deliverable from being achieved or to cause significant delay, increase in cost, or unacceptable reduction in quality. Please note that the risks listed here are only a preliminary indication of the possible risks and their probability and likely level of impact. A more detailed risk assessment would be required in order to establish a more accurate understanding of the risks facing the project.

Annex A – List of References

Relevant standards and references are highlighted below and include:

Code	Discipline	What does it offer
BS 31000	Risk Management	Code of practice and guidance for the implementation of BS ISO 31000
BS 65000	Organisational Resilience	Guidance on organisational resilience
BS 11200	Crisis Management	Guidance and good practice
ISO 22301	Emergency Management	Requirements for incident response
ISO 22301	Business Continuity Management	Management Systems Requirements
ISO 22313	Business Continuity management	Management Systems Guidance
AE/SCNS/ NCEMA 7000	Business Continuity Management Standard –	Specifications for a Management System
BS PD 25222	Business Continuity Management	Guidance on Supply Chain Continuity

PD 25666	Business Continuity Management	Guidance on Exercising and Testing for Continuity and Contingency Programmes
BS ISO / IEC 27031	Information Technology – Security techniques	Guidelines for Information and Communications Technology readiness for Business Continuity
ISO / IEC 24762	Information Technology – Security Techniques	Guidelines for Information and Communications Technology Disaster Recovery Service
GPG 2013	Business Continuity Management	Business Continuity Institute Good Practice Guidelines 2013

Annex B – Glossary of Key Terms

Initials	Meaning	Comment
AOR	Area of Responsibility	
BAU	Business As Usual	
BCM	Business Continuity Management	
BCMS	Business Continuity Management System	
BIA	Business Impact Analysis	
BSI	British Standards Institute	
C&CM	Crisis and Continuity Management	
CMP	Crisis Management Plan	
CMT	Crisis Management Team	
CoP	Community of Practice	
DNS	Domain Name System / Server	
DR	Disaster Recovery	
ECC	Emergency Control Centre	EOC – Emergency Operations Centre
ELT	Executive Leadership Team	
HSSE	Health, Safety, Security, Environmental	
ICT	Information Communications Technology	

Initials	Meaning	Comment
ISO	International Standards Organisation	
IT	Information Technology	
ITCM	Information Technology Continuity Management	Often known as "IT Disaster Recovery"
ITDR	IT Disaster Recovery	More often known as ITCM
KPI	Key Performance Indicator	
MRT	Mutual Response Team	
MTPD	Maximum Tolerable Period of Disruption	Sometimes known as Maximum Acceptable Outage – MAO
RPO	Recovery Point Objective	Tolerable data loss
RTO	Recovery Time Objective	
SME	Subject Matter Expert	
SPA	Single Point of Accountability	
SPoF	Single Point of Failure	
TNA	Training Needs Analysis	

Annex C – Definitions

Term	Definition
Competence	Ability to apply knowledge and skills to achieve intended results.
Continual improvement	Recurring activity to enhance performance (ISO 22300).
Corrective action	Action to eliminate the cause of nonconformity and to prevent recurrence (ISO 22300).
Document	Information and its supporting medium (paper, magnetic, electronic, optical disk, photograph, master sample.
Effectiveness	Extent to which planned activities are realised and planned results achieved (ISO 22300).
Internal Audit	Audit conducted by, or on behalf of, the organisation itself for management review and other internal purposes, and which might form the basis for an organisation's self-declaration of conformity.
Management System	Set of interrelated or interacting elements of an organisation to establish policies and objectives, procedures and processes to achieve those objectives
Nonconformity	Non-fulfilment of a requirement (ISO 22300)
Policy	Intentions and direction of an organisation as formally expressed by its top management (what and why)

Procedure	Specified way to carry out an activity or a process (ISO 9000) (how and with what resources)
Record	Statement of results achieved or evidence of activities performed
Top Management	Person or group of people who directs and controls an organisation at the highest level
Vendor	The party in the supply chain that makes goods and services available to companies or consumers. The term vendor is typically used to describe the entity that is paid for the goods that are provided, rather than the manufacturer of the goods. A vendor, however, can operate both as the supplier of goods (seller) and the manufacturer.

As of 2024 this is, more or less, where a CIO and CISO should have managed to get their organisation. Unless the above is, more or less, in place there is not a great deal of point in trying to institute what follows in terms of Mixed Reality Leadership,

SECTION 2

Achieving Mixed Reality Leadership

Chapter 4

A Framework for Mixed Reality Leadership

Introduction

The freedom to lead often comes from managing the detail effectively. So far there has been much management guidance in this book to ensure that, particularly from a resilience perspective, an organisation is in a good place to move forward. After Chapters 2 and 3 are working for the organisation, it is time to take the next steps in Mixed Reality Leadership. The first steps, as always, are to make sure the organisation's vision, mission, strategy and governance are properly in place. For some reason, this is where, often, organisations fail at the outset.

Vision and Strategic Alignment

Define a Mixed Reality Vision

Establish a clear and compelling purpose for integrating physical and virtual environments that aligns with the organisation's values, strategic goals and Enterprise Information Security Plan approach (Chapter 2). This vision should articulate how mixed reality (MR) will drive innovation, enhance operational resilience, and foster ecosystem growth. It should also consider industry trends, competitive advantages, and long-term sustainability, ensuring that the adoption of MR technology creates meaningful value for employees, customers, and stakeholders.

Set Key Objectives

Identify specific, measurable objectives that demonstrate the tangible benefits of Mixed Reality implementation. These may include enhancing operational efficiency through process automation, improving security by leveraging immersive training and real-time threat detection, and fostering a more engaged workforce with interactive collaboration tools. Additionally, consider key performance indicators (KPIs) to track success, such as reduced downtime, increased productivity, or higher employee satisfaction rates.

Develop a Roadmap

Design a structured, phased approach that outlines both short-term and long-term strategies for successful Mixed Reality adoption. This roadmap should include key milestones such as selecting and integrating the right MR technologies, developing a robust infrastructure, and ensuring seamless interoperability with existing systems. Additionally, prioritise workforce upskilling initiatives to equip employees with the necessary digital competencies and foster a culture that embraces technological evolution. Address potential challenges such as resistance to change, cybersecurity risks, and scalability to ensure a smooth and sustainable transition

To effectively communicate the concept of **Mixed Reality (MR) Leadership** to both the **Chief Information Security Officer (CISO)** (also include: Chief Information Office (CIO)r/Chief Digital Officer (CDO)) and the **newest employee**, we need tailored messaging that resonates with their roles, responsibilities, and levels of expertise. Here's how:

For the CISO: Ensuring Security and Governance in MR Leadership

Key Message:

As MR bridges the physical and digital worlds, resilience in general, cybersecurity in particular, data protection, and risk management become more complex. Your role is crucial in ensuring that MR adoption aligns with security best practices, regulatory compliance, and organisational resilience.

How It Affects the CISO:

- **Data Protection:** MR systems collect vast amounts of personal, corporate, and environmental data—ensuring its security is critical. Data management contracts are key.
- **Cybersecurity Measures:** Safeguarding against threats such as data breaches, deepfake attacks, and virtual space hacking is essential. DNS server security is key.
- **Policy Development:** Creating governance frameworks to manage authentication, access control, and ethical use of MR technology. Check that these all align with each other.
- **Resilience Planning:** Preparing for potential risks such as system failures or cyberattacks that could disrupt operations. This can be expensive and time consuming, but the alternative?

Personal Responsibility:

- Define and implement security protocols for MR applications.
- Ensure compliance with data protection laws (e.g., GDPR, CCPA).
- Collaborate with IT teams to assess vulnerabilities in MR infrastructure.
- Educate employees on security best practices in immersive environments.
- Ensure you participate fully in the new Trust environment.

For the Newest Employee: Understanding MR Leadership and Your Role

Key Message:

Mixed Reality enhances the way we work, collaborate, and interact with digital tools. As a new employee, your role is to embrace these technologies responsibly, ensuring a seamless blend between virtual and physical workflows.

How It Affects the Employee:

- **Enhanced Collaboration:** MR tools improve remote teamwork, making communication more immersive.
- **Efficient Learning & Training:** MR-based onboarding and training programs accelerate skill development.
- **Workplace Safety & Security:** Awareness of how to securely interact with MR tools minimises risks.
- **Innovation & Engagement:** Being open to experimenting with MR fosters creativity and engagement.
- **Trust in yourself,** your team and your leadership, and vice versa, is key.

Personal Responsibility:

- Follow organisational guidelines on MR usage.
- Maintain awareness of cybersecurity risks in virtual spaces.
- Use MR tools to enhance productivity while ensuring data integrity.
- Provide feedback on MR experiences to help improve user adoption.
- Ensure you participate fully in the new Trust environment.

Bridging the Gap: A Unified Approach

To align both the CISO and the newest employee, **MR Leadership should be a shared responsibility** that balances security, innovation, and user experience. By fostering a **culture of trust, awareness, training, and collaboration**, the organisation can ensure MR is implemented safely and effectively.

Here's a **detailed implementation plan and training framework** to support of **Mixed Reality (MR) Leadership** across all levels of the organisation, ensuring that both the **CISO** and the **newest employee** understand their roles and responsibilities.

Implementation Plan for Mixed Reality Leadership

This plan outlines a **structured approach** for integrating MR securely and efficiently while ensuring **alignment across leadership, security, and employees**.

Establish Leadership & Governance

Objective: Define clear leadership roles, responsibilities, and security policies for MR adoption.

Actions:

- Form an **MR Governance Committee** with all C-Suite but especially **CISO, CDO/CIO, HR, IT, and Innovation Leaders**. **CEO, CFO and COO must be fully aware.**
- Establish **security policies** for MR usage, including data protection, compliance, and access control.
- Develop **a strategic roadmap** with short-term and long-term goals for MR integration.

Deliverables:

- MR Governance Framework (Roles, Policies, and Best Practices)
- Cybersecurity & Compliance Guidelines for MR Environments

Cybersecurity & Risk Management (Led by the CISO with CEO and CRO)

Objective: Ensure MR solutions align with security standards and protect sensitive data.

Actions:

- Conduct **cyber risk assessments** on MR hardware, software, and networks.

- Implement **access control & authentication mechanisms** (e.g., biometrics, MFA).
- Train employees AND cloud providers on **secure data handling in MR environments**.
- Set up **real-time threat monitoring** for MR platforms.

Deliverables:

- Secure MR Access Management System
- MR Incident Response & Recovery Plan
- Cybersecurity Training Modules for Employees

Employee Onboarding & Training (For All Employees, Including New Hires)

Objective: Provide structured MR training to ensure safe, productive usage.

Actions:

Develop **role-specific MR training modules**:
- **Basic MR Awareness Training** (for all employees)
- **Train, explain, the issue of Trust in an MT environment (for everyone)**
- **Advanced MR Security & Compliance Training** (for IT & Security teams)
- **Leadership & Innovation in MR** (for executives & managers)
  - Implement **interactive MR training simulations** to teach safe usage.
  - Ensure ongoing **feedback loops** where employees report challenges and improvements.

Deliverables:

- MR Training Program (Beginner to Advanced)
- Hands-on MR Simulations for Employees
- Security & Ethical Use Guidelines

Integration into Daily Operations

Objective: Ensure MR tools enhance productivity, collaboration, and innovation.

Actions:

- Deploy MR solutions for **virtual meetings, digital twin simulations, and hands-free workflows**.
- Encourage **cross-functional teams** to experiment with MR for improved processes.
- Implement **MR-based employee engagement programs** to drive adoption.
- Use **real-time analytics** to measure MR's impact on efficiency and engagement.

Deliverables:

- MR Adoption Metrics & Performance Reports
- Best Practices Guide for MR Integration in Workflows
- Organisational Trust

Operations Training Framework for Mixed Reality Leadership

This **tiered training approach** ensures that both the **CISO and employees** receive the knowledge they need at the right level.

Level 1: Basic MR Awareness Training (For All Employees)

Objective: Provide fundamental knowledge of MR technology and workplace applications.

Topics Covered:

- What is Mixed Reality? (Differences between XR, AR, VR, AI & MR)
- How MR is used in the organisation
- Basic security & privacy considerations

Delivery Method: Online course, interactive demos, MR-based tutorials

Level 2: MR Security & Compliance (For IT & Security Teams, Led by the CISO)

Objective: Train employees on securing MR platforms and handling data responsibly.

Topics Covered:

- Cybersecurity threats in MR (Deepfake risks, data breaches, MR phishing)
- Access control & authentication in MR environments
- Data encryption & compliance (GDPR, HIPAA, etc.)

Delivery Method: Live workshops, cybersecurity drills, penetration testing simulations

Level 3: MR Leadership & Innovation (For Executives & Managers)

Objective: Equip leaders with the knowledge to drive MR adoption and innovation.

Topics Covered:

- Strategic impact of MR on business growth
- Managing security & ethical concerns in MR
- Future trends & investment strategies in MR

Delivery Method: Executive briefings, strategy workshops, case studies

And, of course, reinforce the Trust aspect of the organisation from top to bottom.

Measuring Success: Key Metrics & Continuous Improvement

To ensure MR Leadership is effective, track progress using these **Key Performance Indicators (KPIs):**

Security & Compliance Metrics (For the CISO & IT)

- Reduction in MR-related security incidents
- Compliance with data protection regulations
- MR system penetration test success rate

Employee Engagement & Productivity Metrics

- Percentage of employees completing MR training
- Productivity improvements using MR tools
- Employee feedback on MR experience
- Organisational Trust becomes evident

Business Impact Metrics

- Cost savings from MR-driven efficiency
- New innovations & solutions enabled by MR
- ROI on MR investments

Final Thoughts & Next Steps

By implementing this **structured plan and training framework**, the organisation ensures that **Mixed Reality Leadership** is **secure, scalable, and effective** and the whole workforce trusts each other.

(How trust is developed is very much an organisation and leadership specific issue).

Immediate Next Steps:

- Check organisation positioning against Chapter 2.
- **CISO:** Finalise MR security policies & risk assessment.
- **HR & IT:** Launch MR onboarding & training programs.
- **Leadership Team:** Align MR roadmap with business objectives.
- **Employees:** Begin foundational MR awareness training.

Governance and Organisational Structure

- **Mixed-Reality Governance Board (MRGB)** – The Saxton Bampfylde Model
    - Include diverse expertise: technology, human behaviour, risk management, and sustainability.
    - Focus on ethical technology adoption and holistic decision-making.

- **Evolved C-Suite Composition**:
    - Introduce new roles like Chief Mixed Reality Officer (CMRO) and Chief Resilience Officer (CRO).
    - Foster collaboration across technical, strategic, and human-centric functions.

Digital / Data

"We are going to gain traction post-pandemic because of digital."

The COVID-19 pandemic has proven that digital development is at the core of business economy. This is only going to heighten and bring forward a greater growth of and reliance upon digital capabilities. This depth of understanding of how these rapidly will increase the levels of data being generated and the potential this brings to understand and evolve business models and strategies in the future. There must be an understanding of the capabilities, potential and risks at Board level.

Communications / Marketing

"The regular cadence of communication needs to run through the whole business, including the Board."

An area that was emphasised as vitally important, at an Executive level, and integral to drive business continuity and growth in the future is communications and marketing. At a Board level, its strategic importance has also grown and NEDs with senior experience in this area will be sought-after.

Cyber

"It is a major issue and we know it, in my mind we need more knowledge on the Board."

Cyber security is an area of real and growing threat, especially with a far greater increase in channelisation of business and online operations. For many this was an area where more experience, if not specific skills, would be welcomed, particularly in how to manage and mitigate risks. It was also agreed that for specific challenges or threats it could be more beneficial to bring in talent to support as needed.

HR

"HR and human capital needs to come into the boardroom with force."

People and their mental and physical well-being are now a clear point on Board agendas, therefore HR and people development experience is growing in importance for Non-Exec candidates. There must be a particular focus on bringing in those who have experience of dealing with transformation and culture development.

Strategic / Business Continuity

"We need much greater eye on strategy than ethic."

In response to the pandemic, the need for more strategic input at Board level to ensure business continuity and risk management is vital. Experience in delivering strong business continuity procedures or running very senior level risk modelling will be highly sought-after.

China/Asian View

"This really has grown way up in our minds. We now need people with deep knowledge of the region."

With a growing Asian market and continued domination from China in many areas, many highlighted this as an important geography to have understanding of from a Board perspective. It will be important in many sectors to have a real depth of understanding of how these rapidly expanding markets operate. This experience could come from people based in UK or Europe, or equally some of our interviewees reported that they were exploring NED recruitment specifically in those geographies.

Global Experience

"The world has got smaller. Technology gives us the chance to bring more global experience into our boardroom."

The appeal of global experience may be more significant for companies with international customer-bases, but even those more focused on UK or smaller, more geographically contained markets felt that this knowledge can bring different and useful perspective to the Board.

AI / Machine Learning

"Business really must be more aware of tech impact and anticipation and what impacts and opportunities this will bring."

The inevitable proliferation of automation, artificial intelligence and machine learning at an operational level will have impacts across business performance, productivity and efficiency as well as labour requirements. It will be increasingly important to have this knowledge represented at Board level.

Audit and Regulatory

"A greater emphasis on technical skill, such as audit, is going to become more important."

A continuously evolving audit and regulatory landscape is a reality for many sectors, and Boards must be able to support and deliver what is required at a technical level. However, there is an increasing need for Boards to bring more balance in the way customers, shareholders and staff are listened and responded to, which requires a more flexible attitude to strategic decision making.

Employee Voice

"We really need the employee voice in the boardroom."

This was an area that there was a growing appetite to introduce more clearly into the Board makeup, extending beyond the Executive level. Whether this be in a greater presence on sub committees, rather than specifically on the full Board, it was felt that this representation must be increased.

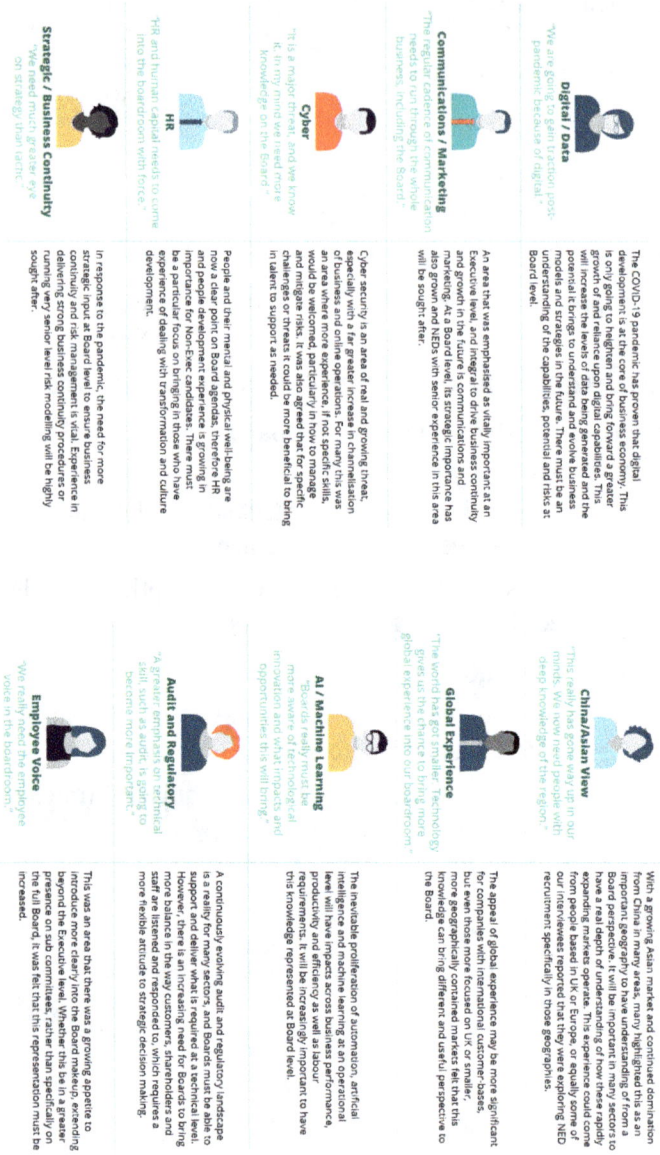

Figure 12: Saxton Bampfylde Board Model

Zero Trust vs. Total Trust Frameworks

- **Virtual Zero Trust**:
    - Implement strict authentication, least privilege access, and continuous monitoring.
    - Use AI-powered tools for real-time threat detection in virtual environments.

- **Physical Total Trust**:
    - Build an empowering culture where employees feel trusted and valued.
    - Use tools like transparent communication and participative leadership to reinforce trust.
    - Build an emotionally intelligent, empathic and mutually supportive workforce.

Systems Thinking and Ecosystem Integration

- **Adopt a Systems Approach**:
    - Map interdependencies between teams, technologies, and stakeholders.
    - Use simulations and digital twins to understand impacts and test decisions.
    - Note: This often runs counter to an ISO standard approach – you have to have a combined ISO standard approach.

- **Foster Ecosystem Collaboration**:
    - Engage external partners, customers, and regulators to create shared value.
    - Leverage platforms that facilitate seamless interaction and integration.
    - Understand, engage, manage and control your supply chain.

Cybersecurity and Cyber-resilience as a Human-Centric Issue

- **Awareness Programs**: Train employees on recognising and mitigating cyber risks.
- **Behavioural Analytics**: Use AI to monitor behavioural patterns for early detection of threats.
- **Human-Centred Policies**: Create security protocols that are intuitive and minimise user friction. All based around Trust.
- **Trust**: this process should be part of building a mutually trusting organisation.

Advanced Technology Integration

- **Blockchain for Supply Chains**:
  - Use blockchain to ensure traceability and reduce inefficiencies in supply chain management.
  - Integrate smart contracts for automated compliance and accountability.
  - Make sure contracts are aligned.

- **AI and Biotech Solutions**:
  - Employ AI for predictive analytics, decision support, and process automation.
  - Leverage biotech for health monitoring, sustainability, and innovation in physical spaces.

Chapter 5

Risk Management, Resilience and Mixed Reality Hardening

Introduction

Risk management is central to leading a successful Mixed Reality organisation. Traditionally risk management has not successfully managed both/all sides of the Mixed Reality equation. Risks on the virtual side of organisations have either been played down, ignored, or suffered from poor management. At the same time few organisations have the sort of integrated hardening (resilience plus) suggested in previous chapters. This chapter seeks to show a way forward in directing and managing the risk and mixed reality hardening of the organisation So, to start with:

- **Assess Risk Appetite**:
  - Risk appetite sits at the apex of an organisational approach to risk. Regularly evaluate organisational tolerance for technological, operational, and market risks.

- **Proactive Resilience Building (Integrated Hardening)**:
  - Develop adaptive/agile crisis management protocols.
  - Simulate mixed-reality threat scenarios to stress-test systems.

Future Impact on Organisational Leadership:

Extended Reality (XR), Augmented Reality (AR), Virtual Reality (VR):and Artificial Intelligence (AI),

These technologies will transform decision-making, training, and collaboration. AI will provide data-driven insights, enabling leaders to make smarter, faster decisions. AR and VR will enhance virtual communication, immersive training, and global teamwork, allowing leaders to foster stronger connections in distributed teams. Leaders will need to embrace a holistic tech-savvy mindset and foster a culture of continuous learning.

Biotechnology:

Advances in biotechnology will reshape industries like healthcare, agriculture, and manufacturing. Leaders must be prepared to navigate ethical considerations, regulatory landscapes, and cross-disciplinary innovations. A strong focus on sustainability and social responsibility will be essential as biotech solutions impact global challenges like food security and disease prevention.

Ecosystems and Hyperconnectivity:

Leadership will shift from competition to collaboration within ecosystems of organisations, startups, and other entities. Building partnerships and leveraging interconnected networks will become key. Leaders must foster trust, adaptability, and shared value creation while navigating complex interdependencies.

Agile and Adaptive Planning:

In an era of rapid change and uncertainty, traditional long-term planning will give way to agile frameworks. Leaders must cultivate resilience, empower teams to respond dynamically to change, and emphasise iterative planning. Adaptive leadership skills, like emotional intelligence and decision-making under ambiguity, will be critical for sustaining competitive advantage.

Key Takeaway:

Organisational leaders of the future must become visionary, adaptable, and collaborative, harnessing emerging technologies and methodologies to thrive in a complex and rapidly evolving landscape.

- **Scenario Planning**:
  - Create dynamic plans that accommodate multiple potential futures.
  - Use AI-driven tools for forecasting and trend analysis.
- **Iterative Decision-Making**:
  - Break initiatives into smaller, adaptable stages for quicker pivots.

Culture and Leadership Development

- **Leadership Training**:
  - Train leaders to operate in mixed reality environments with emotional intelligence, technical acumen and employee trust.
- **Culture of Innovation**:
  - Encourage experimentation and risk-taking in adopting new tools and methods.
- **Diversity and Inclusion**:
  - Prioritise diverse perspectives in decision-making to foster creativity and equity.

Monitoring, Adaptation and Continuous Improvement

- **Key Performance Indicators (KPIs)**:
    - Track progress on metrics like security incidents, employee engagement and trust, and ecosystem contributions.

- **Feedback Loops**:
    - Use real-time feedback from employees, stakeholders, and customers to refine strategies.

- **Tech Audits**:
    - Regularly evaluate the performance and ethical implications of mixed-reality technologies.

Chapter 6

Cyber Threats to Mixed Reality Leadership

Two of the authors' (Hyslop & White, 2024) with the 2nd year undergraduates of University of Buckingham (2024) work on the invisible apocalypse is a companion to this chapter,

State and Non-State Actor Threats

The military doctrines of China, Russia, Iran, North Korea, the United States, and NATO encompass a range of strategies, including significant emphasis on cyber warfare. Here is a summary of each nation's doctrine with a particular focus on their cyber warfare components:

China: China's military strategy integrates cyber warfare as a critical element of its overall defence and offense capabilities. The People's Liberation Army (PLA) has developed sophisticated cyber units tasked with both defensive and offensive operations. These units focus on cyber espionage, intellectual property theft, and potential disruption of enemy information systems. China's approach to cyber warfare is comprehensive, aiming to establish information dominance in any potential conflict.

Chinese Cyber Warfare Doctrine

China's military doctrine is rooted in the concept of **"Active Defence"**, which emphasises strategic deterrence and pre-emptive measures to secure national interests. Key aspects include:

Strategic Goals:

- **Preservation of Sovereignty**: Protect territorial integrity, including Taiwan, the South China Sea, and border regions.
- **Global Influence**: Position China as a dominant global power through both military and economic means.
- **Technological Superiority**: Build advanced capabilities in AI, quantum computing, hypersonic missiles, and space technology.

Key Principles:

- **Information Warfare**: The doctrine prioritises "information dominance," focusing on using data, networks, and cyber tools to gain an edge in conflicts. Cyber and electronic warfare are key components.
- **Unrestricted Warfare**: Coined by Chinese military theorists, this strategy involves leveraging all domains of conflict—economic, political, psychological, and technological—beyond traditional military engagement.
- **Dual-Use Technologies**: China integrates civilian technologies (e.g., 5G, AI) into its military, blurring the line between commercial and defence industries.

Cyber Warfare:

- China views cyberspace as a battlefield where dominance is essential for national security.
- The **Strategic Support Force (SSF)** is a dedicated branch responsible for cyber espionage, information operations, and electronic warfare.
- Chinese cyber operations focus on:
  - **Espionage**: Stealing intellectual property and military secrets.

- ○ **Disruption**: Targeting adversary critical infrastructure.
- ○ **Disinformation**: Spreading narratives to influence public opinion globally.

Mixed Reality Warfare:

China's doctrine incorporates mixed warfare methods, including:

- Economic, trade and financial coercion (e.g., Belt and Road Initiative influence).
- Legal warfare (leveraging international laws for strategic purposes).
- Psychological operations (shaping global perceptions of China's rise).
- Ideological, religious and racial warfare.
- Supra-national and diplomatic warfare.
- Critical Infrastructure warfare.
- Sanction warfare.
- Economic Aid Warfare.
- Resource, Knowledge and Technological warfare.
- Ecological and Water warfare.
- Legal and regulatory warfare.
- Criminal/Smuggling/Migration warfare.
- Social Warfare.
- Drug warfare..

Russia: Russia views cyber warfare as an essential tool for achieving its strategic objectives. The Russian military doctrine emphasises the use of cyber capabilities to conduct information operations, including propaganda dissemination and disruption of adversary command and control systems. Russia has been implicated in various cyber-attacks targeting critical infrastructure and political institutions in other countries, reflecting its focus on leveraging cyber tools for geopolitical influence. Russia blurs the boundary between state actors and organised crime.

Russian Cyber Warfare Doctrine

Russia's military doctrine is deeply influenced by its historical focus on defence against perceived encirclement by NATO and the West. It emphasises a mix of traditional military strength and asymmetric tactics.

Strategic Goals:

- **Defend Sovereignty**: Protect Russia's territorial integrity and sphere of influence, particularly in Eastern Europe and Central Asia.
- **Geopolitical Influence**: Reassert Russia as a global power capable of challenging NATO and the U.S.
- **Deterrence**: Maintain a credible nuclear deterrent while enhancing conventional and unconventional capabilities.

Key Principles:

- **Non-Linear Warfare**: Russia embraces the concept of "Gerasimov Doctrine," a blend of military and non-military tactics. It emphasises achieving objectives through subversion, cyber operations, and psychological manipulation.
- **Strategic Depth**: Focus on controlling buffer zones (e.g., Ukraine, Belarus) to ensure strategic depth against Western threats.
- **High-Technology Warfare**: Prioritise advanced weapons systems, including hypersonic missiles, electronic warfare systems, and integrated air defence.

Cyber Warfare:

- Cyber capabilities are central to Russia's strategy for asymmetrically countering Western superiority.
- The **GRU (Main Intelligence Directorate)** and **FSB (Federal Security Service)** lead cyber operations.
- Russian cyber objectives include:
    - **Disruption**: Attacking critical infrastructure (e.g., power grids, financial systems).

- ○ **Election Interference**: Using cyber tools to influence political outcomes in adversary states.
- ○ **Espionage**: Gathering intelligence from Western governments and organisations.
- ○ **Hybrid Cyber Tactics**: Combining cyber attacks with disinformation campaigns to destabilise adversaries.

Hybrid Warfare:

Russia's doctrine heavily integrates hybrid warfare methods, including:

- **Disinformation**: Using state-controlled media (e.g., RT, Sputnik) and social media to influence global narratives.
- **Proxy Conflicts**: Supporting paramilitary groups and separatist movements (e.g., in Ukraine and Syria).
- **Economic Warfare**: Leveraging energy supplies (e.g., natural gas) as a geopolitical tool.

Comparative Analysis of Cyber Warfare Strategies

- **China**: Emphasises long-term strategic espionage, intellectual property theft, and disinformation aimed at reshaping global perceptions of China's rise.
- **Russia**: Focuses on short-term, high-impact operations like disrupting elections, infrastructure sabotage, and spreading chaos through hybrid tactics.

Both nations share a belief in the decisive role of cyber and information warfare in modern conflicts, but their strategies reflect their unique geopolitical goals and historical contexts.

Iran: Iran has significantly advanced its cyber warfare capabilities over the past decade. The Iranian military doctrine incorporates cyber operations as a means to counter technologically superior adversaries. Iranian cyber units have been involved in attacks targeting financial institutions, critical infrastructure, and private sector entities, aiming to deter adversaries and project power within the region.

North Korea: North Korea's military strategy heavily relies on asymmetric warfare tactics, with cyber warfare playing a pivotal role. The country has developed a dedicated cyber warfare unit known as Bureau 121, responsible for conducting cyber espionage, financial theft, and disruptive attacks against critical infrastructure. North Korea's cyber operations are designed to offset its conventional military limitations and exert influence on the global stage.

United States: The United States' military doctrine recognises cyberspace as a distinct warfighting domain. The U.S. has established the United States Cyber Command (USCYBERCOM) to oversee cyber operations, focusing on defending national interests against cyber threats and, when necessary, conducting offensive cyber operations. The U.S. aims to deter adversaries by maintaining robust cyber capabilities and integrating them into broader military strategies.

NATO: NATO's strategic concept includes the recognition of cyber threats as a significant concern for collective security. The alliance has developed policies and capabilities to enhance cyber defence among member states, promoting information sharing, resilience, and coordinated responses to cyber incidents. NATO's approach to cyber warfare emphasises defence and deterrence, ensuring that the alliance can operate effectively in the face of evolving cyber threats.

In summary, cyber warfare has become an integral component of military doctrines worldwide. Each of these nations and alliances has developed strategies to incorporate cyber capabilities into their military operations, reflecting the increasing importance of cyberspace in modern warfare

Chapter 7

Implementing Mixed Reality Leadership

There are no illusions from hereon about the difficulties of implementing Chapters 2 and 3, let alone Mixed Reality Leadership. Nevertheless if organisations are to survive the coming revolution it has to be done, and fast.

Foundation Building:

- Establish the governance framework.
- Develop the vision and define the role of mixed reality in the organisation.

Integration and Training:

- Deploy initial mixed-reality technologies.
- Train leaders and employees to operate effectively in hybrid environments.

Scaling and Optimisation:

- Scale successful initiatives across the organisation.
- Continuously refine strategies based on real-world feedback and evolving technologies.

Sustained Leadership and Innovation:

- Foster a culture of ongoing innovation and adaptability.

- Build partnerships to remain at the forefront of mixed-reality advancements.

Strategic Outcomes

- Enhanced organisational resilience.
- Improved trust and collaboration in hybrid environments.
- Streamlined operations and innovative problem-solving.
- Sustainable value creation for stakeholders.

Chapter 8

Leadership Training in Mixed Reality Environments

Emotional Intelligence (EQ) in Mixed Reality Leadership

Emotional intelligence remains crucial for navigating relationships, inspiring trust, and fostering collaboration in mixed-reality settings. It requires self-awareness and training in recognising emotions and biases. This is particularly the case in virtual interactions where non- verbal cues may be reduced or absent. Reflective practices such as journaling or feedback sessions help build the necessary awareness.

Empathy and tough compassion are required emotional intelligence traits. The ability to 'read a room' in both physical and virtual environments is important. Training on recognising employee stress, particularly from mixed reality challenges, is another requirement.

Leaders must be adaptable and therefore must be equipped with tools to respond flexibly to unexpected disruptions such a virtual breakdowns or rapid tech changes.

Communication skills are writ large with a need for clarity and conciseness in digital communication (e.g., emails and virtual meetings). Storytelling becomes a more important skill in order to inspire and motivate teams across physical and virtual settings.

Intellectual curiosity is strongly linked to emotional intelligence (EI) and is a crucial component of it. Studies indicate that intellectual curiosity can predict higher EI, as it fosters open-mindedness, empathy, and adaptability. In rapidly changing environments and ecosystems, such as those with mixed reality leadership, intellectual curiosity is essential. It enables individuals to navigate complex situations, embrace new ideas, and understand diverse perspectives, thereby enhancing their emotional intelligence and overall effectiveness in dynamic organisational settings.

Psychological and Social Impact of Mixed Reality Leadership

Introduction

Mixed Reality (MR) environments, which blend physical and digital worlds through augmented reality (AR) and virtual reality (VR), are transforming workplaces across industries. While these technologies offer enhanced collaboration, efficiency, and engagement, they also introduce unique psychological challenges and effects for both leaders and employees.

Cognitive Load and Adaptation

Working in MR environments demands significant cognitive resources as individuals must process both real and virtual stimuli. This increased cognitive load can lead to mental fatigue, impacting decision-making and productivity. Leaders must be mindful of designing workflows that balance MR interaction with cognitive recovery time.

Presence and Social Connection

MR fosters a sense of presence that can enhance team cohesion despite geographical distances. However, it also poses challenges related to social cues and nonverbal communication. Employees may struggle with interpreting virtual body language or experience a diminished sense of real-world interaction, leading to feelings of isolation or disconnection.

Leadership in MR Environments

Leading in MR spaces requires a shift in traditional management styles. Effective virtual leadership involves clear communication, emotional intelligence, and the ability to foster trust without physical presence. Leaders must adapt by leveraging MR tools to maintain engagement and motivation while ensuring inclusivity in virtual spaces.

Stress and Well-being

Prolonged exposure to MR can contribute to eye strain, motion sickness, and mental fatigue. Additionally, the blurred boundaries between work and personal life in MR settings may increase stress levels. Organisations should establish guidelines to mitigate these risks, such as implementing mandatory breaks and ergonomic design principles.

Ethical and Psychological Considerations

MR introduces ethical concerns related to privacy, surveillance, and data security. The psychological impact of being constantly monitored in a virtual space can lead to anxiety and reduced job satisfaction. Companies must establish transparent policies to protect employees' rights and mental well-being.

Conclusion

While MR environments offer innovative opportunities for remote work and collaboration, they also present significant psychological challenges. Leaders must proactively address cognitive load, social connection, well-being, and ethical concerns to foster a positive and sustainable MR workplace. Thoughtful implementation and continuous evaluation of MR's psychological effects will be crucial in shaping the future of work.

Overcoming Virtual Fatigue and Cognitive Overload in MR Leadership

Mixed Reality leaders face unique challenges, including virtual fatigue and cognitive overload due to prolonged exposure to digital environments. To combat these issues, leaders should:

- **Implement Structured Breaks:** Regular breaks from MR interactions can help reduce fatigue and maintain focus.
- **Optimise Workflows:** Simplifying MR tasks and using intuitive interfaces can minimise cognitive strain.
- **Encourage Physical Movement:** Alternating between MR and real-world tasks can reduce eye strain and physical discomfort.
- **Enhance Digital Well-being Strategies:** Incorporating mindfulness techniques, blue light reduction, and ergonomic MR setups can support mental and physical health.
- **Leverage AI Assistance:** Using AI-driven automation can streamline repetitive tasks and alleviate cognitive load.

Stress and Well-being

Prolonged exposure to MR can contribute to eye strain, motion sickness, and mental fatigue. Additionally, the blurred boundaries between work and personal life in MR settings may increase stress levels. Organisations should establish guidelines to mitigate these risks, such as implementing mandatory breaks and ergonomic design principles.

Ethical and Psychological Considerations

MR introduces ethical concerns related to privacy, surveillance, and data security. The psychological impact of being constantly monitored in a virtual space can lead to anxiety and reduced job satisfaction. Companies must establish transparent policies to protect employees' rights and mental well-being.

Conclusion

While MR environments offer innovative opportunities for remote work and collaboration, they also present significant psychological challenges. Leaders must proactively address cognitive load, social connection, well-being, and ethical concerns to foster a positive and sustainable MR workplace. Thoughtful implementation and continuous evaluation of MR's psychological effects will be crucial in shaping the future of work.

Technical Acumen for Mixed-Reality Leadership

Mixed Reality Leadership demands a baseline understanding of key technologies, coupled with the ability to leverage them strategically. This is a key skill. It does not mean that the leader has to be a qualified high tech individual but the leader must be sufficiently broad in understanding how the organisation fits together.

In terms of digital literacy leaders need to be familiar with tools like AR/VR platforms, blockchain, AI applications, and collaboration software (e.g., Microsoft Teams, Slack, or Miro). Experimentation can take place in workshops or sandbox environments for experimentation.

Data driven decision making is important in mixed reality situations. Leaders must know how to interpret analytics dashboards, and performance metrics from virtual systems. Focus on skills such as predictive analytics, trend spotting and scenario planning..

Cybersecurity Awareness is essential. An understanding of zero-trust principles and data privacy regulations. Leaders must be trained on identifying and mitigating social engineering attacks.

- Develop leaders' understanding of zero-trust security principles and data privacy regulations.
- Include training on identifying and mitigating social engineering attacks.

Challenges and Opportunities in Training

- Teach leaders to assess ROI for emerging technologies, balancing innovation with business needs.
- Encourage a partnership mindset with IT and innovation teams to co-create solutions.

Key Training Modalities and Best Practices

- **Workshops and Seminars**:
    - ○ Conduct in-person or virtual sessions focusing on hybrid leadership challenges.
- **AR/VR Simulations**:
    - ○ Use immersive tools to train leaders in real-time mixed-reality scenarios, such as virtual team management or crisis response.
- **Mentorship and Peer Learning**:
    - ○ Pair emerging leaders with experienced mentors who have successfully navigated hybrid environments.
- **Continuous Learning Platforms**:
    - ○ Offer access to resources like LinkedIn Learning or Coursera for self-paced technical and soft-skill development.

Leaders should be prepared to address challenges unique to hybrid and mixed-reality environments:

- **Building Inclusive Cultures**:
    - ○ Train leaders to ensure equity between in-office and remote employees.
    - ○ Emphasise the importance of creating spaces for all voices, both physical and virtual.
- **Boundary Management**:
    - ○ Offer guidance on setting boundaries for work-life balance, especially for virtual teams.
    - ○ Teach techniques for managing "always-on" expectations.

- **Conflict Resolution**:
    - Provide tools for identifying and resolving misunderstandings in text-based or asynchronous communications.
    - Role-play conflict scenarios in hybrid settings.
- **Compassionate Team Working:**
    - Ensure and establish balanced teamworking across the organisations.

Defining Success in Mixed Reality Leadership Training

- Leaders who excel at managing diverse, distributed teams.
- Enhanced employee satisfaction and retention, driven by empathetic and effective leadership.
- Increased organisational agility and resilience, supported by leaders who understand both human dynamics and technological advancements.

Chapter 9

Transformational Leadership in the Mixed Reality Age

The closest traditional leadership style to this mixed-reality leadership model would be **Transformational Leadership**, but with significant modern enhancements to account for the complexity of hybrid environments and advanced technology integration. Here's why:

Visionary Thinking and Strategic Adaptation

Transformational leaders focus on inspiring, motivating, and empowering teams to achieve goals, innovate, and adapt. This aligns well with the requirements of mixed-reality leadership, as both emphasise:

Visionary Thinking:

- Both styles require a compelling vision for the future. In mixed-reality leadership, this includes leveraging virtual and physical spaces to achieve organisational goals.

Empowering Others and Organisational Change

- Mixed-reality leaders, like transformational leaders, prioritise employee growth and autonomy, trusting their teams to operate effectively across hybrid environments.

Adaptability and Change Management:

- Transformational leaders thrive in dynamic conditions, as do mixed-reality leaders who navigate rapid technological and societal shifts.

Trust Frameworks and Relationship Focussed Leadership

- Emotional intelligence, a hallmark of transformational leadership, is crucial in fostering trust, collaboration, and empathy in both physical and virtual spaces.

Intellectual Curiosity

- Need to enable to provide insightful viewpoints of looking at hybrid environments and ecosystems from adaptable and flexible perspectives, assists with change, innovation, sustainability and effectiveness.

Enhancements Beyond Transformational Leadership

While transformational leadership is the closest traditional style, mixed-reality leadership introduces modern enhancements that go beyond its scope:

Technical Acumen:

- Transformational leadership doesn't inherently emphasise technological expertise. Mixed-reality leaders must be digitally literate and strategically adept at leveraging technologies like AI, blockchain, and AR/VR.

Systems Thinking:

- Mixed-reality leadership requires a systemic view of interconnected ecosystems—teams, technologies, and external stakeholders. Transformational leadership traditionally focuses more on organisational culture and goals than broader systems integration.

Trust Frameworks:

- Mixed-reality leaders balance **virtual zero trust** (security protocols) and **physical total trust** (empowering employees), which is more nuanced than transformational leadership's broad emphasis on trust-building.

Servant and Democratic Leadership

- Servant and democratic leadership sit beside transformational leadership as the guiding leadership styles for Mixed Reality leadership. This type of approach helps to get over the clear difficulties presented in re-orienting organisations away from traditional approaches to ensure the Saxton Bampfylde board model, and the subsequent required actions describe herein, can be achieved.

Cybersecurity and Risk Awareness for Leaders

- Mixed-reality leaders focus on addressing cybersecurity as a human and organisational issue, an area transformational leadership does not typically address.

Agile Leadership in Mixed Reality Environments

- Mixed-reality leadership incorporates agile, iterative planning to navigate the uncertainties of hybrid and technological landscapes. Traditional transformational leadership operates more on broad visionary planning.

Other Related Leadership Styles

Mixed-reality leadership also draws elements from other leadership models:

- **Servant Leadership**: Focus on empowering teams, building trust, and prioritising employee well-being.
- **Situational Leadership**: Adapting leadership style to fit team

needs and circumstances, particularly in hybrid or mixed-reality environments.

- **Digital Leadership**: Emphasises leveraging technology to drive transformation, closely related to mixed-reality leadership's technical component.

Conclusion

Transformational leadership is the foundation, but mixed-reality leadership expands upon it to include:

- Advanced technological integration.
- Enhanced focus on ecosystems and cybersecurity.
- New frameworks for hybrid work and planning.

Chapter 10

Training and Development for Mixed Reality Leadership

Core Competencies for Mixed Reality Leaders

Leadership training must evolve from traditional frameworks to include skills, tools, and mindsets essential for navigating mixed-reality landscapes.

Traditional Leadership Training Focus:

- Emphasis on soft skills like communication, collaboration, and motivation.
- General management skills (e.g., delegation, decision-making).
- Limited integration of technology, often focused on productivity tools.

Mixed Reality Leadership Training Focus:

- Comprehensive inclusion of advanced technologies (AI, blockchain, AR/VR).
- Training in systems thinking and ecosystem collaboration.
- Preparing leaders for hybrid and distributed workforces.
- Enhanced emphasis on agility, cybersecurity, and trust frameworks.
- Compassionate Teamworking

Core Components of Mixed Reality Leadership Training

Understanding the Key Components of Mixed Reality

- **The Physical World**
- **The Virtual World**
- **The Metaverse**
- **Vulnerabilities and Threats**
- **Enemy/Competitive Doctrines**
- **Competitive Intelligence, Marketing and Product Development**

Emotional Intelligence in Mixed Reality Work

- **What to Teach**:
  - Building empathy in digital-first interactions.
  - Managing team dynamics when communication is partially virtual.
  - Recognising and addressing employee burnout in hybrid settings.
- **How to Teach**:
  - Virtual role-playing and simulations using AR/VR to model scenarios like conflict resolution in virtual meetings or hybrid project coordination.

Digital and Cyber Literacy and Technology Adaptation

- **What to Teach**:
  - Understanding and applying tools like blockchain for supply chains, AI for decision-making, and AR/VR for team collaboration.
  - Familiarity with cybersecurity best practices and protocols.

- **How to Teach**:
    - ◦ Offer sandbox environments where leaders can experiment with emerging technologies.
    - ◦ Partner with tech providers to deliver hands-on workshops tailored to organisational needs.

Agile and Systems Thinking

- **What to Teach**:
    - ◦ Iterative planning methods that emphasise adaptability.
    - ◦ Mapping and managing interdependencies across organisational systems.
- **How to Teach**:
    - ◦ Conduct scenario planning exercises to simulate real-world challenges in hybrid ecosystems.
    - ◦ Use digital twins (virtual replicas of systems) for experimentation and decision modelling.

Mixed Reality Collaboration and Communication

- **What to Teach**:
    - ◦ Strategies for creating equity between in-office and remote employees.
    - ◦ Mastering virtual presentation and storytelling techniques.
- **How to Teach**:
    - ◦ Simulate team interactions with a mix of physical and virtual participants.
    - ◦ Use feedback tools to assess clarity, engagement, and impact.

Risk Management and Cybersecurity Awareness

- **What to Teach**:
    - ◦ Risk Appetite and Risk Management

- Balancing virtual zero trust with physical total trust.
- Cyber risk as a human and organisational challenge, not just a technical one.

- **How to Teach**:
  - Integrate cybersecurity scenarios into leadership decision-making simulations.
  - Offer cross-disciplinary sessions involving IT, HR, and compliance teams.

Metrics for Evaluating Leadership Training

- **What to Teach**:
  - Leading partnerships across diverse ecosystems, including suppliers, customers, and regulators.
  - Driving shared value creation in collaborative networks.

- **How to Teach**:
  - Case studies on successful ecosystem integration in real-world settings.
  - Workshops with cross-functional teams and external stakeholders.

The Mixed Reality Leadership Accelerator Programme

AR/VR/AI-Based Immersive Training

- Create virtual simulations of complex leadership scenarios.
- Examples: Crisis management in a hybrid environment or onboarding remote teams.

Gamification

- Use gamified experiences to teach decision-making, resource allocation, and team management.
- Example: A game where leaders navigate a mixed-reality

workplace while balancing employee needs and technological demands.

Blended Learning Models

- Combine online, in-person, and on-demand resources for flexibility.
- Use platforms like Coursera, LinkedIn Learning, or organisation-specific learning management systems (LMS).

Peer Learning and Mentorship

- Encourage experienced leaders to mentor emerging ones, sharing insights on adapting to hybrid challenges.

Continuous Learning Platforms

- Provide access to real-time updates on new technologies, hybrid best practices, and leadership strategies.
- Use AI-driven personalised learning systems to tailor content to individual leaders' roles and needs.

Metrics for Success in Leadership Training

Mixed-reality leadership training should measure:
- **Behavioural Change**: Improved ability to engage and inspire hybrid teams.
- **Technical Competence**: Confidence in using AR/VR tools, data analytics platforms, or cybersecurity measures.
- **Team Feedback**: Increased employee satisfaction with leadership in hybrid settings.
- **Organisational Impact**: Enhanced resilience, innovation, and collaboration across ecosystems.

Example Training Program: The "Mixed Reality Leadership Accelerator"

- Program Structure:

- **Phase 1: Foundational Learning**
  - Online modules on emotional intelligence, cybersecurity basics, and digital tools.

- **Phase 2: Interactive Simulations**
  - AR/VR environments where leaders manage hybrid teams or navigate crises.

- **Phase 3: Mentorship and Peer Learning**
  - Pair leaders with mentors for real-world insights and advice.

- **Phase 4: Capstone Project**
  - Leaders design and present a mixed-reality strategy for a specific organisational challenge

Chapter 11

Governance and Global Regulation in Cyberspace

Global Challenges in the Digital and Cyber Era

Global regulation in the physical, virtual, and metaverse worlds is not co-ordinated and is therefore different in different locales. The United States prioritises individualism and innovation, while Europe emphasises privacy and data protection, resulting in different approaches to cyber challenges. The further east of Europe one goes the laxer, for example and as a generalisation, is the regulation of data until you reach China when all data is controlled by the state. Changes in the world order....

Key Regulatory Frameworks by Region

United States of America

The U.S. adopts a sectoral approach to cybersecurity, with a mix of federal and state laws. The items of legislation are: The Cybersecurity Information Sharing Act (CISA), Computer Fraud and Abuse Act (CFAA), and state-level privacy laws like the California Consumer Privacy Act (CCPA). The regulation focus is: protecting critical infrastructure, fostering public-private partnerships, and ensuring personal data privacy. The important challenges are: balancing individual privacy with national security and free speech rights.

There are other corporate compliance regulations of importance. This is an overview of key U.S. governance laws and regulations that apply to various types of organisations, spanning corporate governance, financial accountability, privacy, and industry-specific compliance:

Corporate Governance and Financial Accountability

These laws ensure, or are supposed to ensure, transparency, accountability, and ethical behaviour in organisations:

- **Sarbanes-Oxley Act (SOX)**: Mandates stringent financial reporting and internal controls for publicly traded companies. It addresses:
  - Accurate financial disclosures.
  - Independent auditing requirements.
  - CEO/CFO accountability for financial statements.

- **Dodd-Frank Wall Street Reform and Consumer Protection Act**: Strengthens financial sector regulation to prevent systemic risks. Key provisions include:
  - Executive compensation disclosures.
  - Whistleblower protection.
  - Enhanced risk management for financial institutions.

- **Securities Act of 1933 & Securities Exchange Act of 1934**: Require truthful securities disclosures and prohibit fraud in the securities markets.
- **Foreign Corrupt Practices Act (FCPA)**: Prohibits bribery of foreign officials and mandates accurate financial recordkeeping by organisations engaged in international business.

Data Protection and Privacy Laws

Organisations must comply with regulations protecting personal data and digital privacy:

- **California Consumer Privacy Act (CCPA)**: Governs data privacy rights for California residents, including:
  - Right to know, delete, and opt-out of data sales.
  - Transparency in data usage.
- **Health Insurance Portability and Accountability Act (HIPAA)**: Regulates healthcare organisations' handling of patient data to ensure confidentiality and security.
- **Gramm-Leach-Bliley Act (GLBA)**: Requires financial institutions to protect consumer financial data and notify users about data-sharing practices.
- **Children's Online Privacy Protection Act (COPPA)**: Protects children under 13 by requiring parental consent for data collection.
- **Cybersecurity Information Sharing Act (CISA)**: Encourages sharing of cybersecurity threat information between private companies and the federal government.
- Payment Card Industry Data Security Standard

Employment and Labour Laws

Regulations to ensure fair treatment of employees and compliance with workplace standards:

- **Fair Labour Standards Act (FLSA)**: Establishes minimum wage, overtime pay, and child labour protections.
- **Equal Employment Opportunity Laws (EEO)**: Enforced by the EEOC, these include protections against workplace discrimination under Title VII of the Civil Rights Act, the Americans with Disabilities Act (ADA), and the Age Discrimination in Employment Act (ADEA).
- **Occupational Safety and Health Act (OSHA)**: Ensures safe and healthful working conditions.

Environmental Regulations

Governance related to environmental responsibility:

- **Clean Air Act (CAA)** and **Clean Water Act (CWA)**: Mandate environmental compliance in industries to prevent pollution.
- **Resource Conservation and Recovery Act (RCRA)**: Regulates hazardous waste management.
- **Corporate Sustainability Reporting**: While not mandatory, ESG (Environmental, Social, and Governance) reporting frameworks are increasingly critical for investors.

Tax Compliance

- **Internal Revenue Code (IRC)**: Enforces tax compliance for all organisations, including nonprofits, through IRS regulations.
- **Tax Cuts and Jobs Act (TCJA)**: Implements changes affecting corporate tax rates and international taxation.

Nonprofit and Charitable Organisation Governance

- **Internal Revenue Code Section 501(c)(3)**: Establishes tax-exempt status requirements for nonprofits.
- **State Nonprofit Corporation Laws**: Govern registration, reporting, and operational transparency at the state level.

Industry-Specific Governance

- **Federal Financial Institutions Examination Council (FFIEC)**: Sets standards for financial institutions' operations and IT governance.
- **Food and Drug Administration (FDA) Regulations**: Enforce compliance in pharmaceutical and food industries.
- **Federal Communications Commission (FCC) Rules**: Regulate telecommunications and broadcasting industries.

Cybersecurity and Critical Infrastructure

- **Federal Information Security Modernisation Act (FISMA)**: Requires federal agencies and contractors to follow stringent cybersecurity protocols.
- **National Institute of Standards and Technology (NIST) Cybersecurity Framework**: Voluntary guidance for organisations to manage cybersecurity risks.

Importance of Governance Compliance

This is a bit of a list, to put it mildly, but is of great importance to the Board, CEO, and C-Suite members. These people need to keep across these issues, are the ones that should keep them awake at night and are the ones that could send them to jail.

Adhering to these laws and regulations is vital for:

- **Avoiding Penalties**: Noncompliance can lead to fines, sanctions, and reputational damage.
- **Building Stakeholder Trust**: Transparency and accountability foster investor and public confidence.
- **Operational Efficiency**: Structured governance enhances decision-making and reduces risks.

Organisations must stay updated on regulatory changes and implement robust compliance frameworks tailored to their industry and size

European Union

The European Union (EU) leads the world in stringent (?) cyberspace regulations:

- **Key Frameworks**: General Data Protection Regulation (GDPR), Network and Information Security Directive (NIS2), and Digital Services Act (DSA).
- **Focus Areas**: User privacy, platform accountability, content moderation, and combating disinformation.

- **Enforcement**: Strict penalties for violations ensure compliance but raise operational challenges for multinational platforms.

Key European Union Governance Laws and Regulations

Corporate Governance and Financial Accountability

EU regulations emphasise transparency, shareholder rights, and ethical business practices:

- **EU Corporate Sustainability Reporting Directive (CSRD)**:
    - Requires large companies to report on environmental, social, and governance (ESG) matters.
    - Expands on the Non-Financial Reporting Directive (NFRD) and aligns with the EU's Green Deal goals.
- **Shareholders Rights Directive (SRD II)**:
    - Strengthens shareholder influence over company governance.
    - Enhances transparency of remuneration policies and proxy advisory firms.
- **Markets in Financial Instruments Directive (MiFID II)**:
    - Regulates investment firms to increase market transparency and investor protection.
- **Statutory Audit Directive**:
    - Standardises auditing practices across member states to ensure high-quality financial reporting.

Data Protection and Privacy Laws

The EU leads globally in robust data protection standards:

- **General Data Protection Regulation (GDPR)**:
    - Applies to all organisations processing personal data of EU citisens, regardless of location.

- Key principles: data minimisation, consent, transparency, and accountability.
- Strict penalties for non-compliance (up to €20 million or 4% of annual global turnover).

- **ePrivacy Directive** (soon to be replaced by the ePrivacy Regulation):
  - Governs the confidentiality of electronic communications and the use of cookies.

- **Data Governance Act**:
  - Promotes secure sharing of non-personal data among businesses, public institutions, and researchers.

Employment and Labour Laws

EU labour regulations prioritise worker rights, safety, and equality:
- **Working Time Directive**:
  - Limits maximum working hours (48 hours per week) and mandates minimum rest periods.

- **Equal Treatment Directives**:
  - Ensure non-discrimination in employment based on gender, ethnicity, age, disability, or religion.

- **Health and Safety at Work Directive**:
  - Establishes minimum workplace safety standards across industries.

- **European Works Council Directive**:
  - Requires multinational companies to establish councils for employee consultation on transnational matters.

Environmental and Sustainability Regulations

The EU is at the forefront of environmental governance:

- **EU Taxonomy Regulation**:
  - ◦ Establishes a classification system for environmentally sustainable economic activities.
- **European Climate Law**:
  - ◦ Legally binds the EU to become climate-neutral by 2050.
- **Emissions Trading System (ETS)**:
  - ◦ Cap-and-trade system to reduce greenhouse gas emissions.
- **Waste Framework Directive**:
  - ◦ Establishes waste management and recycling standards.

Financial Sector Governance

The EU's financial regulations aim to ensure market stability and protect investors:

- **Banking Union Regulations**:
  - ◦ Comprise the Single Supervisory Mechanism (SSM) and the Single Resolution Mechanism (SRM) for EU banks.
- **Capital Requirements Regulation (CRR)** and **Directive (CRD)**:
  - ◦ Strengthen banks' resilience and ensure capital adequacy.
- **Anti-Money Laundering Directive (AMLD)**:
  - ◦ Sets measures to combat money laundering and terrorist financing, including Know Your Customer (KYC) rules.
- **Insurance Distribution Directive (IDD)**:
  - ◦ Regulates insurance product distribution to protect consumer rights.

Cybersecurity and Critical Infrastructure

Governance around cybersecurity and infrastructure resilience is growing:

- **Network and Information Security Directive (NIS2)**:

- Expands cybersecurity requirements for critical infra-structure and key service providers.
- Focuses on risk management, incident reporting, and cross-border collaboration.

- **Digital Operational Resilience Act (DORA):**
  - Mandates ICT risk management for financial institutions.

- **Cybersecurity Act:**
  - Introduces an EU-wide cybersecurity certification frame-work for IT products and services.

Tax Compliance and Anti-Competition Laws

- **Common Consolidated Corporate Tax Base (CCCTB)** (proposed):
  - Aims to simplify corporate taxation within the EU.

- **State Aid Rules:**
  - Prevent governments from distorting competition through unfair subsidies.

- **EU Competition Law:**
  - Includes Articles 101 and 102 of the Treaty on the Func-tioning of the EU (TFEU), addressing anti-competitive agreements and abuse of market dominance.

Digital and AI Governance

- **Digital Services Act (DSA)** and **Digital Markets Act (DMA):**
  - Regulate online platforms to ensure transparency, accountability, and fair competition.

- **Artificial Intelligence Act (2023):**
  - Establishes risk-based regulations for AI systems, focus-ing on safety, privacy, and non-discrimination.

Importance of Compliance with EU Governance

Adherence to EU regulations ensures:

- **Legal Certainty**: Minimises the risk of penalties and reputational harm.
- **Market Access**: Compliance is essential for operating in the EU's single market.
- **Sustainability Goals**: Aligns organisations with the EU's ambitious environmental and social objectives.
- **Investor Confidence**: Transparent governance practices attract international investment.

Organisations operating in or interacting with the EU must implement robust compliance frameworks, engage in proactive monitoring of regulatory updates, and prioritise transparency and sustainability in their governance practices.

United Kingdom

Key UK Governance Laws and Regulations

Corporate Governance and Financial Accountability

UK governance laws emphasise transparency, accountability, and stakeholder interests:

- **UK Corporate Governance Code**:
  - Applies to companies listed on the London Stock Exchange.
  - Emphasises principles of board effectiveness, shareholder engagement, and long-term value creation.
  - Encourages a comply-or-explain approach for flexibility.

- **Companies Act 2006**:
  - The primary legislation governing company law in the UK.

- Covers directors' duties, shareholder rights, and corporate reporting.
- Mandates strategic reports for larger companies to include ESG factors.

- **Bribery Act 2010**:
  - Establishes strict anti-corruption measures, including corporate liability for failure to prevent bribery.

- **UK Stewardship Code**:
  - Encourages institutional investors to act in the best long-term interests of beneficiaries by promoting responsible investment and engagement with investee companies.

Data Protection and Privacy Laws

The UK enforces robust data protection regulations, largely aligned with the EU:

- **UK General Data Protection Regulation (UK GDPR)**:
  - Derived from the EU GDPR post-Brexit, with similar principles of transparency, accountability, and consent.
  - Applies to organisations processing personal data of UK residents.
  - Includes penalties of up to £17.5 million or 4% of annual global turnover for non-compliance.

- **Data Protection Act 2018**:
  - Supplements UK GDPR with additional provisions, including national security exemptions and age-appropriate design standards.

- **Privacy and Electronic Communications Regulations (PECR)**:
  - Governs electronic marketing, cookies, and communications privacy.

Employment and Labour Laws

The UK maintains comprehensive labour protections:
- **Equality Act 2010**:
    - Consolidates anti-discrimination laws and promotes equal opportunities in employment and services.
- **Employment Rights Act 1996**:
- Covers employee rights, including notice periods, redundancy, and unfair dismissal protections.
- **Health and Safety at Work Act 1974**:
    - Ensures workplace safety and mandates risk assessments.
- **Modern Slavery Act 2015**:
    - Requires larger companies to report efforts to eliminate slavery and human trafficking in supply chains.

Environmental and Sustainability Regulations

The UK has ambitious goals for environmental governance and sustainability:
- **Climate Change Act 2008**:
    - Legally binds the UK to achieve net-zero greenhouse gas emissions by 2050.
- **Environment Act 2021**:
    - Sets legally binding targets for air quality, biodiversity, water, and waste management.
    - Introduces enhanced reporting obligations for companies on environmental impact.
- **Streamlined Energy and Carbon Reporting (SECR)**:
    - Mandates large organisations to report energy usage, carbon emissions, and energy efficiency measures.

Financial Sector Governance

Much of the UK financial sector, particularly in the City, is run as subsidiaries or partners of major USA banks. It is therefore important to understand which USA financial compliance and regulatory issues apply in addition, or instead of, UK rules.

The UK's financial regulations focus on market stability and investor protection:

- **Financial Services and Markets Act 2000 (FSMA):**
    - Provides the framework for financial regulation, overseen by the Financial Conduct Authority (FCA) and Prudential Regulation Authority (PRA).
- **Banking Act 2009:**
    - Introduces a special resolution regime to manage failing financial institutions.
- **Anti-Money Laundering Regulations:**
    - Implements the UK's AML framework, including Know Your Customer (KYC) requirements.
- **Senior Managers and Certification Regime (SM&CR):**
    - Ensures accountability of senior executives in financial services firms.

Cybersecurity and Digital Governance (needs update)

Cybersecurity is a growing focus in UK governance:

- **Network and Information Systems (NIS) Regulations 2018:**
    - Requires operators of essential services and digital service providers to implement robust cybersecurity measures.
- Computer Misuse Act 1990:
    - Criminalises unauthorised access to computer systems and data.

- **UK Online Safety Act** (2023):
    - Seeks to regulate social media platforms and protect users from harmful content, with a focus on children's safety. (This is the one that led to J.D, Vance's famous comment to Keir Starmer in April 2025 that UK was not a bastion of free speech!)

Tax and Anti-Avoidance Regulations

- **Finance Acts**:
    - Annually updated to reflect the government's tax policies, covering corporation tax, VAT, and personal income tax.
- **Tax Avoidance Disclosure Rules (DOTAS)**:
    - Requires the disclosure of tax avoidance schemes to HMRC.
- **Offshore Tax Compliance Rules**:
    - Includes measures to combat tax evasion through offshore entities.

Sector-Specific Governance

- **UK Stewardship Code**:
    - Promotes responsible investment practices among institutional investors.
- **Ofgem, Ofcom, and other regulators**:
    - Govern specific industries like energy, telecommunications, and utilities.
- **Charity Governance Code**:
    - Offers guidance for trustees of charitable organisations to ensure transparency, accountability, and effectiveness.

Importance of Governance Compliance in the UK

Adhering to UK governance laws is essential for:

- **Risk Mitigation**: Avoiding legal penalties and reputational damage.
- **Stakeholder Confidence**: Building trust among investors, employees, and customers.
- **Market Competitiveness**: Aligning with global governance standards enhances market access.
- **Sustainability Leadership**: Compliance with environmental and social governance fosters long-term growth.

Organisations operating in the UK must prioritise compliance through proactive monitoring, robust internal controls, and continuous training of leadership and employees.

China

Key China Governance Laws and Regulations

China's cyberspace governance is state-controlled:
- **Key Laws**: Cybersecurity Law, Data Security Law, and Personal Information Protection Law (PIPL).
- **Regulation Model**: Strict content censorship, data localisation, and heavy government oversight of digital platforms.
- **Global Impact**: China's model promotes "cyber sovereignty," influencing other authoritarian states.
- **Blockchain**: China is a global leader in Blockchain patents (at over 250 000). It is an assumption that these patents will assist China create an independent and secure Internet.

India

Key India Governance Laws and Regulations

India is enhancing its regulatory landscape:
- **Key Developments**: IT Act 2000, proposed Digital Personal Data Protection Bill (DPDPB), and the CERT-In guidelines for incident reporting.

- **Focus Areas**: Data protection, content moderation, and regulation of social media intermediaries.
- **Challenges**: Striking a balance between regulatory enforcement and safeguarding free speech.

Russia

Key Russia Governance Laws and Regulations

Russia follows a centralised approach to cyberspace governance:

- **Key Frameworks**: Sovereign Internet Law and Yarovaya Laws.
- **Regulation Characteristics**: Heavy surveillance, internet traffic control, and suppression of dissent.
- **Geopolitical Influence**: Russia's strategy underpins its disinformation campaigns and cyber warfare capabilities.
- **152: The Federal Law on Personal Data**

North Korea

Key North Korea Governance Laws and Regulation

North Korea maintains one of the most restrictive cyber environments globally:

- **Regulation Overview**: No open internet; access is restricted to a highly monitored intranet (Kwangmyong).
- **Cyber Operations**: North Korea's government engages in cyber espionage and financial hacking for regime sustenance.

Iran

Key Iran Governance Laws and Regulations

Iran combines strict control with active cyber operations:

- **Key Features**: Internet filtering, platform bans, and state-led cyber campaigns.

- **Digital Sovereignty**: Efforts to create a "National Internet" separate from the global web.

In a Mixed Reality (MR) world, where digital and physical environments merge, social media platforms—especially those with fewer controls and fact checks—will play a complex role in leadership and governance. Companies like **Apple, Google, Microsoft, and Meta (Facebook)** will not just be tech providers but also key power players shaping social, political, and economic structures. Here's how:

Control Over Information & Public Perception

- With fewer fact checks, these platforms can become **breeding grounds for misinformation**. In MR, where digital overlays alter real-world experiences, biased or false narratives could be **engineered to manipulate public perception**.
- Political leaders and governments will increasingly **depend on these platforms** for mass communication, making them central to decision-making.

Algorithmic Influence on Governance

- Leadership in MR worlds will not just be about policies but **who controls the algorithms**.
- Companies like Meta and Google will shape **what people see, how they interact, and even what they believe** through AI-driven feeds and immersive MR experiences.
- In nations with weak regulations, tech companies might **override traditional governance**, essentially **becoming shadow governments**.

Digital Citizenship & Identity Control

- MR will likely require users to have **persistent digital identities**. Tech giants could act as **de facto governments**, controlling access to virtual spaces, citizenship, and rights within MR environments.
- With fewer controls, companies might **sell or exploit identity**

data, making users more vulnerable to surveillance or social engineering.

Decentralisation vs. Corporate Domination

- On one hand, MR can empower decentralised governance (e.g., blockchain-based social systems).
- On the other hand, without proper regulations, Big Tech could monopolise these worlds, controlling economies (via digital currencies, NFTs) and **dictating laws within virtual spaces**.

The Risk of an Unregulated "Reality"

- MR allows companies to design **customised realities**—potentially **isolating users in echo chambers**.
- Without regulations, they could influence **elections, policymaking, or social movements** by curating immersive propaganda.

Conclusion: Who Governs the New Reality?

Tech giants will shape governance in MR more than traditional governments, especially if **fact-checking and regulatory controls remain weak**. The challenge will be **finding a balance** between innovation and **preventing corporate overreach**, ensuring that MR serves as a tool for democracy rather than manipulation. See the opening statements of this book.

Impact of Facebook's Change in Fact-Checking Policy

Facebook's shift on fact-checking in early 2025 may have significant implications:

- **Global Influence**: With a user base spanning most regulatory regions, Facebook's policies can indirectly affect compliance with local disinformation and content moderation laws.
- **Erosion of Trust**: Fact-checking reversals could undermine

public trust in digital platforms, complicating adherence to stringent laws like the EU's DSA.

- **Regulatory Challenges**: In regions like India and the U.S., weaker fact-checking may clash with initiatives to curb fake news and election interference.

- **Empowerment of Authoritarian Models**: Reduced fact-checking may inadvertently align with state-controlled narratives in countries like China, Russia, and Iran.

- **Catalyst for Regulation**: This volte-face could prompt stricter regulatory interventions globally to ensure platform accountability and combat misinformatittom of Formon.

Regional Approaches to Big Tech & Governance

- **Western Approach (U.S./Europe)**
  - The U.S. leans toward a **corporate-driven, free-market approach**, where Big Tech has immense power over political narratives (as seen in the Trump era).
  - **Europe**, however, is more cautious, with the **EU leading in regulations** like GDPR and the Digital Services Act, pushing back against disinformation and monopolies.

- **East Asian Approach (China, Japan, South Korea)**
  - **China** takes a **government-controlled, highly censored approach**, regulating Big Tech (Alibaba, Tencent, ByteDance) to **serve state interests** rather than corporate power.
  - **Japan & South Korea** have a **hybrid model**, balancing free markets with strict digital governance.

- **West Asian Approach (Middle East, India, Russia)**
  - **Russia** and some Middle Eastern nations **use Big Tech for state-driven narratives** rather than allowing corporate free-for-alls.
  - **India** is still finding its footing but has a **rapidly evolving regulatory environment** that swings between digital freedom and government intervention.

The World Economic Forum's Warning: Disinformation as the No.1 Risk

The **WEF labelling disinformation as the top global risk** is significant. In an MR world, where immersive digital environments can shape perceptions even more deeply than social media, the dangers multiply.

Key Risks of Disinformation in MR:

- **Algorithmic Reality Manipulation:** In MR spaces, **AI-driven propaganda** could create **fully immersive "false realities"**, reinforcing echo chambers.

- **Election & Policy Influence:** The power of **deepfake avatars, AI-driven discourse, and virtual misinformation** could destabilise democracies.

- **Corporate and State Power Struggles:** The **fight between corporate control (Big Tech) and state control (governments)** over digital spaces will define geopolitics.

- **Economic Warfare & Digital Colonialism:** Tech giants could **exploit developing nations** by controlling MR platforms and **dictating economic policies** through digital currencies and trade.

Authors' Take: A Corporate vs. Government Battle for Control

- **Trump-era Big Tech dominance** showed the danger of corporate-run politics. Now, the question is **whether states can reclaim governance** or if we enter a new era of **"Digital Oligarchy"**.

- **WEF is right to flag disinformation as a top risk**, but the **solution isn't just more regulation—it's about global digital governance models** that balance innovation, privacy, and truth.

Chapter 12

Mixed Reality Leadership in Critical Infrastructures and Critical Information Infrastructures

Mixed Reality Leadership for Critical Infrastructure Sectors

Overview

Critical Infrastructure (CI) and Critical Information Infrastructure (CII) sectors require innovative governance and management approaches due to increasing complexity, digitalisation, and evolving threats. Mixed Reality Leadership (MRL) integrates virtual, augmented, and physical environments to enhance decision-making, situational awareness, and resilience.

Key Components of MRL for Critical Infrastructure Sectors:

- **Augmented Situational Awareness**
  1. Real-time data visualisation and predictive analytics for risk assessment.
  2. Digital twins for scenario planning and response simulation.

- **Remote Collaboration & Crisis Management**
  1. Virtual command centres integrating AI-driven insights.

    2. Cross-sectoral and international coordination using MR-enhanced communication tools.

- **Training & Workforce Development**
  1. Immersive simulations for leadership training in crisis scenarios.
  2. AI-driven coaching for decision-making under uncertainty.

- **Cyber-Physical Resilience**
  1. MR-enabled cybersecurity monitoring and response.
  2. Enhanced asset management through virtual inspections and predictive maintenance.

Sector-Specific Applications

Sector	Mixed Reality Leadership Application
Energy	Digital twins for grid management, MR for cyber-physical security monitoring.
Water	Remote MR-assisted pipeline inspections, AI-driven leak detection.
Transportation	Smart traffic control, virtual emergency response training.
Health	Remote MR-assisted surgeries, hospital infrastructure resilience.
Telecommunications	MR network diagnostics, immersive disaster recovery training.
Civil Nuclear	Virtual radiation hazard simulations, MR for maintenance training.
Defence	Augmented battlefield visualisation, MR for war-gaming simulations.

Sector	Mixed Reality Leadership Application
Finance	MR-driven fraud detection, immersive cybersecurity exercises.
Food	Supply chain MR analytics, immersive regulatory compliance training.
Government & Policy	Virtual policymaking simulations, MR-enabled legislative collaboration.
Space	MR for satellite maintenance, immersive astronaut training.
Chemicals	Hazardous material handling simulations, MR for emergency drills.
Emergency Services & Crisis Response	Real-time situational awareness overlays, MR-enabled triage training.

Foundation Economy Sectors

The foundational economy (see Chapter 1) encompasses essential goods and services like utilities, healthcare, education, and social care, which support everyday life. It impacts society by ensuring access to vital resources, fostering social equity, and enhancing economic stability. This economy supports organisations of all sizes by providing a reliable infrastructure for operations. Mixed reality leadership, integrating AI, AR, VR, and XR, is fundamental from a human-centric perspective. It enhances collaboration, training, and decision-making, enabling leaders to navigate complex environments and drive innovation. For example, educational leaders can use mixed reality simulations to practice handling challenging situations, such as conferences with parents or coaching teachers. This method helps develop leadership skills in a low-risk setting, providing immediate feedback and opportunities for reflection.

This synergy ensures sustainable growth and adaptability in diverse organisational contexts.

Foundational economy sectors include essential services that support everyday life, such as:

- Utilities (energy, water, sewerage)
- Healthcare
- Education
- Social care
- Food processing and retailing
- Transport networks (rail, bus)
- Telecommunications networks.

These sectors are crucial for societal well-being and economic stability, providing the infrastructure necessary for all types of organisations to thrive.

Conclusion

Mixed Reality Leadership is essential for CI sectors to enhance resilience, efficiency, and crisis response. Governments and industries must formally integrate MR technologies into governance frameworks to improve security, sustainability, and preparedness.

Chapter 13

Ethical Considerations in Mixed Reality Leadership

Introduction

Mixed Reality (MR) Leadership involves leading organisations through the integration of **physical** and **digital** environments. This approach presents **ethical challenges** across governance, privacy, surveillance, and AI-driven bias. Below are examples of how **directors, managers, and individuals** can handle these challenges in both **personal and professional contexts**.

Ethical Implications of Leadership and Governance

Challenge: In mixed reality environments, leaders must balance innovation with ethical decision-making, ensuring fairness, inclusion, and responsible use of technology.

Professional Context

- **For Directors:** A CEO of a global company using virtual collaboration tools (like Meta's Horizon Workrooms) must ensure that AI-driven avatars do not reinforce discrimination based on gender, race, or disability. Policies must be in place to promote **ethical virtual representation and inclusivity**.
- **For Managers:** A manager in an **AI-powered hiring platform**

(e.g., Pymetrics, HireVue) must prevent bias in VR-based interviews, ensuring that **AI doesn't favour certain accents, facial features, or behaviours** that could lead to discrimination.

- **For Individuals:** Employees using MR environments (like Microsoft Mesh) for work meetings must practice **ethical behaviour in virtual spaces**—for example, avoiding manipulative deepfakes or identity misrepresentation.

Personal Context

- ✓ A **university professor** teaching in a **VR-enabled classroom** must ensure that digital interactions are ethical and don't exclude students with disabilities.

- ✓ A **social media influencer** using AR filters must acknowledge how **beauty-enhancing AI tools** create **unrealistic standards**, potentially affecting followers' self-esteem.

Privacy, Surveillance, and Digital Rights Concerns

Challenge: In mixed reality, vast amounts of personal data (eye movements, emotions, speech patterns) are collected. Ensuring **privacy and digital rights** becomes critical.

Professional Context

- **For Directors:** A CTO of a **VR-powered workplace** (e.g., Accenture's metaverse office) must ensure that employee **eye-tracking data and facial expressions** are not exploited for marketing without consent.

- **For Managers:** A retail company implementing **AI-powered surveillance in stores** (e.g., Amazon Go) must ensure customer behaviour tracking complies with **GDPR or CCPA** regulations.

- **For Individuals:** A **remote worker** using a VR office tool must be aware of how much of their biometric data (e.g., voice tone, facial tracking) is stored and who owns it.

Personal Context

- ✓ A **parent** buying an **AR learning app** for their child must check how the company handles **children's biometric data**, preventing exploitation.

✓ A **gamer** using an **AR headset** must ensure that **location tracking** is disabled if they don't want companies harvesting movement patterns.

Bias in AI-Driven Tools

Challenge: AI tools in mixed reality can reinforce **racial, gender, and socio-economic bias**, leading to **unfair decisions** in hiring, governance, and social interactions.

Professional Context

- **For Directors:** A board implementing **AI-driven financial predictions** must ensure that the system doesn't **favour wealthy customers** over marginalised groups when approving loans.
- **For Managers:** A manager using **AI-driven employee monitoring tools** (e.g., Microsoft Viva) must ensure that productivity metrics don't **unfairly penalise neurodivergent workers** who may perform better under flexible schedules.
- **For Individuals:** A job applicant using a **VR interview assessment** tool must be aware that AI **voice and accent analysis** may introduce bias against non-native English speakers.

Personal Context

✓ A **content creator** using AI-generated avatars should verify that the system doesn't **default to Eurocentric features**, ensuring **diverse representation**.

✓ A **consumer** using AI-driven fashion recommendations must check whether **bias in AI models** leads to exclusion of certain body types or cultural clothing styles.

Conclusion: Responsible Mixed Reality Leadership

Mixed reality leaders must ensure **ethical governance, data privacy, and AI fairness** in both personal and professional settings.

As **directors, managers, and individuals**, staying informed and applying **transparent policies** will help build a **more inclusive and responsible digital future**.

Ethical Implications of Leadership and Governance

Case Studies:

Virtual Workplace Misconduct in Meta's Horizon Workrooms

Challenge: Employees using VR meeting spaces have reported instances of **unethical behaviour, such as virtual harassment**. Unlike physical spaces, VR makes it difficult to establish clear boundaries, making governance complex.

Leadership Response: Meta introduced a **"personal boundary" feature**, ensuring that avatars **can't invade personal space** unless explicitly permitted.

AI-Powered Hiring Discrimination in VR Interviews

Challenge: Some companies use **AI-driven VR interviews** to analyse **eye movements, speech tone, and body language,** but these systems have been found to **discriminate against neurodivergent or disabled candidates**.

Leadership Response: IBM and Microsoft have developed **ethical AI hiring guidelines**, ensuring **AI models are trained on diverse datasets** to reduce bias.

Key Challenges

- **Regulating behaviour in virtual environments** (e.g., preventing misconduct in VR spaces).

- **Ensuring transparency** in **AI-driven decision-making** (e.g., in hiring or promotions).

Establishing Ethical Oversight for Emerging Technologies (e.g., AI-generated Managers).

Best Practices for Leaders & Individuals:

- **For Directors:** Establish **Virtual Code of Conduct policies** and **AI Ethics Committees** to oversee decision-making.
- **For Managers:** Provide **VR ethics training** to employees and ensure AI-powered decisions are **auditable**.
- **For Individuals:** Be aware of **digital workplace rights**, and report **ethical violations** in virtual settings.

Privacy, Surveillance, and Digital Rights Concerns

Case Studies

Eye-Tracking Surveillance in VR Headsets

Challenge: Companies like Meta and Apple use **eye-tracking in VR headsets** to analyse where users look. This data can be used for **personalised ads**—raising concerns about **corporate surveillance**.

Leadership Response: Privacy advocates have pushed for **user control over biometric data**, and **some regulators require "opt-in" consent** for eye-tracking.

Amazon's AI-Powered Employee Surveillance

Challenge: Amazon warehouse workers have reported **AI-driven cameras monitoring their every move**, penalising **bathroom breaks** and minor inefficiencies.

Leadership Response: Amazon faced backlash and implemented **less invasive AI monitoring** while increasing **human oversight** of AI decisions.

Key Challenges

- **How much digital surveillance is too much?** (Balancing security vs. privacy).
- **Who owns biometric data?** (Users, corporations, or governments?).
- **What protections exist for digital workers?** (Especially in VR workplaces).

Best Practices for Leaders & Individuals

- **For Directors:** Adopt **privacy-first policies** and implement **data transparency laws** (e.g., allowing users to access/delete personal data).
- **For Managers:** Limit **excessive AI surveillance** and ensure employees **understand how they're being monitored**.
- **For Individuals:** Use **privacy tools** (like VPNs, encrypted communication), and **review terms of service** for apps collecting biometric data.

Bias in AI-Driven Tools

Case Studies:

Racial & Gender Bias in AI Hiring Algorithms

Challenge: AI tools used by **companies like Amazon** for recruitment were found to **favour male candidates** because historical hiring data was **biased against women**.

Leadership Response: Amazon scrapped its AI hiring tool and developed **human-AI hybrid decision-making models** to **prevent bias from being amplified**.

Bias in Facial Recognition & Digital Avatars

Challenge: Some **VR platforms and AI-generated avatars** default to **Eurocentric features**, failing to represent diverse users.
Leadership Response: Microsoft and Google introduced **inclusive AI datasets** to ensure **diverse digital representation**.

Key Challenges

- **How do we ensure AI doesn't inherit human biases?**
- **How do we make AI-driven leadership more inclusive?**
- **How do we hold companies accountable for biased AI decisions?**

Best Practices for Leaders & Individuals:

- **For Directors:** Implement **AI fairness audits** and **diverse AI training datasets** to reduce bias.
- **For Managers:** Advocate for **human oversight** in AI-driven decision-making.
- **For Individuals:** Be aware of **how AI systems assess you** (e.g., in hiring, finance) and **demand transparency** in AI decisions.

Final Thoughts: Leading Ethically in the Digital Age

Mixed Reality Leadership requires balancing **technological advancement with ethics, privacy, and fairness.** By **adopting responsible governance, privacy-first policies, and unbiased AI** practices, directors, managers, and individuals can **create a safer, more ethical digital future**.

Action Plan for Ethical Mixed Reality Leadership

This **action plan** provides a structured approach for **directors, managers, and individuals** to navigate **ethical governance, privacy, and AI bias** in **Mixed Reality (MR) environments**.

Ethical Leadership & Governance

Challenge: Preventing unethical behaviour in virtual environments and ensuring responsible leadership in AI-driven workplaces.

Actions for Directors (CEOs, Executives, Policymakers)

- **Develop a Virtual Code of Conduct:** Define **ethical behaviour guidelines** for employees in MR spaces (e.g., no harassment in VR, transparency in AI hiring).
- **Create an AI Ethics Committee:** Establish a diverse **advisory board** to oversee **AI decision-making** (e.g., AI hiring, VR workplace monitoring).
- **Implement AI Transparency Rules:** Require that **AI-driven HR decisions** (promotions, hiring) include a **human review process**.
- **Regulate Deepfake & Identity Fraud Risks:** Enforce policies to **prevent misuse of AI-generated avatars** for impersonation.

Actions for Managers (HR, Team Leads, Middle Management)

- **Train Employees on Digital Ethics:** Conduct **workshops on VR ethics** (e.g., avoiding discriminatory AI decisions, respecting digital identity).
- **Monitor AI Bias in Employee Evaluations:** Ensure AI doesn't **unfairly penalise workers** based on background, gender, or disability.
- **Use Transparent AI Decision Tools:** Adopt AI systems that **allow employees to challenge unfair decisions** (e.g., wrongful performance reviews).

Actions for Individuals (Employees, Freelancers, Users)

- **Know Your Rights in Virtual Workplaces:** Demand clarity on **how AI tracks your performance** in MR environments.
- **Report Ethical Violations in VR Spaces:** Use platforms' reporting tools if you **experience misconduct** (e.g., harassment in VR meetings).

- **Understand AI's Role in Hiring & Promotion:** Ask employers how **AI hiring tools evaluate candidates** and push for **human oversight** in decisions.

Privacy, Surveillance & Digital Rights

Challenge: Preventing excessive **AI surveillance** and ensuring users control their **biometric data** in MR environments.

Actions for Directors (CEOs, Executives, Policymakers)

- **Establish Privacy Regulations for VR Workplaces:** Mandate **"opt-in" policies** for AI tracking of **eye movement, facial expressions, and speech patterns**.
- **Ensure Data Transparency:** Require companies to **disclose what biometric data is collected** and **who has access** to it.
- **Limit AI Employee Monitoring:** Set **clear boundaries** on workplace surveillance (e.g., tracking productivity only during work hours).

Actions for Managers (HR, Team Leads, Middle Management)

- **Use Ethical AI Surveillance:** Avoid using **highly intrusive AI tools** (e.g., AI that tracks bathroom breaks).
- **Ensure Employees Can Opt Out:** Give workers the option to **disable AI tracking features** in MR tools (e.g., VR eye-tracking data).
- **Protect User Privacy in VR Meetings:** Ensure **MR platforms don't record conversations** without consent.

Actions for Individuals (Employees, Freelancers, Users)

- **Check Privacy Settings on MR Devices:** Disable **excessive tracking** (e.g., Meta's eye-tracking ads).
- **Use Encrypted Virtual Communication Tools:** Choose **privacy-focused platforms** for virtual work.
- **Push for Digital Rights in Workplaces:** Advocate for **GDPR-style protections** in MR workplaces to control your **own data**.

AI Bias & Fairness in MR Environments

Challenge: Preventing discrimination in AI-driven decisions (e.g., biased hiring, unfair workplace evaluations, racial/gender bias in avatars).

Actions for Directors (CEOs, Executives, Policymakers)

- **Mandate Bias Audits for AI Systems:** Require **regular AI fairness checks** to prevent **discriminatory outcomes**.
- **Develop Inclusive AI Training Data:** Ensure AI is trained on **diverse data sets** to avoid **reinforcing racial or gender bias**.
- **Ban AI-Only Hiring Decisions:** Require **human review of AI hiring** and performance evaluation decisions.

Actions for Managers (HR, Team Leads, Middle Management)

- **Monitor AI-Driven Hiring for Bias:** Check if AI **favours certain accents, genders, or backgrounds** in hiring decisions
- **Ensure Fair Representation in MR Avatars:** Use **inclusive AI models** that offer diverse **skin tones, disabilities, and cultural attire**.
- **Advocate for AI Explainability:** Employees should be able to **challenge AI-driven decisions** (e.g., why they were rejected for a promotion).

Actions for Individuals (Employees, Freelancers, Users)

- **Understand How AI Evaluates You:** Ask employers how **AI-based evaluations work** (e.g., is your **eye contact in VR** being judged for promotions?)
- **Call Out AI Bias in MR Spaces:** Report issues if **AI-generated avatars exclude certain ethnicities or genders**.
- **Use Ethical AI-Powered Tools:** Choose platforms that **prioritise fairness and transparency** in MR experiences.

Final Steps: Implementing Ethical Mixed Reality Leadership

Immediate Actions (Next 30 Days)

Directors: **Establish an AI Ethics Policy** & conduct **AI Bias Audits**

Managers: **Train teams on AI fairness** & ensure **AI transparency in evaluations**

Individuals: **Review MR privacy settings** & **demand AI decision transparency**

Long-Term Strategy (6-12 Months)

Companies: **Develop AI Oversight Committees** & adopt **inclusive AI models**

Governments: **Pass regulations on AI hiring & biometric data privacy**

Users: **Push for ethical MR governance & privacy protections**

Final Thought: Building a Responsible Mixed Reality Future

Mixed Reality Leadership is about balancing **innovation with ethics, privacy, and fairness**. By taking proactive steps today, **directors, managers, and individuals** can **shape a more inclusive, fair, and secure digital future**.

Chapter 14

The Next Supercycle

Definition of a Supercycle

A supercycle represents a prolonged period of profound transformation driven by technological advancements, societal changes, and shifts in economic paradigms. These cycles reshape industries, governments, and daily life.

Core Drivers of Global Transformation

Core Drivers of Global Transformation

Global transformation is shaped by interconnected technological, economic, political, environmental, and social forces. These core drivers define the trajectory of change and impact critical infrastructures, governance, and societal resilience.

Technological Innovation & Digitalisation

- **Artificial Intelligence & Automation** – Reshaping industries, labour markets, and decision-making.
- **Quantum Computing & Advanced Cybersecurity** – Revolutionising encryption and data security.
- **5G & Beyond** – Enabling hyper-connectivity and real-time global communication.

- **Mixed Reality & Metaverse** – Transforming education, healthcare, and workspaces.
- **Biotechnology & Synthetic Biology** – Advancing healthcare, agriculture, and environmental solutions.

Geopolitical Shifts & Power Dynamics

- **Multipolar World Order** – Shift from US-led dominance to emerging powers like China, India, and regional blocs.
- **Geoeconomics & Resource Competition** – Control over critical minerals, rare earth elements, and energy markets.
- **Cyber & Hybrid Warfare** – Increasing threats to national security through digital and disinformation campaigns.

Climate Change & Environmental Sustainability

- **Extreme Weather Events** – Rising risks of floods, droughts, and wildfires.
- **Energy Transition & Decarbonisation** – Shift towards renewables, hydrogen, and nuclear energy.
- **Sustainable Development & Circular Economy** – Reduction of waste, carbon footprint, and resource exploitation.

Economic Disruptions & Financial Evolution

- **De-Dollarisation & New Financial Systems** – Rise of CBDCs (Central Bank Digital Currencies) and decentralised finance (DeFi).
- **Automation & Workforce Displacement** – Need for reskilling and new economic models (e.g., Universal Basic Income).
- **Supply Chain Resilience & Deglobalisation** – Shift towards regional production hubs and nearshoring.

Demographic & Societal Transformations

- **Aging Populations & Workforce Challenges** – Increasing strain on healthcare, pensions, and productivity.
- **Urbanisation & Smart Cities** – Growth of megacities with AI-driven infrastructure.

- **Human Enhancement & Transhumanism** – Merging of biology and technology for cognitive and physical augmentation.

Space Exploration & Extra-Terrestrial Expansion

- **New Space Race** – Competition between nations and private enterprises (SpaceX, Blue Origin, China).
- **Asteroid Mining & Lunar Colonisation** – Potential for resource extraction beyond Earth.
- **Space-Based Energy & Defence Systems** – Future potential for space-based solar power and security initiatives.

Health & Biosecurity Challenges

- **Global Pandemics & Health Crises** – Need for resilient healthcare systems and rapid-response biotechnology.
- **Genomics & Personalised Medicine** – Precision treatments and AI-driven diagnostics.
- **Mental Health & Cognitive Well-being** – Addressing stress, burnout, and digital overload.

Governance, Regulation & Ethical Challenges

- **AI & Ethical Dilemmas** – Governance of autonomous systems, biases, and algorithmic decision-making.
- **Surveillance & Digital Freedoms** – Balancing security with privacy rights.
- **Global Governance & Institutional Reforms** – Redefining international cooperation and regulatory frameworks.

Conclusion

The convergence of these drivers is reshaping the global order, demanding adaptive leadership, innovation, and resilience strategies. Proactive governance, sustainable development, and technological foresight will be critical in navigating the future of global transformation. (And this list does not really cover the impact of Trump's USA leadership.)

Societal Implications and Organisational Impact

Societal Implications & Organisational Impact of Global Transformation

The accelerating pace of global transformation presents profound implications for society and organisations. Leaders must prepare for shifts in employment, governance, ethics, and public trust while ensuring organisational agility, resilience, and innovation.

Implications

Workforce Disruptions & The Future of Work

Job Displacement & Reskilling Demands

- AI, automation, and robotics will displace millions of jobs, requiring large-scale workforce reskilling (see Chapter 1).
- Growth in new industries (e.g., AI ethics, cybersecurity, space tech) will demand new skill sets.

Rise of the Gig & Digital Economy

- Traditional 9–5 jobs will decline, replaced by flexible, remote, and AI-assisted work structures.
- Hybrid work models will become standard, affecting urban economies and corporate real estate.

Income Inequality & Digital Divide

- Disparities in AI accessibility, automation-driven job losses, and unequal education will widen wealth gaps.
- Governments may consider Universal Basic Income (UBI) as a response to economic shifts.

Social & Political Response:

- ✓ Policies for reskilling, digital inclusion, and fair AI implementation.

✓ Expansion of remote work infrastructure and upskilling initiatives.

Governance, Ethics & Privacy Challenges

- **AI Governance & Algorithmic Bias**

- AI-driven decision-making could reinforce systemic inequalities if not ethically managed.
- Governments and regulators will push for AI transparency, fairness, and accountability.

Surveillance vs. Privacy Dilemmas

- Nations will implement mass surveillance for security and pandemic control, raising privacy concerns.
- The tension between security (biometric tracking, AI policing) and civil liberties will intensify.

Decentralisation of Power

- Blockchain and Web3 will decentralise governance, reducing corporate and government control over data.
- Digital currencies (CBDCs, Bitcoin) will challenge traditional banking systems.

Social & Political Response:

✓ Stricter AI regulation and digital rights advocacy.
✓ Adoption of decentralised finance (DeFi) and digital identity systems.

Global Stability & Security Risks

Cyberwarfare & Mixed Reality Threats

- Cyberattacks on critical infrastructure (energy, healthcare, finance) will increase.
- AI-powered disinformation campaigns will influence elections and global narratives.

Climate-Driven Migration & Resource Conflicts

- Rising sea levels and extreme weather will trigger mass displacement.
- Competition for water, minerals, and arable land may lead to geopolitical tensions.

Space Militarisation & AI-Led Warfare

- Space will become the next battleground for national security dominance.
- AI-driven autonomous weapons will pose ethical and legal challenges.

Social & Political Response:

- ✓ Strengthening cybersecurity and critical infrastructure resilience.
- ✓ Diplomacy and global cooperation on AI, space, and environmental security.

Health, Well-being & Social Behaviour Shifts

Rise of Bioengineering & Longevity Science

- Genetic modification, CRISPR, and longevity treatments will redefine human health.
- Ethical concerns over designer babies and human augmentation will spark debate.

Mental Health & Cognitive Overload

- Digital addiction, AI-driven work stress, and social isolation will increase.
- Demand for mental health solutions (e.g., neurotech, mindfulness AI) will rise.

Changing Social Norms & Relationships

- Virtual interactions will replace physical ones, affecting human relationships.
- AI companionship and digital influencers will challenge traditional human connections.

Social & Political Response:

- ✓ Regulations on biotech and human enhancement.
- ✓ Greater investment in mental health and social resilience programs.

Organisational Impact

Business Model Disruptions & Competitive Pressures

AI-First Companies Will Dominate

- AI-native businesses will have a competitive advantage in decision-making, automation, and analytics.
- Traditional companies must integrate AI or risk obsolescence.

Hyper-Personalisation & Data Monetisation

- Consumer expectations will shift toward AI-driven, personalised experiences.
- Data will become the most valuable asset, leading to ethical concerns over ownership and use.

Decentralisation & Blockchain Impact

- Decentralised platforms (Web3, DAOs) will challenge traditional corporate structures.
- Businesses must rethink trust, governance, and value exchange models.

Organisational Strategy:

✓ Shift towards AI-driven, data-centric business models.

✓ Invest in blockchain-based security and transparency.

Workforce & Organisational Culture Transformation

Human-AI Collaboration Will Reshape Jobs

- AI and automation will augment (rather than replace) human jobs, requiring redefined roles.
- Organisations must foster AI literacy and build hybrid human-AI teams.

Demand for Continuous Learning & Adaptability

- Employees will require ongoing upskilling due to rapid tech evolution.
- Companies must invest in AI-powered learning platforms and adaptive training.

Workforce Diversity & Inclusion in a Digital World

- The shift to remote work will diversify talent pools globally.
- Organisations must ensure inclusive digital workspaces and fair AI hiring.

Organisational Strategy:

- Develop AI-enhanced learning programs for workforce agility.
- Foster an AI-augmented work culture with ethical AI policies.

Cybersecurity & Digital Trust Challenges

Increased Cybersecurity Risks

- AI-driven cyberattacks will target financial, healthcare, and governmental sectors.
- Organisations must strengthen cybersecurity protocols with AI-driven threat detection.

Consumer Trust in AI & Data Usage

- Ethical concerns over AI-driven decision-making will require corporate transparency.
- Companies must ensure compliance with global data privacy laws (e.g., GDPR, CCPA).

Regulatory Complexity & Compliance

- Governments will impose stricter AI, cybersecurity, and data privacy laws.
- Organisations must adopt AI-compliance monitoring tools and regulatory foresight.

Organisational Strategy:

- ✓ Implement AI-powered cybersecurity measures.
- ✓ Build consumer trust through transparency and ethical AI governance.

Sustainability & Corporate Responsibility

Green Technologies & Carbon Neutrality

- Companies will face pressure to adopt carbon-neutral business models.
- Investment in sustainable technologies (hydrogen, circular economy) will become a priority.

ESG (Environmental, Social, Governance) Standards

- Regulatory bodies will enforce stricter ESG compliance.
- Organisations must integrate sustainability metrics into core business operations.

Supply Chain & Resource Ethics

- Ethical sourcing and responsible AI will define brand reputation.
- Companies must leverage blockchain for transparent supply chains.

Organisational Strategy:

✓ Adopt sustainability-focused innovations (green AI, carbon capture tech).

✓ Align corporate strategies with ESG and ethical sourcing standards.

Conclusion: Future-Ready Leadership & Organisational Adaptability

For Society:

◆ Policymakers, educators, and businesses must **collaborate** to ensure ethical AI, privacy, and sustainable economic models.

◆ Governments must establish **global AI governance frameworks** and promote equitable digital transformation.

◆ New educational models must prepare future generations for AI-driven workplaces.

For Organisations:

◆ Leaders must **embrace agility, innovation, intellectual curiosity and ethical leadership** to navigate disruption.

◆ AI, sustainability, and cybersecurity should be at the **core of strategic decision-making**.

- Future-proofing through **workforce adaptability, regulatory compliance, and risk intelligence** is key.

The future belongs to leaders who anticipate change, act decisively, and build resilient, ethical, and AI-powered organisations.

Strategic Leadership Responses

Strategic Response for Organisational Leaders to Global Transformation Drivers

Organisational leaders must adopt a proactive, adaptive, and resilient approach to navigate global transformation. This requires strategic foresight, digital agility, sustainable practices, and robust risk management. Below is a structured response to each driver of transformation:

Embrace Technological Innovation & Digitalisation

Strategic Response:

- **Invest in AI & Automation** – Enhance productivity while upskilling employees.
- **Leverage Quantum & Cybersecurity Advances** – Build next-gen data protection mechanisms.
- **Adopt 5G & IoT Solutions** – Improve operational efficiency and decision-making.
- **Utilise Mixed Reality & Digital Twins** – Enhance training, collaboration, and risk simulations.

Action Plan:

- Create a **Chief AI Officer (CAIO)** role for innovation leadership.
- Implement **AI-driven decision-support systems** for real-time insights.
- Develop **cyber resilience frameworks** to counter evolving threats.

Navigate Geopolitical Shifts & Global Power Dynamics

Strategic Response:

- **Diversify Supply Chains** – Reduce reliance on single-source regions.
- **Enhance Geopolitical Risk Intelligence** – Leverage AI-driven predictive analytics.
- **Strengthen Cyber & Hybrid Warfare Defences** – Implement robust cybersecurity and disinformation countermeasures.
- **Build Strategic Partnerships** – Engage in multi-stakeholder alliances for stability.

Action Plan:

- Establish a **Geopolitical Risk Unit** (included 3rd Party Risk) within the organisation.
- Monitor **trade policy, sanctions, and regulatory shifts** proactively.
- Develop **cross-border contingency plans** for trade disruptions.

Adapt to Climate Change & Sustainability Imperatives

Strategic Response:

- **Integrate ESG (Environmental, Social, and Governance) Frameworks** – Align with global sustainability standards.
- **Invest in Renewable Energy & Circular Economy Models** – Reduce carbon footprint.
- **Develop Climate Resilience Strategies** – Implement AI-driven climate risk analytics.
- **Advance Sustainable Finance & Green Investments** – Drive long-term value creation.

Action Plan:

- Appoint a **Chief Sustainability Officer (CSO)** to oversee green initiatives.

- Commit to **net-zero targets and carbon offset strategies**.
- Utilise **climate scenario planning** for business continuity.

Manage Economic Disruptions & Financial Evolution

Strategic Response:

- **Adopt Decentralised Finance (DeFi) & CBDC Readiness** – Future-proof financial transactions.
- **Strengthen Financial Resilience** – Diversify revenue streams and risk mitigation strategies.
- **Invest in Workforce Upskilling & Automation** – Address job displacement risks.
- **Develop Crisis-Resistant Business Models** – Build operational agility.

Action Plan:

- Monitor **emerging financial trends**, including cryptocurrency regulations.
- Develop **alternative financial models** for crisis periods.
- Foster **financial literacy programs** for employees and stakeholders.

Address Demographic & Societal Transformations

Strategic Response:

- **Embrace AI-Augmented Workforces** – Leverage human-machine collaboration.
- **Prepare for Generational Workforce Shifts** – Adapt leadership to Gen Z and future talent dynamics.
- **Implement Smart City & Urbanisation Solutions** – Align with emerging megacity trends.
- **Champion Human Enhancement & Digital Well-being** – Address ethical implications.

Action Plan:

- Design **inclusive work policies** catering to diverse workforce demographics
- Invest in **lifelong learning programs** to keep employees future-ready.
- Develop **AI-driven HR analytics** for optimised workforce planning.

Engage in Space & Extra-Terrestrial Strategies

Strategic Response:

- **Monitor Space Commercialisation Trends** – Identify industry impact opportunities.
- **Enhance Satellite & Space Data Utilisation** – Improve business intelligence.
- **Prepare for Space-Based Communications & Security** – Strengthen global connectivity strategies.
- **Invest in Aerospace Collaborations** – Explore space industry partnerships.

Action Plan:

- Explore **satellite-driven data analytics** for operations optimisation.
- Develop **resilient infrastructure solutions** for space-based technologies.
- Engage in **public-private partnerships** for space-related advancements.

Strengthen Health & Biosecurity Preparedness

Strategic Response:

- **Adopt AI-Driven Health Monitoring** – Ensure workplace well-being.
- **Develop Pandemic & Biosecurity Protocols** – Enhance organisational resilience.
- **Invest in Personalised Medicine & Genetic Advancements** – Align with healthcare trends.
- **Support Mental Health & Cognitive Well-being** – Foster a high-performance culture.

Action Plan:

- Implement **real-time health analytics** for risk assessment.
- Design **remote healthcare support systems** for employees.
- Partner with **biotech firms** for workforce health solutions.

Advance Governance, Ethics & Regulatory Compliance

Strategic Response:

- **Develop AI Ethics & Governance Frameworks** – Ensure responsible AI deployment.
- **Balance Privacy & Security Concerns** – Align with global data protection laws.
- **Strengthen Institutional Trust & Transparency** – Foster responsible leadership.
- **Reinforce Global Compliance & Policy Adaptation** – Stay ahead of regulatory changes.

Action Plan:

- Establish a **Digital Ethics & Compliance Task Force**.
- Engage in **regulatory foresight exercises** to anticipate legal shifts.
- Develop **AI-driven compliance monitoring systems**.

Conclusion: The Leadership Imperative

Organisational leaders must adopt **agility, resilience, and innovation** as core leadership traits to navigate global transformation. By **leveraging emerging technologies, strengthening governance, embracing sustainability, and proactively mitigating risks**, leaders can **future-proof their organisations** and drive long-term success.

Key Leadership Priorities:

- **Invest in AI, sustainability, and digital transformation.**
- **Develop geopolitical foresight and supply chain resilience.**
- **Enhance crisis preparedness, cybersecurity, and workforce adaptability.**
- **Champion ethical leadership and responsible innovation.**

The Future Belongs to Leaders Who Anticipate, Adapt, and Act!

Next Supercycle

The next supercycle, already emerging in the USA, will consist of and be driven by:
- **Artificial Intelligence (AI)**: The integration of AI into nearly every sector, revolutionising decision-making, automation, and human-machine collaboration.
- **Biotechnology**: Advances in genetic engineering, CRISPR, and synthetic biology, enabling precision medicine and potentially extending human lifespan.
- **Renewable Energy Transition**: The move towards sustainable energy systems, including solar, wind, and advancements in battery technologies.
- **Quantum Computing**: Transforming problem-solving capabilities across fields like encryption, materials science, and logistics.
- **Space Exploration**: Private and public investments driving space colonisation, resource mining, and satellite-based technologies.
- **Geopolitical Shifts**: Emerging economic powers and the

realignment of global trade, coupled with tensions over data sovereignty and cybersecurity.

- **Demographic Changes**: Aging populations in developed nations and youthful demographics in emerging economies influencing consumption patterns and innovation.

These developments increase the technical challenges to mixed reality leadership way beyond the requirements for today's traditional organisational leaders.

Societal Implications

- **Workforce Transformation**: Automation and AI will displace some jobs while creating demand for new skills, necessitating education reform.
- **Ethical Challenges**: Debates around privacy, bias in AI, and the ethical use of biotechnology will grow more urgent.
- **Global Inequality**: Disparities in technological access may widen the gap between nations and social classes.

Opportunities and Risks

- **Opportunities**: Unprecedented innovations in healthcare, climate mitigation, and connectivity could elevate quality of life worldwide.
- **Risks**: Concentration of power among tech giants, cyber warfare, and environmental consequences from poorly managed technologies could undermine progress.

Strategies for Adaptation

Amy Webb emphasises the need for:

- **Scenario Planning**: Organisations and governments must prepare for multiple futures by identifying signals and trends early.
- **Collaboration**: Cross-disciplinary and international cooperation

to address global challenges like climate change and cyber threats.

- **Ethical Frameworks**: Proactively establishing regulations and norms to guide the development and deployment of disruptive technologies.

The next supercycle is a period of immense potential and challenge, demanding strategic foresight, ethical vigilance, and global cooperation to navigate successfully.

Organisational Planning for the Next Supercycle

If we look at the leadership needs for the next supercycle then this book would align with anticipated needs:

Chapter 15

Organisational Planning for the Next Supercycle

Agile and Adaptive Leadership Models

- **Flat Hierarchies**: Encourage decentralised decision-making to improve responsiveness to rapidly changing conditions.
- **Empowerment**: Equip mid-level leaders with decision-making authority to act quickly and innovatively.
- **Dynamic Leadership Development**: Build leadership pipelines that prioritise adaptability, emotional intelligence, and cross-disciplinary skills.

Strategic Foresight and Scenario Planning

- **Trend Analysis**: Integrate tools and processes to monitor emerging technologies, societal changes, and geopolitical trends.
- **Scenario-Based Strategies**: Develop flexible plans for multiple potential futures to mitigate risks and capitalise on opportunities.
- **Continuous Learning**: Foster a culture of ongoing education for leaders to stay ahead of disruptive trends.

Building Resilient and Sustainable Organisations

- **Crisis Management Protocols**: Prepare leaders for managing disruptions, whether from climate events, technological upheavals, or cyber threats.
- **Sustainable Practices**: Embed environmental, social, and governance (ESG) goals into core leadership strategies to align with societal and regulatory expectations.
- **Digital Resilience**: Strengthen cybersecurity leadership and preparedness for potential attacks or system failures.

Workforce Transformation and Future-Proofing Leadership

- **Upskilling and Reskilling**: Anticipate shifts in skill demands by investing in employee training programs.
- **Human-Machine Collaboration**: Prepare leaders to guide teams that include AI-driven tools and systems, ensuring harmonious integration.
- **Employee Empowerment**: Encourage participative decision-making and cultivate a culture of innovation across all organisational levels.

Cultural and Ethical Leadership

- **Fostering Trust**: Build organisational cultures grounded in transparency, accountability, and trust to navigate uncertainties.
- **Ethics in Innovation**: Ensure leaders champion ethical frameworks for the adoption of technologies like AI and biotechnology.
- **Inclusion and Diversity**: Lead with an emphasis on equity and inclusion to foster innovation and align with global societal trends.

Global Collaboration and Multi-Stakeholder Engagement

- **Cross-Border Partnerships**: Collaborate with governments, NGOs, and other organisations to address shared global challenges such as climate change and cybersecurity.
- **Platform Thinking**: Develop ecosystems that connect partners, suppliers, and consumers for mutual benefit.
- **Stakeholder Leadership**: Engage actively with all stakeholders, from employees to communities, to build a shared vision and commitment.

Data-Driven Decision Making and AI Integration

- **Real-Time Analytics**: Utilise AI and big data for informed decision-making and early identification of trends.
- **Predictive Tools**: Leverage technology to anticipate disruptions and design proactive responses.
- **Metrics for Innovation**: Shift focus from traditional performance metrics to ones that measure adaptability, innovation, and resilience.

Leadership Mindset and Development

- **Curiosity and Lifelong Learning**: Cultivate leaders who are open to experimentation and continuous improvement.
- **Emotional Intelligence (EI)**: Train leaders to navigate the complexities of workforce emotions, uncertainty, and ethical dilemmas.
- **Visionary Leadership**: Inspire and guide organisations by articulating a clear, compelling vision for thriving in the supercycle.

Anticipated Challenges for Leadership

- Resistance to Change: Overcoming inertia in traditional organisations.

- Balancing Innovation with Ethics: Ensuring rapid innovation does not outpace moral and regulatory frameworks.
- Navigating Complexity: Managing the interdependence of technologies, markets, and geopolitical shifts.

Conclusion

To meet the challenges of the next supercycle, organisations must prioritise leadership that is agile, inclusive, ethical, and globally minded. Forward-thinking planning, combined with investments in people and technology, will be critical to thriving in this transformative era

Chapter 16

The Automation, Statistical and Big Data Paradoxes and Mixed Reality Leadership

Automation Paradox and Mixed Reality Leadership

The **automation paradox** refers to the phenomenon where increasing levels of automation in systems, rather than reducing the need for human involvement, can sometimes increase the demand for human skills and oversight. This paradox arises because automation, while streamlining and enhancing efficiency, also introduces complexities that require human intervention in unexpected or critical situations.

Key Aspects of the Automation Paradox:

- **Increased Complexity**:
  - Automated systems often rely on sophisticated algorithms and interconnected components. When they fail or encounter edge cases, troubleshooting these systems requires specialised human expertise.

- **Overreliance and De-skilling**:
  - As automation takes over routine tasks, humans might become less practiced or skilled in performing those tasks manually. This can make it harder for them to step in effectively during emergencies or system failures.

- **Heightened Monitoring Needs**:
  - Automated systems require vigilant monitoring to ensure proper functioning. Humans must oversee processes, audit outputs, and validate decisions made by machines, especially in high-stakes scenarios like aviation, healthcare, or finance.

- **Unexpected Failures**:
  - Automation cannot always account for novel, ambiguous, or extreme conditions. Human operators are needed to handle these situations, but they may face challenges due to reduced familiarity with manual operations.

- **Trust and Accountability**:
  - When systems automate critical decisions, there's often a need for humans to validate or override these decisions. Ensuring accountability and maintaining trust in automated systems requires human judgment and intervention.

Examples of the Automation Paradox:

- **Aviation**: Modern aircraft are highly automated, with autopilot systems handling much of the flight. However, pilots are still required to monitor the systems and take over during emergencies. Accidents have occurred when pilots, unpractised in manual control, struggled to manage crises after automation failed.

- **Healthcare**: AI-driven diagnostic tools can enhance accuracy, but doctors still need to interpret AI recommendations and apply contextual judgment. Misdiagnoses may occur if medical professionals blindly rely on AI without cross-verifying.

- **Finance**: Algorithmic trading automates buying and selling decisions, but humans are required to manage risks and intervene during market anomalies like "flash crashes."

Mitigating the Automation Paradox:

- **Training and Upskilling**: Regular training ensures that humans retain the skills needed to intervene when automation fails.

- **Designing with Human Oversight**: Automated systems should be designed to include clear roles for human operators, with intuitive interfaces and decision-support tools.
- **Balanced Automation**: Automation should focus on augmenting human capabilities rather than entirely replacing them, ensuring collaboration between humans and machines.

The automation paradox highlights the importance of maintaining a human-centric approach to technology, ensuring that automation enhances rather than undermines human competence and control.

The Automation Paradox & The Statistical Paradox in Mixed Reality Leadership

Both the **Automation Paradox** and the **Statistical Paradox** pose unique challenges in **Mixed Reality Leadership (MRL)**. Understanding these paradoxes is essential for leadership teams managing organisations that integrate physical and virtual environments.

The Automation Paradox and Mixed Reality Leadership

Definition: As automation improves, human intervention is needed **less frequently**, but when required, the situations are **more complex**—making errors more likely.

Key Issues for Mixed Reality Leadership Teams:

Over-Reliance on Automation in Mixed Reality Workplaces

Issue: AI-driven virtual environments (e.g., automated HR hiring, AI-powered collaboration tools) reduce human workload, but when **failures occur, human operators may lack the expertise** to intervene effectively.

Solution: Ensure human oversight by maintaining a mix of **manual control** and **automated functions** in MR systems. Example: **Pilots still require flight training** even with advanced autopilot systems.

Skill Degradation in a Fully AI-Driven Mixed Reality Workplace

Issue: Employees who work in **highly automated MR environments** (e.g., VR-driven logistics, AI-powered performance reviews) **lose critical problem-solving skills** because AI handles most tasks.

Solution: Rotate employees between automated and manual roles to ensure continuous learning. Example: **Doctors using AI diagnostic tools** should still practice manual diagnosis to **retain critical thinking skills**.

Human-AI Collaboration Risks in Virtual Workspaces

Issue: AI decision-making in **virtual leadership roles** (e.g., AI-driven project managers) can lead to **human disengagement**, where employees **blindly trust AI without critically evaluating decisions**.

Solution: Implement Explainable AI (XAI) in MR systems to make AI decisions transparent. Employees must understand **how AI-driven workplace evaluations, promotions, and feedback work**.

The Statistical Paradox and Mixed Reality Leadership

Definition: When analysing data at a macro level, patterns may **mislead** decision-makers due to hidden biases, misinterpretation, or aggregation errors.

Key Issues for Mixed Reality Leadership Teams:

AI-Driven Bias in MR Workspaces

Issue: AI analytics in MR environments can **misinterpret statistical correlations**—leading to unfair HR decisions. Example: **AI tracking "low engagement" in VR meetings** may penalise **neurodivergent employees** who interact differently.

Solution: Use intersectional data analysis to ensure **AI-powered analytics are fair**. Example: Instead of just tracking "average engagement," look at **multiple behavioural indicators** to reduce bias.

Simpson's Paradox in Virtual Hiring & Performance Analytics

Issue: AI-driven hiring tools may suggest **certain groups perform worse** in job assessments, but when analysed by subgroup (gender, ethnicity, region), the pattern **reverses**—misleading HR teams.

Solution: Disaggregate AI data in hiring decisions to **check for hidden bias**. Leadership should **audit AI tools** to prevent biased decision-making.

Flawed Data Interpretation in MR Decision-Making

Issue: AI-powered dashboards in MR environments can **present misleading statistics**, influencing leadership decisions based on **aggregated but misleading insights**.

Solution: Train MR leaders in statistical literacy to properly interpret AI-generated reports, ensuring decisions are based on **accurate, contextual data**.

The Big Data Paradox and Mixed Reality Leadership

The **Big Data Paradox** refers to the counterintuitive phenomenon where increasing the amount of data does not necessarily lead to better insights or decision-making. Instead, as datasets grow, issues such as noise, bias, spurious correlations, and computational complexity can obscure meaningful patterns. In some cases, more data can lead to *overfitting*, misleading conclusions, or decision paralysis.

Big Data Paradox in Mixed Reality Leadership

In the context of **Mixed Reality (MR) Leadership**, where leaders use augmented reality (AR), virtual reality (VR), and artificial intelligence (AI) to manage teams and make decisions, the **Big Data Paradox** presents unique challenges:

- **Information Overload:** Leaders in MR environments have access to vast amounts of real-time data, including biometrics, performance analytics, and immersive simulations. However, without proper filtering, this abundance of data can overwhelm decision-making.

- **False Patterns & Biases:** MR systems leverage AI to generate insights, but the quality of these insights depends on how data is collected and processed. If training datasets contain biases, MR leaders might make decisions based on misleading trends.

- **Cognitive Load & Decision Fatigue:** Immersive MR environments require leaders to process multisensory information. Too much data can lead to cognitive overload, reducing the leader's ability to focus on critical insights.

- **Trust in AI & Automation:** Many MR leadership applications integrate AI-driven decision support systems. If leaders blindly trust AI-generated recommendations without critical analysis, they risk falling into the Big Data Paradox—where more data leads to less accurate or less actionable decisions.

Overcoming the Big Data Paradox in MR Leadership

To mitigate this paradox, MR leaders must:

- **Prioritise Data Quality Over Quantity:** Focus on collecting and analysing relevant, high-quality data rather than excessive amounts.
- **Leverage AI for Smart Filtering:** Use AI to highlight key insights while avoiding unnecessary noise.
- **Balance Data with Human Judgment:** Ensure human intuition and experience complement data-driven insights.
- **Develop Data Literacy:** Train MR leaders to interpret and challenge AI-generated recommendations critically.

By understanding and addressing the Big Data Paradox, MR leaders can harness the power of data-driven decision-making without falling into its traps

Leadership Strategy for Managing These Paradoxes

Establish a Human-AI Collaboration Framework

- ✓ Ensure AI-driven MR workplaces always include **human oversight and training** to **prevent skill degradation**.
- ✓ Use **Explainable AI (XAI)** to keep decision-making **transparent**.

Audit AI Data for Bias and Misinterpretation

- ✓ Disaggregate AI-driven insights to **prevent statistical paradoxes** from leading to biased decisions.
- ✓ Regularly **test AI hiring tools and performance analytics** to detect **Simpson's Paradox-type errors**.

Maintain Employee Skills & Critical Thinking

- ✓ Rotate employees between **automated and manual roles** to ensure they **retain problem-solving abilities**.
- ✓ Provide **ongoing statistical literacy training** for leadership teams.

Final Thought: Balancing AI and Human Judgment in MR Leadership

Mixed Reality Leadership must **balance automation with human expertise** while ensuring AI **does not mislead decision-making** through statistical paradoxes. By implementing **AI transparency, continuous skill training, and robust data audits**, leaders can **navigate these challenges effectively**.

Policy Framework for Managing the Automation & Statistical Paradoxes in the Aviation Industry

Mixed Reality Leadership (MRL) in aviation requires **balancing AI automation, human expertise, and data-driven decision-making** while addressing the **Automation Paradox** and the **Statistical Paradox**. This policy framework ensures that aviation leaders, regulators, and employees **maintain safety, efficiency, and fairness** when integrating AI and Mixed Reality (MR) technologies.

Addressing the Automation Paradox in Aviation

Challenge: Increased automation in aviation reduces pilots' manual flying time, but when failures occur, human intervention is needed in highly complex scenarios—leading to **skill degradation** and slower responses in emergencies.

Policy Actions for Aviation Leadership Teams

Flight Training & Human Oversight

- ✓ **Mandate Regular Manual Flying Hours** – Require pilots to complete a **minimum number of manual flight hours per month**, even in highly automated cockpits.
- ✓ **Simulated Mixed Reality (MR) Emergency Training** – Integrate **VR-based emergency drills** where pilots handle **AI system failures** without autopilot assistance.

AI Transparency in Automated Flight Systems

- √ **Implement Explainable AI (XAI) for Cockpit AI** – Ensure that automated flight systems **display clear explanations** for AI-driven adjustments (e.g., weather-based autopilot deviations).
- √ **Require "Human-in-the-Loop" Override Systems** – Aviation AI systems must allow **instant manual override** to prevent excessive reliance on automation.

Preventing Skill Degradation Among Flight Crews

- √ **Introduce Mixed Reality Decision-Making Simulations** – Use **AR/VR cockpit environments** to train pilots on **complex manual flight scenarios** they rarely encounter.
- √ **Rotate Pilots Across Manual & Automated Flight Roles** – Ensure that pilots operate a mix of **automated and manual aircraft** regularly.

Addressing the Statistical Paradox in Aviation

Challenge: AI-driven data analysis in aviation (e.g., predicting pilot fatigue, aircraft maintenance needs, passenger behaviour) can lead to **misleading conclusions** due to aggregation errors or biased algorithms.

Policy Actions for Aviation Leadership Teams

Avoiding Misinterpretation of AI-Driven Safety Data

Disaggregate AI Flight Data by Context – Ensure that AI-generated safety insights **do not generalise across different aircraft models, weather conditions, or pilot experience levels**.

Mandate Regular Audits of AI-Powered Safety Alerts – Check for **false positives** or **hidden biases** in AI risk assessments (e.g., AI falsely flagging certain flight routes as "high risk").

Bias Reduction in AI-Based Aviation Hiring & Training

Ensure AI-Based Pilot Assessments Are Bias-Free – AI-powered pilot evaluation tools must be **tested for fairness across gender, ethnicity, and neurodiversity**.

Audit AI Flight Crew Scheduling Systems for Unintended Bias – Prevent scheduling algorithms from **unfairly disadvantaging certain groups** (e.g., female pilots getting fewer international routes due to AI misinterpretations).

Improving Passenger Data Analytics Without Statistical Bias

Check for Simpson's Paradox in Passenger Data Analysis – Avoid misleading insights when analysing **on-time performance, customer satisfaction, or airline efficiency**.

Require Transparency in AI-Driven Ticket Pricing & Customer Service AI – Ensure AI-driven airline pricing and service recommendations **do not disproportionately disadvantage lower-income passengers**.

Leadership Strategy for Managing These Paradoxes in Aviation

Immediate Actions (Next 3-6 Months)

Airlines: **Mandate human oversight & regular manual flying hours**

Aviation Regulators: **Implement AI bias audits for safety, hiring & ticketing algorithms**

Pilots & Crews: **Train in MR-based emergency scenarios to retain manual skills**

Long-Term Strategy (6-24 Months)

- Aviation Companies: **Deploy Explainable AI (XAI) in cockpit automation & AI scheduling systems**
- Governments: **Establish legal frameworks for AI bias audits in aviation hiring & passenger analytics**
- Employees: **Engage in continuous AI ethics & MR training to adapt to evolving automation**

Final Thought: Ensuring Safe & Fair Aviation Leadership in the AI Era

Mixed Reality Leadership in aviation must **balance automation with human expertise**, ensuring pilots retain **manual skills** while preventing **biased AI decisions** in hiring, scheduling, and safety analytics

Similar approaches are required in defence, finance and health.

Chapter 17

Case Studies Aviation, Defence, Finance, and Health, Oil and Gas

Introduction

Aviation, Defence, Finance and Health are amongst the most highly regulated organisations. Primary research undertaken at the University of Buckingham and Buckinghamshire New University has revealed some practical support for many of the ideas in this book.

Aviation

The International Civil Aviation Organisation has had a very positive impact on facilitation and security worldwide. International Air Transport Association somewhat less. Co-author John Greaves comments, for context, as follows on his recent experiences post the 2025 Heathrow resilience failure and its specific and more general impact in the USA:

'The aviation section cries out for emotional input which is not appropriate for this book, I would, however, like to comment to the extent that the overarching sector has squeezed a pint into a quart and yet when, normally, such actions are taken in a business sector you would expect to see improved profits, or at least lower costs, neither of these are consistently met by the US carriers' profitability, though their costs decline as the offering is reduced. The airports, where the income from activities, and the offset of

third-party providers has done nothing for any parties except reduce competency to the lowest cost of labour and customer service to near zero, unless you are rated a premium passenger. Imagine a two tier or three tier Walmart shopper, where you are only allowed to be in a particular part of the store and have to buy everything at the store price or do not enter.

The Aviation sector is a myriad of misinformation. At my local airport, the same at ORD and CLT, the information screens are controlled by the airport MIS, not the carriers. There is no info feed between carrier and airport except via the ATC for traffic purposes and even then it is the actual flight not the corporate feed. Information to passengers on delays, causes of same and likely solution time is indiscriminate and arbitrary. At MLB yesterday the 06.22 flight finally left at 12.05 pm, the only AA communication was "Sorry for delay" and periodic possible departure times. The 12.08 left on time, the 13.10 was delayed to 17.04 pm. aging equipment, oversold flights, stressed crew, and many missed connections were met by an offer to passengers of a 300 USD credit if you changed your flight voluntarily, There must be a better way. There is a train... the tracks exist but the carrier is AMTRAK, a local service train disguised as an express that takes 12 to 14 hours to travel what I drive in 8 or less with fuel and comfort stops. The air carriers however lobby against trains, and even if they did not to simply expand AMTEAK milk trains is not a solution. Express trains between Miami and Charlotte in under 4 hours and no intermediate stops would be an innovative and green solution, apparently in US Airlines the green of it all is dollars not environment.' Clearly, still much to do!

Aviation's Conformity to the Saxton Bampfylde (2021) Board Model in the Context of Mixed Reality Leadership (MRL)

As aviation organisations navigate digital transformation, their leadership structures must evolve to incorporate emerging technologies and new governance frameworks. The **Saxton Bampfylde (2021) Board Model** provides a benchmark for evaluating board attributes in the aviation industry. When viewed through the lens of **Mixed Reality Leadership (MRL)**, which emphasises decision-making in hybrid physical-virtual environments, additional insights emerge regarding the industry's adaptability and preparedness for future challenges.

Summary of Aviation Board Attributes

Aviation organisations were assessed against ten **Saxton Bampfylde (2021) Board attributes**, including Digital/Data, AI/ML, Cybersecurity, Strategy, Global Operations, and Employee Voice. The findings reveal varying degrees of conformity, with **Airbus, Changi Airport, and Heathrow** demonstrating strong alignment, while **low-cost airlines and some regulatory bodies lag behind**.

Key Observations:

- **Strategic Alignment vs. Operational Execution**: ICAO demonstrates high-level strategic thinking but faces challenges in operational execution, particularly in cybersecurity and employee voice. This gap is critical in MRL settings where **virtual and real-world operations must be seamlessly integrated**.

- **Lack of Digital, Cyber, and AI Preparedness**: Across organisations, **cybersecurity and AI capabilities are underdeveloped**, exposing vulnerabilities in an era where **augmented intelligence and immersive analytics are essential for leadership decision-making**.

- **Regulatory Challenges in MRL Integration**: Organisations like **FAA and UK CAA follow traditional board structures**, limiting their ability to **leverage MR simulations for risk assessment, training, and real-time crisis management**.

- **Legacy vs. Digital-First Airlines**: While **Boeing and Airbus have digital integration strategies**, low-cost carriers like **EasyJet and Whizz Air lack robust cyber and data governance frameworks, making them susceptible to digital threats**.

MRL Implications for Aviation Leadership

The concept of **Mixed Reality Leadership (MRL)** is crucial for aviation leaders to effectively manage **physical and virtual interactions, data-driven decision-making, and AI-augmented operations**. The study's findings highlight three key MRL challenges:

Virtual Governance and Decision-Making

- **Current State:** Many aviation boards operate using **traditional governance models,** with limited use of **virtual reality (VR) for simulations** and **augmented reality (AR) for real-time decision-making**.
- **MRL Application:** Boards should implement **MR-powered strategy rooms** for scenario planning, crisis simulations, and digital twin modelling to align strategy with operational realities.

AI-Augmented Risk Management

- **Current State:** Risk assessment remains **fragmented**, with **AI/ML capabilities unevenly distributed** across aviation organisations.
- **MRL Application:** AI-driven MR dashboards should be integrated into board-level decision-making, enabling real-time monitoring of cybersecurity threats, operational efficiency, and compliance metrics.

Cybersecurity and Digital Resilience

- **Current State:** The biggest weaknesses in the Saxton Bampfylde analysis are **cybersecurity, digital/data governance, and employee voice**.
- **MRL Application:** Implement **Hybrid Hardening©**, a resilience approach combining **real-world cybersecurity protocols with MR-driven cybersecurity training and simulations** to address digital vulnerabilities.

Recommendations for Aviation Boards in an MRL Context

1. **Adopt MR-Based Leadership Training:** Use **immersive leadership training programs** to prepare executives for complex decision-making in digital-physical hybrid environments.

2. **Enhance AI-Driven Governance:** Implement AI-augmented boardroom analytics to provide real-time insights into **operational risks, financial health, and security threats**.

3. **Strengthen Cyber and Digital Competencies:** Recruit board members with expertise in **cybersecurity, AI, and digital transformation** to bridge the existing skill gaps.

4. **Leverage Digital Twins for Aviation Strategy:** Utilise digital twin technology to **simulate fleet management, airport operations, and regulatory compliance scenarios**.

5. **Improve Employee Voice Through MR Collaboration Tools:** Deploy **VR-based employee engagement platforms** to ensure workforce participation in strategic decision-making.

Conclusion

The aviation industry's leadership structures must evolve to integrate **MRL principles**, ensuring boards are **digitally competent, cyber-aware, and AI-augmented**. Organisations that successfully incorporate **MR technologies into governance, strategy, and operational decision-making** will lead the future of aviation. The adoption of **Hybrid Hardening© strategies** will be critical in reinforcing digital resilience while enhancing organisational agility in mixed reality environments.

Enhancing Aviation Security through Mixed Reality (MR) Integration

Executive Summary

The aviation sector is at a critical inflection point where cyber and physical threats are increasingly interlinked, amplified by the growing digitisation of aircraft systems, airport infrastructure, and supply chains. Mixed Reality (MR) presents a transformative opportunity not only to address these threats but to reshape security culture, improve training, and enhance resilience across the aviation ecosystem. This briefing outlines the current security landscape, key vulnerabilities, and actionable MR-enabled strategies tailored for strategic oversight and governance.

Overview of Threat Landscape

Cybersecurity and Digital Threats

- **Digital Flight Manuals and Avionics**: Risk of data tampering, ransomware, and malware due to digital integration.
- **In-Flight Entertainment Systems (IFE)**: Frequently unpatched and potentially vulnerable to lateral cyber intrusions.
- **Engine and Manufacturer Data Exchange**: Real-time telemetry transmission introduces potential interception and manipulation risks.
- **Manufacturing Supply Chain**: Component tracking, software updates, and insider risks due to global sourcing.

Physical Security Issues

- **Airport Infrastructure**: Documented cases of poor cyber resilience (e.g., Heathrow, U.S. airport attacks).
- **Aircraft Manufacturing Facilities**: Threats include unauthorised physical access, sabotage, and compromised digital twins.
- **Pilot Health and Performance**: Digital overload and reduced physical interface may affect situational awareness and decision-making.

Strategic Recommendations for MR Integration

Cybersecurity Training & Simulations (via MR)

- Deploy VR-based red-teaming simulations for cyber incidents.
- Embed immersive training for all levels of staff, including non-technical employees.

- Conduct virtual rehearsals for multi-layer attack scenarios (e.g., concurrent cyber and physical breaches).

Secure Supply Chain Transparency

- Integrate **blockchain and RFID** tracking with MR visual overlays.
- Enable maintenance crews to authenticate aircraft parts in real-time.
- Visualise life cycle data and supply chain provenance via AR dashboards.

Enhancing Cockpit and Pilot UX

- Use MR to fuse analog and digital cues, reducing cognitive overload.
- Create MR environments for pilot mental health monitoring and stress-response training.
- Simulate high-pressure scenarios to identify weak points in human-machine interaction.

Airport Emergency and Crowd Management

- MR-guided simulations for physical evacuation, cyber lock-downs, and hybrid attacks.
- AR wearables for security staff to direct crowds using real-time hazard overlays.
- Training modules for biometric screening and behavioural anomaly detection.

Executive-Level Risk Visualisation

- Develop MR-enabled strategy rooms for C-suite decision-makers.
- Visualise cyber threat maps, maintenance statuses, geopolitical alerts, and more.
- Adopt Saxton Bampfylde board frameworks enhanced with immersive analytics.

Governance & Implementation Recommendations

- **Establish an MR Security Task Force** with cross-functional expertise (cybersecurity, operations, HR, compliance).
- **Pilot MR training and simulation programs** at flagship locations.
- **Partner with MR and blockchain solution providers** that meet aerospace-grade standards.
- **Conduct quarterly MR readiness reviews** embedded within existing governance structures.
- **Measure ROI** through key security KPIs: incident response time, training effectiveness, compliance rates.

Conclusion

Mixed Reality is more than a technology—it is a strategic enabler of resilience, situational awareness, and cultural transformation. For board members, investing in MR is not simply a response to today's risks, but a proactive posture toward the complexity of tomorrow's aviation ecosystem.

If we apply the same approach to defence, finance and health then a summary of the requirements of Mixed Reality Leadership in a similar context would be:

Defence, Finance, and Health Sectors' Conformity to the Saxton Bampfylde (2021) Board Model in the Context of Mixed Reality Leadership (MRL)

Introduction

As organisations in defence, finance, and health navigate digital transformation, their leadership structures must evolve to incorporate emerging technologies and new governance frameworks. The Saxton Bampfylde (2021) Board Model provides a benchmark for evaluating board attributes across these industries. When viewed through the lens of Mixed Reality Leadership (MRL), which emphasises decision-making in hybrid physical-virtual environments, additional insights emerge regarding adaptability and preparedness for future challenges.

Summary of Board Attributes

Defence, finance, and health organisations were also assessed against ten Saxton Bampfylde (2021) Board attributes, including Digital/Data, AI/ML, Cybersecurity, Strategy, Global Operations, and Employee Voice. The findings reveal varying degrees of conformity, with institutions like NATO, the Bank of England, and Mayo Clinic demonstrating strong alignment, while smaller regulatory bodies and legacy institutions lag behind.

Key Observations

Defence Sector

- **Strategic Alignment vs. Operational Execution:** NATO and the UK Ministry of Defence (MoD) exhibit strong strategic alignment but face challenges in operationalising MRL, particularly in cybersecurity and AI-driven threat intelligence.
- **Cyber and AI Preparedness:** While cybersecurity is a high priority, AI and digital integration remain fragmented, affecting real-time decision-making and threat response.
- **Regulatory Constraints in MRL Integration:** Traditional command structures limit the adoption of MR simulations for training, battlefield analysis, and crisis response.

Finance Sector

- **Legacy vs. Digital-First Institutions:** While major banks (e.g., HSBC, JPMorgan) have robust AI-driven governance strategies, some financial regulators lack MR-powered risk assessment frameworks.
- **Cybersecurity and Data Governance Gaps:** The finance sector faces increasing cyber threats, yet MR-based cybersecurity simulations and fraud detection tools remain underutilised.

- **MRL in Crisis Scenarios:** Financial institutions lag in using MR for crisis simulations, stress testing, and real-time fraud analytics, leading to slower responses to emerging risks.

Health Sector

- **Integration of AI and MR in Decision-Making:** Leading institutions like Mayo Clinic and NHS Digital have begun integrating AI and MR for patient diagnostics, yet many healthcare boards lack cyber and digital expertise. This deficiency is a key problem in the UK's NHS.
- **Operational Challenges in MR Adoption:** Hospitals and regulatory bodies (e.g., the FDA) are slow to adopt MR-powered telemedicine, affecting emergency response capabilities.
- **Cybersecurity Concerns:** Digital patient records and AI-driven diagnostics introduce security vulnerabilities that require MR-based resilience training.

MRL Implications for Leadership in Defence, Finance, and Health

MRL is crucial for leaders in these industries to effectively manage physical and virtual interactions, data-driven decision-making, and AI-augmented operations. The study's findings highlight three key MRL challenges:

Virtual Governance and Decision-Making

- **Current State:** Many organisations operate using traditional governance models, with limited use of MR for strategic planning and crisis management.
- **MRL Application:** Institutions should implement MR-powered strategy rooms for real-time risk analysis, predictive modelling, and policy simulations.

AI-Augmented Risk Management

- **Current State:** AI-driven risk assessment remains fragmented across industries, with varying levels of investment in predictive analytics.
- **MRL Application:** AI-integrated MR dashboards should be used at the board level for monitoring cybersecurity threats, economic stability, and healthcare outcomes.

Cybersecurity and Digital Resilience

- **Current State:** Cybersecurity remains the weakest area in the Saxton Bampfylde model analysis, affecting data integrity, fraud prevention, and national security.
- **MRL Application:** Implement **Hybrid Hardening©**, a resilience approach combining real-world cybersecurity protocols with MR-driven cybersecurity training and simulations.

Recommendations for Boards in an MRL Context

1. **Adopt MR-Based Leadership Training:** Use immersive leadership training programs to prepare executives for complex decision-making in digital-physical hybrid environments.
2. **Enhance AI-Driven Governance:** Implement AI-augmented boardroom analytics to provide real-time insights into operational risks, financial stability, and security threats.
3. **Strengthen Cyber and Digital Competencies:** Recruit board members with expertise in cybersecurity, AI, and digital transformation to bridge the existing skill gaps.
4. **Leverage Digital Twins for Strategic Planning:** Utilise digital twin technology to simulate military operations, financial market fluctuations, and healthcare system responses.
5. **Improve Employee Voice Through MR Collaboration Tools:** Deploy VR-based engagement platforms to enhance workforce participation in policy and strategic decision-making.

Conclusion

Leadership structures in defence, finance, and health must evolve to integrate MRL principles, ensuring boards are digitally competent, cyber-aware, and AI-augmented. Organisations that successfully incorporate MR technologies into governance, strategy, and operations will be better positioned to navigate future challenges and drive innovation in their respective fields.

Mixed Reality (MR) Leadership in a Blockchain + RFID-Driven World

Some disambiguation is required on Blockchain. There are two forms of blockchain the currency management tool, now referred to as DeFi or digital electronic finance and enterprise blockchain, a source of immutable data so essential to the modern commerce platform and as a valid replacement for the now almost 70-year-old information technology criteria referred to as Turing methodology.

This book is concerned with enterprise blockchain – that is not to say that FinTech blockchain has no place as it is a potential corridor between the smart contract and its currency principles, its financial tooling, and that of the delivery model contained within supply chain technology today.

Examples of blockchain effectiveness particularly with regard to immutable data, are already legend yet pushback on adoption is still common. This may be the human resistance to change and yet herein we find no option but to change from the boardroom through leadership into C level management level and to blue collar all of which align themselves with the objective enshrined in this publication allowing for a successful enterprise in the years to come.

Blockchain provides an essential avenue between the smart contract and the smart delivery. It allows for suppliers who indulge in nefarious, illegitimate, illegal practices to be in effect prevented from doing so at the first instance rather than the last instance. In our forthcoming training modules these will be fully demonstrated including corporate credentials and corporate references who have benefited from the implementation of enterprise blockchain and in so doing resulted in billions, yes, billions of dollars of savings.

Human recognition of our need to become more environmentally friendly, green, allows us to recognise blockchain as one of the most green-friendly tools available to the enterprise of the modern era.

Now to turn to another essential tool of mixed reality RFID, a technology that from its inception in the early 1990s, subject to regulation, has grown into a multibillion-dollar industry identifying assets as diverse as aircraft components, oil platforms, transportation modules, shirts in your local Walmart, and the suitcase you

carry on the plane. Radio frequency identification has required an unparalleled assimilation into that regulated by the International Telecommunications Union (Radio), and the standards industry, designed to encourage innovation and implementation on a global scale.

RFID today for the user is governed by the standards of ISO IEC SC 31 whose governing tenets are those of parts 18001 through 9. These police the utilisation and delivery of almost every current implementation that we may not easily recognise as RFID, contactless payment, Apple Pay, the tag on the shirt you bought in a retailer, the sensor tag that alerts the refinery to overheating in a pipeline, the location of a fire tender on an airport, or of a person in a secure facility or any facility, these deliverables have been developed under a standard format in conjunction with the regulatory agencies and have resulted in significant improvements in supply chain, consumer protection, and asset integrity.

To approach mixed reality without engaging in both Blockchain and RFID as the physical entities of the environment required today is to ignore the realities of 2030 just five years away.

It has not been possible here to discuss the relevancy, impact, and inclusion of standards that allow for assimilable and easily implemented cross environment platforms. It would however form a significant part of training programs going forward.

When supply chains and natural resource operations (like oilfields) are managed through Blockchain, which is the only implementable tool that provides immutable data (for trust, auditability, contracts) and RFID a proven real time asset identifier, including status, (Sensor tags), Location, and includes real time reporting on the asset operational effectiveness (for real-time tracking and identification), the environment shifts from *physical-first* to *virtual-first*.

Leadership in this new paradigm—Mixed Reality Leadership—needs to evolve along several dimensions:

- Strategic Shift: From Physical Oversight to Virtual Orchestration
- Mixed Reality leaders no longer walk the warehouse, refinery, chemical plant, or oilfield—all of which are high risk assets in the 2030 MR scenario—and need to be managed via *digital twins*, *MR dashboards*, and *predictive analytics*.
- Strategic decisions are driven by real-time data, smart contracts, and automated rulesets rather than intuition and experience alone.

Leadership Traits Needed

- Digital literacy and fluency in MR interfaces
- Strategic systems thinking to understand cyber-physical feedback loops
- Comfort with letting go of physical control whilst not relinquishing responsibility

Zero Human Intervention Operations: How Leaders Stay in the Loop

Even in zero-touch systems, leadership must:

- Set autonomous decision frameworks (e.g., thresholds for triggering smart contracts or alerts) Many of these triggers exist though there alrm model is based on an alert to a third party who then determines an appropriate response, the lost time is in milliseconds often is still too long for a 2030 facility.
- Define fail-safes and override protocols when systems go rogue or deviate from norms. Double indemnity is the crux of MR in critical facility management utilising the MR tool set of Blockchain, RFID, AI as the physical activation. There remains a need for the MR aware personnel to facilitate and craft ongoing system engineering

- Govern AI/automation ethics and compliance, ensuring fairness, transparency, and security.

Leadership Roles
- Policy architect – designing the rules AI and automation must follow
- Exception handler – managing edge cases and anomalies
- System steward – maintaining integrity of the digital ecosystem

Control through Visibility: MR + Blockchain + RFID Integration

In a Blockchain-RFID environment:
- RFID tags provide real-world anchors to virtual assets (e.g., barrels of oil, shipping containers)
- Blockchain ensures tamper-proof records, traceability, and smart contract enforcement

MR visualisations (via HoloLens, Meta, Apple Vision Pro, etc.) give leaders immersive insight into supply flows and asset statuses

Leadership Needs:
- Ability to interpret immersive dashboards
- Risk anticipation based on pattern recognition across digital twins
- Understanding trust boundaries (where blockchain guarantees end and real-world fraud could begin)

Human-in-the-Loop Controls: What's Still Needed?

Even in fully automated systems, some level of human oversight remains crucial:
- Auditability: Ensuring human-readable trails exist
- Decision validation: Approving or vetting high-impact decisions (e.g., asset decommissioning, emergency reroutes)
- System learning: Training AI on edge cases from human input

These are not day-to-day ops roles—they're governance and assurance roles.

Cultural & Ethical Leadership

As machines take over execution, human leadership must focus on:
- Ethics of automation (e.g., avoiding bias in smart contracts)
- Transparency with stakeholders
- Change management for workforce adaptation

In Summary: Mixed Reality Leadership Characteristics

Capability	Description
Immersive Situational Awareness	Leading from within MR environments that mirror real-world operations
Digital Governance	Setting policies for blockchain/RFID-driven automation
Exception Management	Remaining accountable for anomalies in autonomous systems
Ethical Oversight	Guarding against misuse of virtual control and automation
Cross-Domain Fluency	Understanding blockchain tech, logistics, supply chain theory, and digital interfaces
Trust Engineering	Ensuring systems remain reliable, transparent, and auditable

Mixed Reality Leadership Model for Onshore and Offshore Oil & Gas Asset Management, Incorporating:

- Blockchain (for secure, auditable operations)
- RFID (for asset tracking)
- Drones (as mobile data collectors and inspectors)
- Mixed Reality (MR) (as the leadership interface)
- Zero human intervention operations (as the endgame)

CASE STUDY: Onshore & Offshore Oil and Gas Asset Management

Core System Architecture

Layer	Function	Tech Used
Physical Layer	Real-world pipelines, rigs, sensors, valves, containers	IoT devices, RFID tags
Data Harvesting Layer	Autonomous collection of data	Drones (aerial & underwater), RFID scanners
Data Integrity & Automation	Tamper-proof tracking, smart contracts	Blockchain (e.g., Hyperledger, Ethereum)
Control & Command Layer	Immersive monitoring & intervention	MR (e.g., HoloLens, Vision Pro)
Leadership Layer	Governance, policy, strategy	Mixed Reality Leadership

MIXED REALITY LEADERSHIP FRAMEWORK

A visual model broken into 4 capability pillars + a control core:

Immersive Situational Awareness (ISA)

Seeing the entire operation—onshore & offshore—without ever setting foot on a rig.
- View 3D digital twins of rigs, tanks, pipelines
- Real-time data overlays from RFID and IoT devices
- Drone-captured visual & thermal feeds streamed into MR
- Predictive maintenance visualised as alerts on holograms

Leadership Role:
"Virtual Field Commander" – Orchestrates operations and interventions via MR

Digital Governance & Rule Architecture

Defining how machines make decisions—before they ever act.
- Smart contracts for fuel allocation, subcontractor access, safety checks
- Permissions for drone access and airspace corridors
- Digital locks/unlocks for valves or pipelines based on real-time data

Leadership Role:
"Automation Architect" – Builds the invisible rulebook for operations

Autonomous Oversight & Exception Management

Let systems run—but know exactly when to step in.
- Drones detect corrosion on offshore rig → auto-log on blockchain → alert in MR

- Valve overpressure → auto-shutdown if rule matches threshold
- Supply delivery delay → flagged for human review if no block-chain record validates transport origin

Leadership Role:
"Exception Strategist" – Handles edge cases, system learning, and override triggers

Ethical & Human Systems Leadership

Just because it's automated doesn't mean it's neutral.
- Prevent smart contract bias in resource allocation
- Ensure drone and RFID tracking aligns with human rights & local law
- Maintain trust with stakeholders about automated systems

Leadership Role:
"Digital Ethicist" – Guards fairness, trust, transparency

CORE: Human-in-the-Loop Assurance

While operations are zero-touch by default, leadership defines where humans must remain involved, such as:
- Regulatory approval gates (e.g., safety inspections, environmental monitoring)
- Ethics reviews for AI decisions
- Manual override protocols for drones or smart contract behaviours

Leadership Role:
"Sentinel of the System" – Ensures the automation never drifts from human values

Drone Use Cases in This Architecture

Drone Role	Example	Integrated Tech
Pipeline Inspection	Drone flies perimeter, reads RFID + camera data	RFID + MR visualisation
Rig Surveillance	Offshore drone inspects rig structure for corrosion or intrusion	Video feed to MR + blockchain event logging
Emergency Response	Drones deployed post-incident to scan for damage before human teams enter	Thermal imaging + IoT data relay
Inventory Validation	Drone counts RFID-tagged barrels, compares to blockchain record	Smart contract triggers if mismatch found

Leadership Summary: Mixed Reality Leadership Capabilities Matrix

Capability	Description	Leadership Action
Immersive Control	Use MR to supervise live ops in virtual space	Orchestrate remote decisions
Automation Governance	Set rules for zero-human systems	Define & test smart contracts
Trust Management	Ensure stakeholder buy-in & auditability	Establish reporting & feedback loops

Capability	Description	Leadership Action
Edge Case Response	Manage exceptions & anomalies	Stay engaged as override authority
Drone Command & Policy	Program drone behaviours & rules	Oversee airspace permissions, safety policies

Strategic Leadership in Mixed Reality Operations for Oil & Gas: Managing Supply Chains and Assets through Blockchain, RFID, and Drones

Executive Summary

As oil and gas operations increasingly integrate advanced digital technologies—Blockchain, RFID, and autonomous drones—a shift from traditional, physically grounded management to immersive, data-driven virtual leadership is emerging. Mixed Reality (MR) Leadership, positioned at the intersection of physical operations and digital oversight, is a critical capability in managing extended supply chains and natural resource assets with minimal human intervention. This report outlines the leadership attributes, controls, and strategic frameworks necessary to enable and govern zero human intervention operations, particularly in onshore and offshore oil and gas environments.

Introduction: The Rise of Virtual Operations

The energy sector is undergoing a digital transformation that replaces manual, on-site processes with virtual, automated systems. Technologies such as Blockchain offer transparent and immutable transaction records, RFID enables real-time tracking of physical assets, and drones provide dynamic data collection from field equipment and infrastructure. Combined with Mixed Reality interfaces, these tools empower leaders to manage operations remotely, in real time, and with unprecedented precision.

Core System Architecture

Layer	Function	Technology Used
Physical Layer	Physical infrastructure, sensors, and tagged assets	IoT devices, RFID tags
Data Harvesting Layer	Real-time data collection	Autonomous drones, RFID scanners
Data Integrity Layer	Verification and logging of operations	Blockchain ledgers, smart contracts
Control Layer	Immersive interface for oversight and action	Mixed Reality (MR) systems
Leadership Layer	Strategic decision-making and governance	MR-enabled leadership frameworks

Mixed Reality Leadership Framework

Immersive Situational Awareness (ISA)

MR leaders operate within digital twins of oil rigs, pipelines, and supply chains, overlaid with real-time data. This enables:

- Visual tracking of RFID-tagged assets
- Drone-sourced video and thermal imaging
- Predictive maintenance alerts

Leadership Role: *Virtual Field Commander* – Directs field operations via immersive dashboards.

Digital Governance & Rule Architecture

Leaders design automated workflows enforced through Blockchain smart contracts. This includes:

- Smart contracts for equipment usage and supplier payments
- Permissions for drone access and automated routing
- Safety logic for pipeline control and equipment locks

Leadership Role: *Automation Architect* – **Defines the rules by which autonomous systems operate.**

Autonomous Oversight & Exception Management

While routine operations run autonomously, MR leaders are responsible for:

- Intervening in system anomalies or conflicts
- Overriding smart contracts when needed
- Analysing exception patterns to improve automation logic

Leadership Role: *Exception Strategist* – Manages edge cases and ensures system adaptability.

Ethical & Human Systems Leadership

Automation must be guided by transparent and ethical oversight, including:

- Fairness in contract design and drone surveillance
- Compliance with labour, environmental, and safety regulations
- Transparency with stakeholders regarding automation boundaries

Leadership Role: *Digital Ethicist* – Ensures responsible and human-centred automation.

Human-in-the-Loop Assurance

Even in zero-touch environments, humans must remain in roles of:
- Auditing and compliance
- Critical approvals (e.g., safety, environmental response)
- Ethical review and legal oversight

Leadership Role: *Sentinel of the System* – Maintains alignment between automation and human values.

Drones in Oil & Gas Operations

Autonomous drones play a central role in digital oilfield management:

Drone Role	Function	Technology Used
Pipeline Inspection	Flight paths over pipelines, RFID verification	RFID, HD video, MR overlay
Rig Surveillance	Corrosion and safety checks offshore	Thermal imaging, blockchain logs
Emergency Response	Remote assessment of hazardous zones	Environmental sensors, live MR feed
Inventory Validation	Drone scans vs. blockchain records	RFID, smart contract triggers

Mixed Reality Leadership Capability Matrix

Capability	Description	Leadership Function
Immersive Control	Leading operations through MR interfaces	Real-time strategic direction
Automation Governance	Designing automated systems and rules	Smart contract and drone policy design
Trust Management	Ensuring system auditability and stakeholder confidence	Oversight of data integrity and transparency
Edge Case Response	Managing anomalies outside normal operation	High-risk decision-making and override control
Ethical Stewardship	Ensuring systems reflect ethical and legal standards	Stakeholder advocacy and policy enforcement

Conclusion

Mixed Reality Leadership is a foundational capability in the next era of oil and gas operations. As the industry shifts to virtualised control through Blockchain, RFID, and autonomous drones, leadership must evolve to provide ethical oversight, strategic orchestration, and systemic governance. Human involvement remains essential—not for routine tasks, but for assurance, accountability, and resilience. This hybrid model of digital-first, human-aware leadership is the cornerstone of future-ready operations.

Chapter 18

The Foundational Economy and SMEs

Introduction

The foundational economy as an example in the UK, it employs 40% of the workforce, and 59.9% within SMEs. In 2024, the latter constitute 99.45% of the UK economy. Working with UK Government Small Business Charter working group, the UK Government funded 'Help to Grow' Management Programme delivered at the University of Hertfordshire Business School, consultancy working with SMEs and researching SMEs has shown some practical support for many of the ideas in this book.

Cyber and Digital Security and Resilience

Challenges:

- Limited budgets and lack of in-house expertise.
- Lack of awareness and understanding of the cyber and digital landscape environments and ecosystems.
- Mixed Reality creates more attack surfaces (e.g., IoT devices, AR/VR/XR interfaces, spatial data).

Leadership Strategies:

- **Adopt a "Secure by Design" mindset:** Leaders must build digital literacy across teams, promoting basic cyber hygiene (multi-factor authentication, data backups, encryption, etc.).
- **Outsource smartly and 3rd Risk Management:** Use reputable **MSPs (Managed Service Providers)** for scalable cybersecurity. This spreads cost and brings expertise.
- **Leverage national support schemes:** Many governments offer **cyber resilience vouchers, toolkits**, or **free cybersecurity training for SMEs.**
- **Zero-trust frameworks** are achievable with tools like **Microsoft Defender for Business** or **Google Workspace security**— tailored and affordable for SMEs.

Digital Transformation

Challenges:

- Balancing the potential of MR with the day-to-day pressures of running a small business.
- Integration of MR with existing and legacy systems (ERP, CRM, POS).

Leadership Strategies:

- **Start small, think modular:** Use MR for targeted functions like remote support (e.g., AR for equipment maintenance), virtual product showcases, or training. Tools like **Microsoft HoloLens, ZapWorks**, or **8thWall** can be introduced in stages.
- **Train through low-cost simulations:** AR/VR training environments reduce travel/training costs and improve retention.
- **Evaluate via risk management:** MR enable the ability to equip SMEs to proactively address threats and opportunities, enhancing decision-making, resilience, sustainability, and strategic growth.
- **Champion a learning culture:** Leaders should embody digital curiosity—use bite-sized, gamified learning platforms like

Coursera, HubSpot Academy, or **XR Bootcamps** to upskill themselves and their teams.

Physical and Virtual Security and Resilience

Challenges:

- Physical threats persist (e.g., retail theft), but now blend with virtual vulnerabilities (e.g., digital overlays that can be hijacked).

Leadership Strategies:

- **Unified threat management:** Invest in hybrid security systems combining **smart CCTV, facial recognition,** and **access control** with real-time analytics, often available via affordable SaaS platforms.
- **Use MR for scenario planning:** AR/VR can simulate breaches or crises (e.g., fire, cyberattack) for training staff in real-time response.
- **Privacy by design:** With MR collecting sensitive spatial data, leaders need to ensure **GDPR (or equivalent)** compliance is built into customer and employee interactions.

Marketing in a Mixed Reality Context

Challenges:

- Competing with large firms in immersive experiences.
- Difficulty in creating MR content on a budget.
- Understand 'Obstructive Marketing'.

Leadership Strategies:

- **Lean into storytelling:** MR isn't just about tech; it's a tool to make local stories, heritage, and customer engagement come alive. Use **low-code/no-code platforms** like **BlippAR** or **Spark AR** to build AR experiences.
- **Partner and collaborate:** Form local alliances with

digital creatives, colleges, or tech hubs to co-create immersive experiences.

- **Measure what matters:** Use built-in analytics from AR platforms (e.g., dwell time, interaction points) to iterate fast and keep spending focused.

Leadership Mindset Shift

To succeed in a Mixed Reality world, SME leaders must:

- **Be facilitators of transformation**, not just decision-makers.
- **Invest in trust, ethics and transparency**, especially with data handling.
- **Systems thinking** with **adaptive, cross-functional teams** provide the structure to act and enable to:
    - Recognise patterns and root causes of risk.
    - Respond quickly and collaboratively.
    - Align risk responses with broader business goals.

In many SMEs, roles overlap, which is a strength in agile MR deployments.

Final Thought

Mixed Reality doesn't need to be expensive to be effective. For SMEs, it's not about competing with Meta or Apple—it's about using immersive tools to enhance trust, efficiency, and experience at a human scale. Leaders who demystify tech and focus on solving *real, local* problems with MR will have a major advantage.

Mixed Reality Leadership Framework for SMEs

Purpose-Driven Integration: Begin with a clear goal

Key Question: *Why MR? What problem are we solving?*

Example	Use MR to...	Leadership Role
Service SME		
Local salon	Virtual try-ons (hair colour, makeup) to boost booking confidence.	Align MR with service value and customer experience.
Cleaning service	VR onboarding for consistent, safe staff training.	Align MR with service value and customer experience.
Consultancy firm	Immersive walkthroughs of strategy proposals to improve client understanding and impact.	Align MR with service value and customer experience.
Product SME		
Builder	Enable clients to visualise home extensions or renovations in 3D before construction begins.	Align MR with product value and customer experience.
Cosmetic Producer	Offer AR try-ons to personalise product selection and boost online engagement.	Align MR with product value and customer experience.
Horticulture	Use MR to simulate garden layouts or plant growth for planning and education.	Align MR with product value and customer experience.

Tip: Start with one simple MR-enhanced touchpoint in your customer journey.

Security and Resilience by Simplicity

Key Principle: *Protect and sustain customer and business data without overcomplication.*

- Use **MR apps with built-in GDPR compliance** and role-based access control.
- Store sensitive content in **encrypted, cloud-based systems** (e.g., Google Workspace or OneDrive with 2FA).
- Execute **cyber / digital risk management** on a monthly basis to support business decision making.
- Run **basic cybersecurity training** quarterly for staff (plenty of free modules from the UK's NCSC, for example).

Leadership Role: Normalise cyber awareness—include it in everyday team conversations.

Lean & Modular Tech Stack

Key Principle: *Use what will expand and scale. Avoid vendor lock-in.*

Tool Type	Examples	Cost-Effective Use
AR content creation	Zappar, BlippAR, Spark AR	Create virtual brochures, promo materials.
VR onboarding/ training	EngageVR, AltspaceVR (or Meta Workrooms)	Staff training for onboarding or soft skills.
Smart scheduling & CRM	HubSpot Free, Calendly, Notion	Integrate MR demos with client interactions.

Leadership Move: Assign a digital champion internally (could be part-time) to manage learning and vendor scouting or engage an Immersive Systems Architect

Human-Centric Marketing

Key Principle: *MR as a storytelling amplifier, not just a gimmick.*
- Use AR business cards or service walkthroughs embedded in brochures.
- Offer **virtual consultations** using 3D room scans or avatar-based interactions (useful for home services, coaching, or wellness).
- Host **micro-events in VR spaces** to build community or teach something—e.g., a wellness SME offering guided meditation in a VR forest.

Leadership Role: Encourage co-creation—get your customers involved in feedback on new MR features.

Trust-Led Leadership Culture

Key Principle: *Empower your team to experiment, but anchor in values.*
- Allow staff to **test MR tools** in low-stakes ways (e.g., internal demos, customer feedback loops).
- Build a **cross-functional task force** for digital initiatives—include frontline staff.
- Reflect on **ethical MR use**: Don't just ask "can we use it?" but "should we?"

Leadership Action: Frame digital transformation as *customer care evolution*, not just tech adoption interfacing with an ISA.

Summary: The MR-SMEs Strategy Compass

Dimension	Leadership Action
Purpose	Identify the pain point MR solves.
Security	Build a security-aware culture using simple tools.
Simplicity	Start lean with scalable, modular tech.
Storytelling	Use MR to deepen emotional connection and trust.
People	Invest in mindset, not just tools—lead with learning.

Conclusion

Mixed Reality Leadership is a fundamental capability in the next incarnation of foundational economy for not solely in the UK, but at all levels globally in the area of operations. As the economic and social activities that require MRL through evolving and emerging technologies require ethical oversight, strategic orchestration, and systemic thinking with the relevant governance. Human involvement remains essential—not for routine tasks, but for a precursor of understanding in the cyber/digital environments and ecosystems, as well as assurance, accountability, and resilience. This hybrid model of digital-first, human-aware leadership is the cornerstone of future-ready operations.

Chapter 19

Critical Thinking and Mixed Reality Leadership

Introduction

In today's evolving digital landscapes for any size of organisation, critical thinking aligned with intellectual curiosity is a foundational skill for Mixed Reality Leadership (MRL). Building on the competencies explored in Chapter 2, leaders must navigate varying environments with associated complexity shaped by Augmented Reality (AR), Virtual Reality (VR), Extended Reality (XR), Artificial Intelligence (AI), and data analytics. These immersive technologies offer powerful tools for collaboration and insight, but they also introduce risks of bias, threats, harms, misinformation, and cognitive overload. Effective MRL teams require leaders who can question assumptions, evaluate data critically, and make informed decisions avoiding poor decision making—skills essential for thriving in mixed reality contexts.

The Importance of Critical Thinking in Mixed Reality Leadership

Key Reasons Why **Intellectual Curiosity is Fundamental in Supporting Critical Thinking** and MRL

Exploration of Emerging Technologies – MRL environments evolve rapidly. Curious leaders are more likely to explore new tools

(AR, VR, AI) and understand their implications, rather than relying on outdated methods.

Questioning Assumptions – Intellectual curiosity fuels the desire to ask *why*, *how*, and *what if*. This helps leaders challenge surface-level insights and uncover deeper truths in immersive, data-rich settings.

Adaptability and Learning – Curious leaders are lifelong learners. They adapt quickly to new platforms, interfaces, and data streams—critical in fast-changing MR environments.

Innovation and Problem-Solving – Curiosity leads to experimentation. In MRL, this means testing new ways to collaborate, visualise data, or simulate scenarios—driving innovation.

Bias Detection and Ethical Awareness – A curious mind is more likely to investigate anomalies, question AI outputs, and explore ethical implications—key to responsible leadership in MR.

Intellectual Curiosity for Critical Thinking Solution: It enables and transforms critical thinking from a reactive skill into a proactive leadership asset.

Key Reasons Why Critical Thinking and Intellectual Curiosity is Crucial in MRL

Avoiding the Big Data Paradox & Information Overload.

MR environments generate **massive amounts of real-time data**, from performance metrics to immersive simulations. Without critical thinking:

Leaders risk being **overwhelmed by data** instead of extracting meaningful insights.

Misleading correlations and biased AI outputs can lead to poor decisions.

Decision paralysis can occur if leaders fail to filter and prioritise information effectively.

Critical Thinking Solution: Leaders must analyse data with skepticism, distinguish between relevant and irrelevant information, apply logical reasoning to extract actionable insights, and reflect to be able learn and adapt.

Challenging AI & Automation Bias

MR leadership often involves AI-driven decision-making tools, predictive analytics, and automated processes. While AI can enhance decision-making, it is not infallible.

AI models may inherit biases from their training data,

AI and immersive simulations may reinforce existing biases if not critically evaluated.

Automated decisions may lack the human nuance required for ethical leadership.

Reality Distortion can blur the line between real and simulated experiences, affecting judgment.

Over-reliance on AI can lead to a lack of accountability in decision-making.

Critical Thinking Solution: Leaders must question AI outputs, cross-validate with human expertise, and ensure ethical considerations are incorporated.

Navigating Virtual Collaboration & Digital Ethics

MR teams operate in virtual and hybrid environments, often crossing cultural and geographical boundaries. This introduces challenges in:

Interpreting digital communication (tone, intent, and context can be lost in virtual spaces).

Ensuring inclusivity and fairness (MR tools must not marginalise or disadvantage certain team members).
Balancing transparency and privacy (e.g., biometric tracking, real-time surveillance in virtual spaces).

Critical Thinking Solution: Leaders must assess the ethical implications of MR technologies, foster an inclusive digital culture, and develop communication strategies that bridge virtual and physical divides.

Making Agile & Adaptive Decisions

The immersive nature of MR can create **hyperreal simulations** that feel convincing but may not always reflect reality. Leaders must:

Differentiate between simulated and real-world risks.

Adapt to rapidly changing information and virtual team dynamics.

Balance short-term operational performance with long-term strategy.

Critical Thinking Solution: Leaders must apply **situational awareness**, continuously question assumptions, and adapt strategies based on evolving circumstances.

Encouraging Innovation While Mitigating Risks

MR provides opportunities for creativity, from virtual prototyping to immersive training. However, leaders must think critically to:

Ensure **innovation aligns with business goals** rather than being driven by technology hype.

Identify **risks associated with virtual experimentation** (e.g., security threats, misinformation, psychological effects).

Balance **risk-taking with responsible leadership** in a virtual setting.

Critical Thinking Solution: Leaders should adopt a **structured problem-solving approach**, weigh risks against benefits, and foster a culture of responsible innovation.

Conclusion: The Critical Thinking Edge in MRL

In a Mixed Reality Leadership team, **critical thinking is the foundation of effective leadership**. Without it, leaders risk falling into the traps of misinformation, automation bias, and digital overload. By actively questioning, analysing, and evaluating the MR landscape, leaders can **make informed, ethical, and innovative decisions that drive success**.

Critical Thinking in a Mixed Reality Leadership (MRL) Environment

Building on **Intellectual Curiosity** support **Critical thinking in an MRL environment** refers to the ability to **analyse, evaluate, and synthesise information from immersive and AI-driven technologies to make sound, ethical, and strategic decisions**. In a world where leaders interact with **virtual simulations, AI-driven analytics, and hybrid digital teams**, they must go beyond traditional decision-making approaches.

In MRL settings, **critical thinking** involves:

Interrogating AI and Data Insights – Questioning the accuracy and biases of AI-generated information.

Managing Virtual and Augmented Realities – Distinguishing between simulated scenarios and real-world implications.

Navigating Ethical and Privacy Concerns – Evaluating the impact of MR technologies on fairness, inclusivity, and personal data protection.

Enhancing Decision-Making in Immersive Environments – Using MR tools to test hypotheses, but maintaining human oversight to prevent over-reliance on automation.

Fostering Digital Communication & Collaboration – Critically assessing virtual team interactions, digital body language, and AI-generated reports.

Teaching Critical Thinking for MRL in Higher Education Business Schools

For organisations requires an integrated approach such as via a comprehensive definition and framework for **teaching critical thinking for Mixed Reality Leadership (MRL)** for higher education business schools, but applies to some other across disciplines in higher education. It applies to prepare future business leaders for MRL environments, **higher education institutions must integrate critical thinking into business curricula** using innovative, immersive learning methods.

Core Pedagogical Strategies

Experiential Learning with MR Simulations

Use **VR business simulations** where students face real-time decision-making challenges in a digital economy.

Implement **AR case studies** where students interact with AI-driven market trends, requiring them to assess data credibility.

Example: A business school could create a VR-based leadership lab where students make high-stakes decisions in an AI-driven company, learning to challenge automation biases.

AI-Powered Debate and Socratic Questioning:

Encourage students to **critique AI-generated reports** in a structured debate.

Use Socratic questioning in MR environments, where virtual mentors challenge students' assumptions. Require students to **justify business strategies** using both AI insights and human intuition.
Example: Students could engage in a VR leadership boardroom

where AI presents conflicting market reports, and they must debate which strategy to pursue.

Ethical and Privacy Decision-Making in MR

Teach **ethical frameworks** specific to AI, VR, and digital surveillance in business.

Introduce **immersive ethics labs**, where students experience real-time dilemmas, such as AI-driven hiring biases or deepfake misinformation risks.

Example: A VR ethics scenario where students must balance employee privacy with real-time productivity tracking in an MR workspace.

Gamified Critical Thinking Challenges

Design **MR-based escape rooms** where students solve real-world business problems by applying critical thinking under time constraints.

Use **AI-driven role-playing** where students assume different leadership roles and make strategic decisions based on incomplete or conflicting data.

Example: An AR simulation where students act as business executives responding to an AI-predicted economic crisis, with limited time to analyse the reliability of data.

Cross-Disciplinary Collaboration

Encourage **tech-business hybrid courses**, where students collaborate with AI developers, ethicists, and data scientists to critically assess MR applications.

Develop **MR consulting projects**, where students work with companies using MR technology to improve leadership decision-making.

Example*:* A partnership with an AR startup where students must critically evaluate the leadership impact of immersive business analytics tools.

Conclusion

In an **MRL-driven world**, business leaders must evolve and maintain **intellectual curiosity to** develop **critical thinking skills that integrate AI, data analytics, and immersive technology**. Higher education business schools should embrace **MR simulations, AI debates, ethics labs, gamification, and interdisciplinary collaboration** to prepare students for the **future of leadership in a digital-first economy**

Chapter 20

Higher Education and Mixed Reality Leadership

Introduction

In a world increasingly shaped by immersive and intelligent technologies, **higher education institutions (HEIs)**, with their broader environments and ecosystems (**HEIEEs**) are at a **decisive crossroads!** In the last few years, the evolving **general-purpose technologies (GPTs)**, including **artificial intelligence (AI)** have already begun reshaping academic landscapes, the full potential of immersive technologies—**augmented reality (AR), virtual reality (VR), and the metaverse**—stays largely untapped.

Mixed Reality Leadership (MRL) offers a transformative framework and evolving mindset for integrating these tools into the heart of HEIs and their HEIEEs. Such as at the doctoral level, where creativity and innovation should thrive, fragmented systems often stifle progress. This chapter explores how MRL can **bridge these gaps**, enabling HEIs to foster intuitive, interdisciplinary, and tech-enabled learning environments. By embracing MRL, HEI leaders can unlock new dimensions of creativity, collaboration, and critical thinking—preparing students, staff and HEIs alike for a future defined by immersive, intelligent ecosystems. **The time to act is now: to lead, not follow, in the next wave of educational transformation supporting all economic activity in a digital-first economy.**

Mixed Reality Leadership: Transforming Higher Education

Mixed Reality Leadership (MRL) is poised to revolutionise Higher Education (HE), just as artificial intelligence (AI) is already doing. However, HE has yet to fully embrace its own digital transformation and must act swiftly to adapt. At the pinnacle of the educational experience are PhD programs, fostering the creative future. Yet, when human creativity is examined through unconnected frameworks, it presents challenges not only to learning but also to AI, augmented reality (AR), virtual reality (VR), and MRL. The following explores this challenge and the opportunities these technologies present.

The Power of "Unconnected Frameworks" in Human Creativity

Creativity often emerges when unrelated ideas intersect—consider Einstein's theory of relativity influenced by train rides or Picasso's Cubism inspired by African masks. These breakthroughs result from intuitive leaps rather than purely logical reasoning.

Challenges for AI, AR, VR, and the Metaverse:

- Can these technologies simulate serendipity?
- Can they foster environments that encourage unexpected connections?
- Can they enhance human intuition by presenting information in non-linear, sensory-rich ways?

How Emerging Technologies Spark Creativity

Augmented Reality (AR) — Blending the Physical and Digital

AR superimposes digital elements onto the real world, fostering novel perspectives and intuitive insights.

Creative Catalyst Example:

- An architect walking through a city street sees digital overlays of historical structures, inspiring a fusion of modern and ancient design elements.

Artificial Intelligence (AI) — Beyond Logical Predictions

AI can generate novel ideas, art, music, or text that humans might not conceive independently, though it lacks true intuition.

Creative Catalyst Example:

- A fashion designer using AI-generated patterns based on obscure mathematical formulas discovers groundbreaking design inspirations.

Virtual Reality (VR) — Immersive Exploration of Abstract Concepts

VR enables users to experience entirely new environments, breaking traditional logical constraints and fostering unique insights.

Creative Catalyst Example:

- A scientist explores a VR model of a black hole, intuitively grasping gravitational forces beyond equations alone.

The Metaverse — A Hub for Serendipitous Interactions

A persistent, shared digital space where diverse ideas, disciplines, and cultures intersect, leading to unexpected creative breakthroughs.

Creative Catalyst Example:

- A musician in Japan spontaneously collaborates with a visual artist from Brazil in a metaverse environment, producing a unique multimedia piece neither could have created alone.

Combining Technologies for Maximum Impact

The real potential of these technologies emerges when they converge:
- AI generates abstract art.
- VR immerses users in it.
- AR places it in real-world settings.
- The Metaverse fosters collaborative refinement.

As we enter a new technological supercycle, additional innovations in AI, biotechnology, and convergent ecosystems will amplify these effects.

The Philosophical Question: Can Technology Truly Emulate Intuition?

While these technologies facilitate environments that stimulate intuitive thought, they cannot replicate deep, subconscious processing. However, they can expand how we experience information:
- **VR** challenges spatial intuition.
- **AR** blends context with imagination.
- **AI** introduces novelty into structured thinking.
- **The Metaverse** mirrors the spontaneous connections that drive human creativity.

Education: Unlocking Intuitive Learning and Creative Exploration

Traditional education often relies on linear, logic-based models. Immersive technologies offer more experiential and interactive approaches.

How These Technologies Enhance Learning:

- **AR:** Projects 3D models into classrooms, making complex concepts tangible.
- **VR:** Enables immersive historical or scientific explorations.
- **AI:** Provides personalised, adaptive tutoring.
- **Metaverse:** Creates global classrooms, exposing students to diverse perspectives.

Real-World Example:

- **Labster VR Simulations:** Allow students to conduct virtual chemistry experiments, enhancing hands-on learning.

Mental Health: Reconnecting with Intuition Through Immersive Therapy

Mental health treatments often require accessing subconscious emotions—an area where immersive technologies excel.

How These Technologies Support Mental Health:

- **AR:** Simulates real-world triggers for controlled exposure therapy.
- **VR:** Provides safe environments for trauma therapy or meditation.
- **AI:** Virtual therapists analyse emotional patterns for deeper self-awareness.
- **Metaverse:** Facilitates global support groups for shared healing.

Real-World Example:

- **Psious VR Therapy:** Uses VR exposure therapy to treat phobias and PTSD.

Artistic Collaboration: A Playground for Intuitive Creation

Artists thrive on breaking patterns and forming unexpected connections—a process amplified by immersive technology.

How These Technologies Spark Artistic Innovation:

- **AR:** Turns physical spaces into interactive art installations.
- **VR:** Provides infinite 3D creative environments.
- **AI:** Generates unconventional prompts for artistic inspiration.
- **Metaverse:** Enables global, real-time artistic collaborations.

Real-World Example:

- **Tilt Brush by Google (VR):** Allows artists to "paint" in 3D space.
- **Travis Scott's Fortnite Concert:** A pioneering metaverse event blending music, visuals, and interactivity.

Higher Education Institutions' Challenges

Higher education faces multiple critical challenges:
- **Enrolment Declines:** Falling student numbers due to demographic shifts and tuition costs.
- **Financial Constraints:** Rising operational costs are straining institutions.
- **Evolving Student Expectations:** Demand for flexible, technology-integrated learning.
- **Political and Social Pressures:** Debates over policies, diversity, and inclusion impact institutions.
- **Affordability and Transparency:** Confusion over real education costs deters prospective students.

The Need for Mixed Reality Leadership in HE

MRL is currently missing from HE leadership and curricula, despite its potential to address these challenges. Some universities offer leadership programs to bridge the gap:

As of now, there are no higher education courses explicitly titled "Mixed Reality Leadership" as defined in 2023. However, several institutions offer programs that integrate leadership training with immersive technologies, preparing leaders to navigate organisations operating across physical, virtual, and metaverse realms.

Notable Programs:

- **Florida International University (FIU):** Offers a course titled "HR Leadership in the Metaverse," guiding HR leaders through the transformation of work environments by the metaverse. The course covers organisational culture, recruitment, learning and development, and remote work within virtual spaces.

- **University of Michigan:** Launched online courses utilising extended reality (XR) technologies, allowing learners to explore virtual environments and acquire skills essential for future professional success.

- **Stanford University:** Provides a course titled "Designing for Extended Realities," equipping students with the skills to design XR experiences critically and intentionally, focusing on human-centred approaches. Stanford has also created the definitive AI Index 2025.

US-Based Higher Education Leadership Programs

- **Harvard Graduate School of Education:** Master's Degree in Higher Education, focusing on leadership and policy.

- **University of Pennsylvania:** Executive Doctorate in Higher Education Management.

- **Vanderbilt University:** Master's Degree in Higher Education Administration.

UK-Based Higher Education Leadership Programs

- **King's College London:** MA in Educational Leadership and Management.

- **Nottingham Trent University:** MSc in Higher Education Management and Leadership.
- **University of Oxford:** MSc in Education (Higher Education).
- **University of Birmingham:** MA in Educational Leadership and Management.
- **University of Manchester:** MA in Educational Leadership.

While these programs may not encompass the full spectrum of "Mixed Reality Leadership" as defined, they offer foundational knowledge and skills pertinent to leading in environments that blend physical and virtual elements.

As the concept of Mixed Reality Leadership gains traction, it's anticipated that more specialised courses will emerge to address the unique challenges and opportunities in this evolving landscape

Recent Developments of Note

This is written in very early March 2025. At the end of February 2025 an HE conference was held in the UK, the Evasys Conference on Student Engagement, at the University of Westminster. Amber Tidmarsh of Keele University was the only speaker to deliver on AI. Mixed Reality Leadership and HE leadership in AI to meet the Prime Minister's Sir Keir Starmer's UK AI Powerhouse agenda was missing.

On the 3rd March 2025 Estonia said:

Estonia is set to become the first country to integrate AI into its national education system.

The initiative is led by the President of Estonia Alar Karis, Ministry of Education and Science led by Minister Kristina Kallas in close cooperation with private sector.

Starting September 2025, all 10th and 11th graders will have access to this AI tool, enhancing learning and teaching experiences.

The initiative builds on Tiger Leap, bringing computers to schools 30 years ago. The aim of AI leap is to prepare students for the AI-driven future.

Conclusion: The Future of Higher Education and Mixed Reality Leadership

By integrating AI, AR, VR, and the Metaverse, HE institutions can foster environments where intuitive creativity flourishes. Addressing financial, technological, and pedagogical challenges requires a new wave of leaders skilled in Mixed Reality Leadership. As technological convergence accelerates, HE must embrace innovation to remain relevant and impactful in the evolving educational landscape.

P.S. The authors recommend the work of Professor Mairead Pratschke.

Chapter 21

Summary

The book explores the concept and construct of Mixed Reality Leadership (MRL), which integrates physical, virtual, augmented, and artificial intelligence realities into leadership frameworks. It addresses key topics such as governance, risk management, organisational values, and strategic threats in a mixed reality context. The book emphasises the importance of adaptable leadership styles and robust governance in the mixed reality environment.

The document is divided into several key parts summarised as:

1. Normative and Crisis Management Principles: Section 1 looks at the context and objectives of management and investigates best practice mechanisms and methodologies commonly used to manage information and coordinate responses. Effective organisational management being a necessary precursor of Mixed Reality Leadership.

2. Normative and Crisis Leadership: Sections 1 and 2 explore team dynamics, potential pitfalls, and the characteristics of effective normative and crisis leadership in a Mixed Reality environment.

3. Normative and Crisis Communications Theory & Practice: Both Sections 1 and 2 examine current and required principles of effective communication, including audiences, content, delivery, and control. They include message preparation, live media interviews, press conference hosting, and presentation techniques.

4. Mixed Reality Leadership: Section 2 covers the complexities of integrating mixed reality, extended reality, augmented reality,

virtual reality, and artificial intelligence into a leadership framework called Mixed Reality Leadership. It addresses key topics such as governance (using the Saxton Bampfylde board model), risk management, organisational values, and strategic threats in a mixed reality context.

5. Leadership Styles: Various leadership styles, including transactional, transformational, servant, autocratic, democratic, laissez-faire, charismatic, situational, bureaucratic, and strategic leadership are examined in both the current and Mixed Reality environments. A review of the strengths and weaknesses of each style highlights that Mixed Reality Leadership should take the best from transformational, servant, democratic, laissez-faire, charismatic, situational, and strategic leadership styles. Effective management remains critical, as does trust, to implementing Mixed Reality Leadership.

6. Strategic Challenges and Opportunities: Critical strategic issues with widespread global implications, requiring immediate attention are identified. Case studies in a number of different sectors are used to highlight issues. The book discusses modern agile conflict, invisible apocalypse, ideological tensions, migration, societal pillars, nuclear proliferation, artificial intelligence, climate change, and evolution. These are all part of the University of Buckingham's current curricula in the Security, Intelligence and Cyber syllabus.

7. Cybersecurity and Business Resilience: A comprehensive cybersecurity risk management strategy, including context and reconnaissance, risk management, cybersecurity attack simulation, emergency response plan, and associated business resilience plan is discussed. It emphasises the importance of creating and maintaining a secure and resilient cybersecurity ecosystems a precursor and continuing underpinning for Mixed Reality Leadership.

The book concludes with a forward-looking analysis of the next technological super cycle, underscoring the urgency of proactive mixed reality leadership in an evolving mixed reality landscape.

Chapter 22

Conclusion

In conclusion:

Preparing for the Future of Leadership in a Mixed Reality World

As organisations increasingly operate across blended realities, the need for adaptable, innovative, and resilient leadership becomes paramount. This book highlights the urgency of proactive Mixed Reality Leadership in an evolving mixed reality landscape. Leaders must be equipped with the skills to navigate the complexities of integrating extended reality, augmented reality, virtual reality, and artificial intelligence into their organisational strategies. By fostering collaboration, trust, resilience, and effective management, leaders can ensure their organisations remain competitive, secure, and adaptable in the face of ever-changing realities.

"Mixed Reality Leadership" therefore provides a comprehensive exploration of the complexities and challenges faced by modern leaders in navigating the intertwined realms of physical, virtual, and metaverse environments. As organisations increasingly operate across these blended realities, the need for adaptable, innovative, and resilient leadership becomes paramount. This book emphasises the importance of integrating governance, risk management, organisational values, and strategic foresight into leadership frameworks to effectively manage the evolving landscape.

The principles of normative (Mixed Reality) and crisis leadership, management and communications theory and practice outlined in this book serve as foundational elements for leaders to respond effectively to mixed reality and emergencies whilst maintaining organisational stability. Additionally, the examination of various leadership styles, including transformational, servant, democratic, laissez-faire, charismatic, situational, and strategic leadership, provides valuable insights into the strengths and weaknesses of each approach, highlighting the necessity of a balanced, trusting, and eclectic leadership style in the new mixed reality context.

As the world moves forward into an era marked by a new super-cycle, rapid technological advancements, cybersecurity threats, and global strategic challenges, the role of Mixed Reality Leadership becomes increasingly critical. Leaders must be equipped with the skills to navigate the complexities of integrating extended reality, augmented reality, virtual reality, and artificial intelligence into their organisational strategies. By fostering collaboration, mutual trust, and resilience, leaders can ensure their organisations remain competitive, secure, and adaptable in the face of ever-changing realities.

Whether you are a leader of an organisation or a leader within an organisation radical change is upon you. As a human you have a choice to either control the technology or let the technology control you. It is hoped that, at least in part, this book helps if you have made the 'stay human approach'. The leader's decisions affect the share/stock price, freedom in a real sense of jail time, profits, longevity, insurance costs (you can bet many a dollar this book will be read by insurance companies), and morale (among the many other issues described herein). 'We' have been here before, to an extent. The shift in resilience thinking of a generation or more ago, especially after 9/11, Deborah Pretty's analyses on catastrophes, survival and share prices, Maitland's work on Organisational Security and new ways of looking at it, have all 'sort of' been here before. It is now more complex, more urgent, and even more vital. It requires an enormous mind set shift(s), particularly in regard to Emotional Intelligence.

Ultimately, "Mixed Reality Leadership" serves as a guide for leaders to embrace the opportunities and mitigate the risks associated with the mixed reality landscape. It underscores the urgency of proactive leadership, continuous learning, and strategic innovation to shape a sustainable and prosperous future for organisations operating in this dynamic environment.

Good luck. Maitland, Amanda, and John.

References/Endnotes

1. Andy Jenkinson's LinkedIn posts are available at: https://www.linkedin.com/in/andy-jenkinson-96210727/?originalSubdomain=uk Last Accessed: 5 May 2025.

2. World Economic Forum (2025) *Future of Jobs Report,* January 2025. Available at: https://reports.weforum.org/docs/WEF_Future_of_Jobs_Report_2025.pdf?_gl=1*tftv9s*_up*MQ..*_gs*MQ..&gclid=Cj0KCQjw4cS-BhDGARIsABg4_J06DswSQL81C5GHsElEYBNX3_oUSG5okGrvj1K4YBj0T7iKUETeH1oaAko2EALw_wcB&gbraid=0AAAAAoVy5F4S-LIUjaMKgX_jJg1PMitbD Last accessed: 27th March 2023.

3. Maitland Hyslop's LinkedIn posts are available at: https://www.linkedin.com/in/dr-maitland-hyslop-8ba0742/?originalSubdomain=uk . Last Accessed: 5 May 2025. Particular reference to October, November and December 2024.

4. Hyslop, M.P. (2007) Critical Information Infrastructures: Resilience and Protection. Springer, Boston, USA.

5. Hyslop, M.P. (2014) Obstructive Marketing. Gower, UK.

6. Hyslop, M.P. (2013) Hardening Organisations. PhD Thesis, Northumbria, UK.

7. Hyslop, M.P. (2020) On War, Reiver, UK.

8. Hyslop, M.P. (2023) The Elephant in the Boardroom Reiver, UK.

9. Hyslop, M.P. and White, D. (2024) The Invisible Apocalypse BUCSIS/Reiver, UK.

10. Hyslop, M.P. (2014) *Obstructive Marketing* Gower, UK.

11. Attributed to Amanda Goodger.

12. This is based on a conversation between Amanda Goodger and Julie Froud, Maitland Hyslop's time as a Local Enterprise Chairman under the UK coalition in the early 2010, and his time with Invest in Britain./Northern Development Company.

13. Robinson,C (2025) Available at: https://www.forbes.com/sites/cherylrobinson/people/cherylrobinson5/ Last Accessed: 5 May 2025.

14. In conversation with ChatGPT4 on 20 March 2025.

15. Kipling, R. *I Keep Six Honest Serving Man.* The Kipling Society, London, UK. Available at: https://www.kiplingsociety.co.uk/poem/poems_serving.htm Accessed: 5 May 2025.

16. Horn, A (2025) 'An Estimated 59% of the global workforce will need reskilling by the year 2030' Available at: https://www.linkedin.com/posts/andreashorn1_%F0%9D%97%94%F0%9D%97%BB-%F0%9D%97%B2%F0%9D%98%80%F0%9D%98%81%F0%9D%97%B6%F0%9D%97%BA%F0%9D%97%AE%F0%9D%98%81%F0%9D%97%B2%F0%9D%97%B1-59-%F0%9D%97%BC%F0%9D%97%B3-%F0%9D%98%81-activity-7310543057068687360-KmRS?utm_source=social_share_send&utm_medium=android_app&rcm=ACoAAABddw4B0aY_dmCBwKcKV1otDhzOo5hfYBA&utm_campaign=gmail Last Accessed: 5 May 2025.

17. World Economic Forum (2025) *'Future of Jobs Report'*, January 2025. Available at: https://reports.weforum.org/docs/WEF_Future_of_Jobs_Report_2025.pdf?_gl=1*tftv9s*_up*MQ..*_gs*MQ..&gclid=Cj0KCQjw4cS-BhDGARIsABg4_J06DswSQL81C5GHsElEYBNX3_oUSG5okGrvj1K4YBj0T7iKUETeH1oaAko2EALw_wcB&gbraid=0AAAAAoVy5F4S-LIUjaMKgX_jJg1PMitbD Last accessed: 5 May 2025..

18. Torys LLP (2022) 'Director and officer liability for cybersecurity breaches in Canada and the U.S.' Available at: https://torys.com/en/our-latest-thinking/publications/2022/04/director-and-officer-liability-for-cybersecurity-breaches-in-canada-and-the-us Last Accessed: 5 May 2025.

19. Royal Military Academy Sandhurst (1959) Serve to Lead: An Anthology.

20. Adams, D. (1959) *A Hitchhikers Guide to the Galaxy*. Del Rey.

21. See Andy Jenkison's posts on LinkedIn for a detailed history of this issue. Available at: https://www.linkedin.com/in/andy-jenkinson-96210727/?originalSubdomain=uk . Last Accessed: 5 May 2025.

22. Webb, A (2025) Emerging Tech Report. Available at: https://www.youtube.com/watch?v=oT33_MrqyHo Last Accessed: 5 May 2025.

23. Source: XXX

24. Source: YYY

25. The Health Insurance Portability and Accountability Act (HIPAA) (1996) Available at: https://www.hipaa.org Last Accessed: 5 May 2025.

26. Sarbanes Oxley Act. (2002) Available at: https://sarbanes-oxley-act.com Last Accessed: 5 May 2025.

27. General Data Protection Regulations (2018) Available at: https://www.gdpreu.org Last Accessed 5 May 2025.

28. HIMSS 7 (2021) Celebrating HIMSS Stage 7 Organisations Advancing Global Health | HIMSS

29. Qatari Financial Centre Regulatory Authority. (2025). Available at: https://www.qfcra.com Last Accessed: 5 May 2025.

30. Wood, R. 2000. *Managing Complexity*. London. Economist Books.

31. IBM (2021) 'IBM Insurance Cloud Architecture.' Available at: https://www.ibm.com/industries/insurance (Last Accessed: 5 May 2025)

32. With thanks to Professor John Gordon, former Visiting Professor of Mathematics, Hertfordshire University, UK, for introducing Maitland Hyslop to this concept some 30 years ago.

33. The New Stack (2021) 'Securing Microservices in Service Mesh,' Available at: https://thenewstack.io/mutual-tls-microservices-encryption-for-service-mesh/ Last Accessed: 5 May 2025,

34. Institute and Faculty of Actuaries (2020) Understanding

blockchain for insurance use cases.' Available at: https://www.
actuaries.org.uk/system/files/field/document/Blockchain-
Workstream-v1.8%20FINAL.pdf Last Accessed:5 May 2025

35. National Institute for Standards and Technology (2025) '
Driving Innovation.' Available at: https://www.nist.gov/ Last
Accessed: 5 May 2025.

36. America's Cyber Defense Agency (2021) 'Einstein'
Available at: https://www.cisa.gov/resources-tools/
programs/national-cybersecurity-protection-system/
einstein#:~:text=EINSTEIN%20serves%20two%20key%20
roles%20in%20FCEB%20cybersecurity.,and%20to%20
help%20the%20private%20sector%20protect%20itself. Last
Accessed: 5 May 2025.

37. World Economic Forum (2021) 'Why we need to move from
Cybersecurity to Cyber Resilience.' Available at: https://www.
weforum.org/stories/2021/11/why-move-cyber-security-to-
cyber-resilience/ Last Accessed: 5 May 2025.

38. World Economic Forum(2025) Global Risks Report, Available
at: https://reports.weforum.org/docs/WEF_Global_Risks_
Report_2025.pdf Last Accessed: 5 May 2025.

39. With thanks to Chris Laing, our former colleague at
Northumbria University, for his assistance on this.

40. With thanks to our associate James Royds FBCI for his
assistance on this.

41. Hyslop, M.P. & White, D (2024) *The Invisible Apocalypse*
BUCSIS/Reiver, UK.

42. US Department of Defense (2024*) Military and Security
Developments Involving The People's Republic of China.
Annual Report To Congress.* Available at: https://media.
defense.gov/2024/Dec/18/2003615520/-1/-1/0/MILITARY-
AND-SECURITY-DEVELOPMENTS-INVOLVING-
THE-PEOPLES-REPUBLIC-OF-CHINA-2024.PDF? Last
Accessed: 5 May 2025.

43. Liang, Q & Xiangsui, W (2004) *Unrestricted Warfare*, Filament
Books, USA.

44. Morgan, E. (2024) 'Eroding Global Stability: The Cybersecurity

Strategies of Russia, North Korea, and Iran.' *Irregular Warfare Initiative*. 19 February.

45. https://irregularwarfare.org/articles/eroding-global-stability-the-cybersecurity-strategies-of-china-russia-north-korea-and-iran/?

46. Gerasimov V. (2016) 'The Value of Science Is in the Foresight.' *Military Review*'. January–February. pp 23—29.

47. Morgan, E. (2024) 'Eroding Global Stability: The Cybersecurity Strategies of Russia, North Korea, and Iran.' *Irregular Warfare Initiative*. 19 February.

48. https://irregularwarfare.org/articles/eroding-global-stability-the-cybersecurity-strategies-of-china-russia-north-korea-and-iran/?

49. Ibid

50. Ibid

51. Berzina, K (2025) 'NATO: Strength in Unity.' German Marshall Fund. 21 January. Available at:https://www.gmfus.org/news/nato-strength-unity?utm_source=chatgpt.com Last Accessed: 5 May 2025.

52. Saxton Bampfylde (2021). 'Evolution or Revolution.' Available at: https://www.saxbam.com/thoughtpiece/evolution-or-revolution/ Last Accessed: 5 May 2025.

53. ICAO (2023). 'Strategic Planning and Digital Governance.' Available at: https://www.icao.int/about-icao/Documents/ICAO%20Transformation%20Secretariat%20Strategy%20V3.0.pdf Last Accessed: 5 May 2025.

54. Xiong, M & Wang, H (2022) 'Digital Twin Applications in the Aviation Industry.' Available at: https://www.researchgate.net/publication/362322649_Digital_twin_applications_in_aviation_industry_A_review Last Accessed: 5 May 2025.

55. Nuclear Regulatory Commission (2024) ' 737 Max Digital lessons Learned Report.'Available at: https://www.nrc.gov/docs/ML2224/ML22241A039.pdf

56. Davis, C. (2025) 'Thriving During The Enrolment Cliff: Navigating 2025's Challenges' *University Business*. 16 January. https://universitybusiness.com/thriving-during-the-enrollment-cliff-navigating-2025s-challenges-in-education/?

57. Insight Staff. (2024) 'Higher Education Faces Challenges: Rising Costs, Declining Enrolment, and Equity Issues.' Available at: https://www.insightintodiversity.com/higher-education-faces-challenges-rising-costs-declining-enrollment-and-equity-issues/? Last Accessed: 5 May 2025.

58. Cassidy, C. (2025) 'Teaching to an empty hall': is the changing face of universities eroding standards of learning?' Available at: https://www.theguardian.com/australia-news/2025/feb/19/teaching-to-an-empty-hall-is-the-changing-face-of-universities-eroding-standards-of-learning? Last Accessed: 5 May 2025.

59. Deloitte (2024) Higher Education Trends. Available at: https://www2.deloitte.com/us/en/insights/industry/public-sector/latest-trends-in-higher-education.html? Last Accessed: 5 May 2025.

60. Horowitch, R (2025) 'The The Secret That Colleges Should Stop Keeping.'

61. https://www.theatlantic.com/ideas/archive/2025/02/college-cheaper-sticker-price/681742 Last Accessed: 5 May 2025.

62. FIU (2025) 'HR Leadership in the Metaverse' Available at:https://career.fiu.edu/classes/hr-leadership-in-the-metaverse/?utm_source=chatgpt.com Last Accessed: 5 May 2025.

63. University of Michigan (2025) Extended Reality Courses. Available at: https://record.umich.edu/articles/u-m-launches-three-online-courses-using-extended-reality/? Last Accessed: 5 May 2025.

64. See Stanford. School, Designing for Extended Realities, Available at: https://dschool.stanford.edu/study/elective-courses/designing-in-extended-realities Last Accessed: 5 May 2025.

65. See Stanford University courses: https://hai.stanford.edu/ai-index/2025-ai-index-report Last Accessed 5 May 2025.

66. See Kings College courses at: https://www.kcl.ac.uk/study/postgraduate-taught/courses/educational-leadership-and-management Last Accessed: 5 May 2025.

67. See Nottingham Business School courses at: https://www.

ntu.ac.uk/course/nottingham-business-school/pr/msc-higher-education-management-and-leadership Last Accessed: 5 May 2025.

68. See Oxford University courses at: https://www.ox.ac.uk/admissions/graduate/courses/msc-education-higher-education? Last Accessed: 5 May 2025.

69. See Birmingham University Courses at: https://www.birmingham.ac.uk/study/postgraduate/subjects/teacher-education-courses/educational-leadership-and-management-ma? Last Accessed: 5 May 2025

70. See Manchester University Courses at: https://www.manchester.ac.uk/study/masters/courses/list/08289/ma-educational-leadership/? Last Accessed: 5 May 2025.

71. Professor Mairead Pratschke. Available at: https://www.linkedin.com/in/maireadpratschke/ Last Accessed: 5 May 2025.

72. Pretty, D. (2008) 'Impact of Crisis Leadership on Shareholder Value', *The BCI Symposium*, Brighton, UK, 9/10 October.

www.ingramcontent.com/pod-product-compliance
Lightning Source LLC
Chambersburg PA
CBHW052110230326
41599CB00055B/5426